Praise for
Connected Capitalism

"What a book! I find myself nodding and smiling, clenching my fists, gnashing my teeth, and laughing while I read. A vital, significant, and deeply personal book, *Connected Capitalism* looks at how we can redeem ourselves as a species, a culture, and a society."
Sunshine Jones, electronic musician

"David Weitzner's voice is a measured, compassionate one as it rises above the din of knee-jerk opinion and judgment. Listen: the man has ideas and he knows how to communicate them."
Nels Cline, Wilco guitarist, composer

"I enjoyed reading David Weitzner's provocative book. Even though I strongly believe that capitalism and competition have provided significant benefits to society, I agree that a successful business also relies on trust and cooperation in its relations with its customers, workers, and suppliers. Weitzner argues that we should think of work within a concept of 'connected capitalism.' The best part of this argument is related to spiritualism – we should not be spiritual but do spiritualism."
Jack M. Mintz, President's Fellow of the School of Public Policy, University of Calgary

Also by David Weitzner

Fifteen Paths: How to Tune Out Noise, Turn On Imagination and Find Wisdom

Strategic Management: Creating Competitive Advantages (co-author)

Corporate Social Responsibility (co-editor)

CONNECTED CAPITALISM

How Jewish Wisdom Can Transform Work

DAVID WEITZNER

New Jewish Press
An imprint of University of Toronto Press
Toronto Buffalo London
utorontopress.com

© David Weitzner 2021

Library and Archives Canada Cataloguing in Publication
Title: Connected capitalism : how Jewish wisdom can transform work /
David Weitzner.
Names: Weitzner, David, author.
Description: Includes bibliographical references.
Identifiers: Canadiana (print) 20200380214 | Canadiana (ebook) 20200380265
| ISBN 9781487508425 (cloth) | ISBN 9781487538217 (EPUB) |
ISBN 9781487538200 (PDF)
Subjects: LCSH: Work – Religious aspects – Judaism. | LCSH: Spirituality. |
LCSH: Work-life balance.
Classification: LCC BM729.W64 W45 2021 | DDC 296.7—dc23

ISBN 978-1-4875-0842-5 (cloth)
ISBN 978-1-4875-3821-7 (EPUB)
ISBN 978-1-4875-3820-0 (PDF)

Printed in Canada

We acknowledge the financial support of the Government of Canada, the
Canada Council for the Arts, and the Ontario Arts Council, an agency of the
Government of Ontario, for our publishing activities.

Canada Council Conseil des Arts
for the Arts   du Canada

ONTARIO ARTS COUNCIL
CONSEIL DES ARTS DE L'ONTARIO
an Ontario government agency
un organisme du gouvernement de l'Ontario

Funded by the   Financé par le
Government   gouvernement
of Canada   du Canada

Canada

To my wife, Alana, whose soulful grace fills me with awe and wonder.

Contents

Acknowledgments

First and foremost, thank you to Ronnie Burkett, Nels Cline, David Frum, Lee Ranaldo, Amelia Sargisson, and Michael Solomon for opening up and sharing their spiritual wisdom with me.

Thank you to Heidi Noble and DJ Schneeweiss for being endlessly reliable sources of inspiring conversation and deep thinking.

This book was significantly improved by the diligent efforts of Rachel Baron and an anonymous academic reviewer, whose insights into prior drafts helped shape the final manuscript for the better.

My editor at University of Toronto Press, Natalie Fingerhut, was an early believer in this project. Her enthusiasm and support empowered me to tell a story that had been dormant in my subconscious for many years now, and I am grateful beyond words.

My literary agent, Lucinda Blumenfeld, has gone above and beyond the call of duty. From flying in to Toronto to help hustle the project to off-hour messaging of optimally timed critical kicks, Lucinda is the invaluable and driven professional every author needs and I am fortunate to have in my corner.

Over the years, I have been blessed by the mentorship of three individuals bearing the dual titles of Rabbi and Professor. They have each shaped my thinking on Judaism and spirituality in substantive ways. While their presence is deeply missed, their spirit is imprinted throughout these pages: Yitzchok Block, Emil Fackenheim, and Zalman Schachter-Shalomi, z"l.

Finally, to my family: Alana, Moishe, Shaindy, and Leah. Thank you for being the sparks of connection that matter most.

Introduction
It's Time for a Different Spirituality

Cooperation Is Spiritual

At a *bar mitzvah* one Saturday morning, I found myself in conversation with a friend who happens to be a Google executive from the local Toronto headquarters. Our discussion focused on an interesting phenomena. Rather than complaining about feeling empty and disconnected at work, as most of us do, this executive shared in passionate detail how seriously his company takes the spiritual well-being of its organizational members.

Amongst other initiatives, Google offers employees abundant access to mindfulness training programs that leave participants inspired and meditation rooms that are nothing less than eye-popping. The company recognizes that there is a problem in many work cultures, and has sought to proactively tackle it head on. Google has created the perfect physical space within its corporate offices in which team members can simply *be*. Google offers meditation courses for those employees who may be unfamiliar with the practice. And it created a culture that is supportive of escaping the madness of work to experience the release afforded by a state of passivity.

My friend emphasized that most of his colleagues use the meditation rooms as they were intended to be used: to momentarily abandon all cares and concerns in order to achieve flashes of deep spiritual awareness. But then he said something that gave me pause. He told me that he felt guilty for recently using the meditation room to make an important business call that required an intensity of focus and silence. While his colleagues "were coming in to the room seeking inner peace and deep meaning" he was "selfishly ruining the vibe by putting my capitalist instincts first."

I thought to myself, isn't this exactly what Google should want its employees to do? Why was he apologizing for using a corporate space for corporate purposes? Even more curiously, why did he view his desire to connect with a person in a meaningful way as something other than spiritual? The reason for this phone call was to continue enhancing a relationship in support of creative cooperative activities. Isn't worldly cooperation as spiritually significant as inner peace?

The short answer is that this anecdote captures the quintessential problem of spirituality at work in the modern era. We have been socialized into viewing business activities as in opposition to spiritual activities. Spirituality is seen as inward and private. Business is outward and public. As a consequence, Western companies have begun embracing mindfulness. They are managing the emotional needs of their employees by allowing them to be spiritual in the meditation room. However, these newly enlightened workers are then expected to return to the main office space and be "business-like." But this approach is totally counterproductive.

Why do many of us see spirituality as distinct and separate from business? As will soon be demonstrated, this certainly was not always the case. What shifts in our culture have influenced the widespread adoption of this unhelpful dichotomy? Indeed, just as the synagogue was the right place for *our* conversation to take place, the meditation room seemed to me to be the perfect place for a relationship-building phone call.

More significantly, I am confident that my spiritual and emotionally intelligent friend instinctively knew this to be the case. That's why he took the call where he did. But he didn't have the language to persuasively express the fact that spiritually meaningful activities can be assertive, active, and cooperative. Progressive decision-makers at Google view spirituality as inward bliss and passivity as the optimal posture for encountering the good. But business activities can be spiritual activities, full of meaning, connection, and wonder. Assertive efforts can be sacred, if we accept a specific burden: the moral responsibility of knowing that when we act, we are connecting ourselves to those who may be impacted by our actions. When work is spiritual, it is also cooperative. It is *doing* with *others*.

The problem with corporate mindfulness is that it is an effort to manage the needs of employees. But spirituality is bigger than that. Experiencing meaning, connection, and wonder means becoming a partner in co-creation, not retreating in passivity. I recognize that this may be somewhat counterintuitive for some, particularly if your only experience of spirituality came while seated on pillows in a meditation room or on a pew in a house of worship. You are very much not alone in this perspective. It even took the famous Hasidic Master Rabbi Moshe Leib of Sassov, who wrestled with the question over two hundred years ago, some time to see the variety of spiritual experiences.

As the story goes, when he first took on a leadership role in his community, he prohibited talking during services at his synagogue. Under the talking ban, some congregants came to synagogue in a cooperative endeavor of prayer. But others, particularly those who weren't feeling the prayers, needed to still show up, keep quiet, and fake it. Before the ban was implemented, people would come to services and find out who needed a job, who was looking for a spouse, who was sick, and other matters of communal importance. With the ban came increased isolation and a decrease in business deals, weddings, and wellness visits in the community.

Eventually, the rabbi realized that there was a higher order of spirituality. Conversation with God was nice. But conversation between people was necessary. One cannot build a sacred community without trust, cooperation, and meaningful relationships. And turning these communal relationships into co-creative partnerships starts with exchanging words. Rabbi Moshe Leib came to see that his action of instituting a ban on conversation was having an impact that he did not expect. He felt responsible for the negative effect it was having on the people in his community. He felt responsible for their pain.

So, the rabbi lifted the ban, recognizing that getting a community together to talk to each other in synagogue was as important a spiritual action as getting together to pray. This story takes on extra meaning as societies across the globe recover from the effects of the COVID-19 pandemic and adjust to the new normal of varying levels of social distancing practices. Individuals being curious about each other and creative in how they might help one another in the everyday challenges of life are the backbone of a cooperative and connected community. What could be more spiritual than a caring community, concerned with the well-being of its members? And why can't that connection be present in our cooperative business activities?

Stop the World, I Want to Get Off

Listening to my enthusiastic friend, I know that Google is right to recognize that navigating the reality of our new economy will require some innovative approaches to human resource management. Many workers are finding it particularly challenging to find stability amidst the craziness of our everyday. The once widely cited expression "That task is above my pay grade," which likely emerged from the military as a respectful deferral to rank, is an anachronism. In the contemporary capitalist corporate work culture, consultants teach executives that the idiom is an excuse used by the lazy, and successful companies need everyone up and down the organizational hierarchy to see each and every problem as their own.

We are expected to be agile risk-takers. We are expected to function in a predictable fashion despite operating in a competitive environment characterized by an accelerated rate of change. Part of the risks we are to assume involves taking ownership of complex challenges that are beyond our individual capabilities to solve. These are problems that demand cooperative responses. We need to find partners of differing and diverse skill sets to work through these challenges with us. But the landscape of who we work with and how is continually shifting under our feet, and has been accelerated by a pandemic that has forced us to rethink the norms of physical contact, leaving us with few opportunities to build these necessary partnerships.

This was made abundantly clear during the onset of the 2020 COVID-19 global public health crisis. While experts will spend the next few years reflecting on what might have been done differently, it became clear very early on that the crisis was exacerbated by failures to coordinate, share information, and respond in a cooperative fashion. For example, the World Health Organization (WHO) was established precisely to serve as a central coordinating body in the event of a global epidemic like this one. After the 2003 SARS crisis, 196 countries signed on to allow WHO to lead the way on containment, emergency declarations, and policy recommendations in future pandemics. But as the 2020 crisis hit, dozens of countries ignored their obligations, failing to report outbreaks. Further, it appears that much of the early advice from WHO, including rejecting calls for travel restrictions and wearing masks in public, were motivated more by political considerations than science, as states that adopted these measures experienced superior outcomes.

On the company level, what the average worker is expected to do in an ordinary day of work at the best of times represents an enormous burden. In challenging times, it becomes an impossibility. The sorry conditions for most workers pre-crisis should never have gotten as bad as they did. Post-crisis is even worse. Many of us continue to find ourselves in contingent employment situations. But we view ourselves as the fortunate ones for still having employment, feeling the pressure to keep quiet and carry on. We are afraid to bring about further disruption, despite the fact that it would be to our benefit. If we are lucky and work for a company that thinks about the spiritual needs of its workers, we enter the meditation room to breathe, be alone for a moment, and savor a passive state. We try to stop the world and get off.

But that is not spiritual work. It is not enough to be managed into a quiet space. We need to be empowered as partners in creation. And I believe it is not too late to demand more from work. We have a unique opportunity to rebuild. I believe that the exploitive business culture that has taken hold in the West can, and must, be resisted. Work needs to be meaningful, creative, and cooperative. And until the arrival of the singularity when all human workers will allegedly be replaced by robots, we are not without the power to bring about the necessary reforms to what we experience in our everyday so that we are cooperative partners. The #MeToo movement has had a demonstrably positive impact on reducing sexual harassment in the workplace, although there is still much work to be done to assure gender equality. And protests arising in the aftermath of the murder of George Floyd on May 25, 2020, in Minneapolis, Minnesota, have stimulated a number of pledges from Corporate America to take action on combatting systemic racism in the workplace, although only time will tell what practical outcomes in improving racial equality will emerge from these commitments. Nonetheless, we have the opportunity to elevate our supposed vulnerabilities to sources of strength. We can go to work to build communities, grow relationships, and shape the world we want. This is what I call doing spiritual work.

Those of us seeking meaning, connection, and wonder – the three pillars of a spiritual experience – in the everyday can harness our physical, mental, and emotional faculties in a practical and uplifting way. My dear mentor, Rabbi Zalman Schachter-Shalomi, affectionately known to his students and colleagues simply as Reb Zalman, wrote the following in his book *Jewish with Feeling*:

The Jewish way of mitzvah encompasses actions that speak to different levels of our psyches. Logical, balanced, healthy action has a place.

Ritual in which we join together in collective witnessing of eternal principles has a place. And decrees that we submit to out of a sense of mystery and even bafflement – these, too, have a place. Judaism, like all world religions, recognizes that *if we are to be transformed, we must appeal not only to the head, but penetrate to our hearts and to our very souls as well.*

Building on this idea, I propose that transforming work into a spiritual experience requires our work lives to, at varying points, provide intellectual meaning, emotional connection, and awe-inducing wonder.

What we need, and what this book offers, is a new approach for thinking about how creating value, initiating change, and encouraging large-scale cooperation is the most important type of spiritual work. This kind of thinking can lay the foundations for a framework that can help us solve many of the socio-economic problems we face today.

With the right framework, we can once again deploy our spiritual capabilities in the context of cooperative work. And by embracing a different type of sacred, we can raise up that which currently seeks to hold us down. The mental, physical, and spiritual can become one, allowing for better strategic decision-making in a disruptive environment, a new way of thinking about purpose in work, and a stronger, more widely and deeply connected cooperative social order. It all begins with meaning, connection, and wonder. Wherever we are in the power hierarchy we need to view spiritual work as an opportunity to form new, hopeful, and transformative partnerships.

We May Not Always Feel It, but We Are Still Spiritual Beings

At each turn, new obstacles are erected that collectively prevent us from finding meaning, connection, and wonder in everyday work. But if more of us were to consciously embrace the type of thinking that can make work spiritual, then maybe even the exploitive elements within the capitalist system itself might change. Maybe we could enact a capitalism driven by curiosity, cooperation, and creativity, where social, cultural, and relational capital are understood to be as necessary for economic exchanges as financial capital.

Even amidst the sense of disconnect brought on by the digital revolution, the forced physical separation necessitated by the pandemic, and the cultural reckoning regarding how we perceive race, our desire for meaning, connection, and wonder has not waned. We may be living through a period of extreme disruption, but our longing for spirituality and community has not been extinguished. Sure, there is sufficient cause for pessimism, as our many digital connections have not created much in the way of meaningful community and racial divides seem more entrenched. But we are not witnessing a wholesale turn to secular materialism. Notwithstanding an increased presence of digital tools and conduits, the power of our analog spiritual faculties has not diminished.

The feelings that arise from meaning, connection, and wonder are so powerful, in fact, that the famed neurologist and Holocaust survivor Viktor Frankl claimed spirituality as the very essence of our humanity. And given how advances in connective technologies have blurred the lines between when we are and are not finding ourselves to be working, a failure to find spirituality at work means losing an essential piece of what it means to be human.

A September 2017 Pew Research survey found that Americans are increasingly claiming to be spiritual, even while their religious identification has declined. Specifically, only 18 per cent of American adults classify themselves as neither spiritual nor religious. Almost half of the American population (48 per cent) self-identify as both religious and spiritual. And more than a quarter of American adults (27 per cent) say they think of themselves as spiritual but not religious, an increase of eight percentage points from polls taken five years earlier.

These findings are, to be candid, a welcome surprise. Turn on cable news and you are likely to hear talking heads characterize the social media–enmeshed society as one of historically unprecedented shallow consumerism and selfishness, operating solely on a mantra of FOMO (fear of missing out). That there is evidence of a growing desire for spiritual self-identification amidst the social, political, and cultural turmoil that our society struggles through is comforting. It's worthwhile to step into the foothold of optimism molded from the quantifiable knowledge that three-quarters of North Americans continue to recognize the importance of seeking meaning, connection, and wonder in their lives. We are still a spiritual people.

A New (Old) Way to Think About Spirituality and Work

In this book we will develop a new (old) spiritual approach to cooperation and work. Our model for how to find meaning, connection, and wonder in ordinary activities will be drawn from the classic teachings of ancient Judaism. However, applying this model will not require the embracing of a Jewish theology. The ideas can be implemented within the context of any paradigm, even one that is wholly secular. But this approach to finding purpose at work will challenge seekers to make connections between seemingly disparate ordinary activities in a manner that may not yet feel natural to those who are used to understanding spirituality as inward bliss and not outward creative, cooperative, and assertive efforts.

This idea of spiritual work is meant to help more people thrive in capitalist environments. It will be built on the pursuit of a higher order of cooperative and transformative human relationships filled with curiosity and wonder. It will encourage us to engage with those who were once strangers, deploy forgiveness for the wrongs of the past where appropriate, and tap into a confident hope for the future.

The inspiration for this approach, and what makes it uniquely Jewish, can be found in a discussion recorded in the Talmud, the ancient collection of a once oral Jewish scholarly tradition that was compiled into writing some 1,500 years ago. The dialogue speculates on what happens during the moments of final judgment, after our bodies have perished and our souls ascend to face their Maker. I have long viewed this exchange as a thought-provoking narrative worthy of consideration by people of all – and no – religious faiths. Whether or not one believes in a soul, or a notion of any form of conscious existence after we die, is irrelevant to appreciating its practical and grounded message.

The primary value of this particular Talmudic discussion is the insightful glimpse it provides into the thinking process of ancient authors wrestling with the biggest question that faces the living: What is the measure of a life lived with purpose? The rabbinic sages decided that the first question asked after death, the most important question that sums up the moral worth of a person's life, will be "Did you conduct your work in good faith?"

Take that in for a minute. How we conduct ourselves in work is identified by these deeply religious scholars as the primary metric for assessing a life well-lived. I know this may be surprising to those not immersed in classical Jewish thinking. In fact, some of us may be instinctively inclined to push back. Could we argue that perhaps the sages were actually most interested in how honest we are in general during our lives, and our work just happens to be a good laboratory in which to effectively test that honesty? I believe there is little evidence with which to support such a spin. The text of the Talmud seems to imply that the highest of spiritual endeavors within the Jewish tradition, the most meaningful of lives, are those occupied by a unique and particular activity of conducting "good-faith" work.

To the ancient rabbinic sages, work contains an inherent sanctity that is of such prime importance, it must be placed prior to inquiries on any other activity. For after this first question, come several others, such as, "Did you set aside fixed time for Torah study?" and "Did you occupy yourself with being fruitful and multiplying?" The question "Did you conduct your work in good faith?" has an aura of holiness. It seems to suggest that work can, and should be, a spiritual activity that can give meaning to a life well-lived.

These fourth-century thinkers were writing in an agrarian economy with limited industrial production. Yet their observations offer an insight that resonates in the disruptive economy of today. They want readers who may encounter the textual recordings of their musings, even hundreds of years later, to know that the first inquiry is not for an account of the sins we avoided while working; not a list of the negative behavior from which we dutifully abstained; not even an account of the non-work-related altruistic endeavors in which we engaged through our work activities. Instead, there is an ultimate need to tell in detail the seemingly mundane story of our actual daily good-faith work interactions in all their messy specifics.

Why would anyone care for such an accounting, unless there is a deep spiritual good to be discovered in the particulars of how we performed the seemingly amoral activities of our work? Placing the question of good-faith work as the ultimate summation of how we lived only makes sense if work and a spiritual practice have the potential to be one and the same. This is not to be found by criticizing business activities or simply delineating a set of rules and prohibitions. It is not a passive approach. The spiritual practice celebrated by ancient Judaism is proactive, cooperative, creative, and based very profoundly in the here and now of the material world.

This means it is no longer meaningful or practical to see business concerns as somehow unique and distinct from spiritual or ethical concerns. The starting point for this approach to spiritual work is rooted in the insights of ancient Jewish thinkers. To get in their headspace, we need to begin by internalizing three notions that were uncontroversial to them, but have fallen out of favor in recent times:

Spirituality is more than inward bliss.

Spiritual pursuits are efforts to attach one's self to an actualized purpose. This inspires actions that will lead to greater communal connections and creative outcomes. To suggest that turning on our spiritual faculties requires us to somehow detach ourselves from the challenges of the material world relegates spirituality to those who dwell in the temples, or high on the mountains. Passive stances are fine on occasion, but cannot be the dominant frame for spirituality. When we seek meaning, connection, and wonder in contemporary work, we need to be encouraged to be assertive, reactive, and cooperative.

Ethics is more than altruism.

Actions that emerge from meaningful work will differ from what we generally regard as the sphere of the moral, like altruism and self-sacrifice. Purposeful work will even demand qualities and character traits that do not, at first glance, have overtly moral significance. These traits can include an entrepreneurial tolerance for risk, an innovative spirit, or a mathematical mindset. Ethics is an urgent call to action in the fast-paced competitive landscape of modern business. Every work decision has ethical implications and bears enormous responsibility. Meeting this burden requires drawing on a wide variety of skill sets and abilities, but most importantly it involves recognizing that every moral action we take binds us to someone else.

Work is more than passive adherence.

Spiritual work changes us, the environment in which we work, and all those who come in contact with us. It is a cooperative endeavor that serves both an ethical and spiritual purpose. As such, it is not about falling in line with higher powers, be they human or divine, but creating new value as co-creators and disrupting old power structures.

We need to start thinking about how we can tell the best possible story of what we do every day in work. We need to explain why it is a good-faith activity, rooted in meaning, fostering connection, and inspiring wonder. And if our work is not a good-faith activity, we need to make it become one. It's time to reflect deeply on how business activities are changing the world we live in – for better or worse – and how we can use our work activities to shape the world we want.

If this sounds like a radical exercise, that's because it is. Capitalism as we know it will be reformed by the actions of spiritual work. If not, it will disappear and be replaced by something wholly new and other that centers relational capital. To use the term coined by media theorist Douglas Rushkoff, the future belongs to those fighting to reclaim *team human*: "The simplest way to understand and change our predicament is to recognize that being human is a team sport. We cannot be fully human, alone. Anything that brings us together fosters our humanity. Likewise, anything that separates us makes us less human, and less able to exercise our will."

The Millennial Dilemma

Despite the findings that the vast majority of us continue to carry an internalized sense of how deeply essential our spiritual faculties are to worldly sense-making, many of us do not see much potential for developing these faculties in the context of our work lives. What are we doing with this widely prevalent desire for spirituality? How do spiritual activities manifest in the digital age? Do most of us treat our spiritual faculties as if they were controlled by an on/off switch, employing a transcendent perspective in some arenas of our endeavors but not others? Just how much of the day is allowed to be imbued with a spiritual hue? Most importantly, are those of us who know how important spirituality is taking the time to craft a dedicated space to find this necessary fulfillment while engaged in work? These are urgent questions with serious implications for the overall health of our society and all of its working members. But of great concern are the struggles of one critical demographic cohort in particular: the millennial generation.

Millennials are the largest generational segment currently in the workforce. They are expected to make up a full 75 per cent of workers before the end of the decade. Their entry into working life coincided with the recession and years of slow growth that followed; as a consequence, millennials experienced less economic growth in their first decade of work than any other generation of North American post-industrial workers. They have lower real incomes and fewer assets than previous generations at comparable ages, as well as higher levels of debt. They are the next generation of leaders, and they have even less reason than their predecessors to see the positive spiritual possibilities of work.

Recent research shared in "The Deloitte Global Millennial Survey 2019" has uncovered that millennials have an increasingly gloomy view about their potential to discover meaning, purpose, or connection within their working lives. Millennials say they are unhappy with traditional social institutions, mass media, slow social progress, their work, government, business leaders, and social media. Millennials are also reluctant to trust current leaders, particularly those who run companies that are not aligned with their values or political views.

Millennials perceive corporations as entities determined to increase their organizational power through whatever means necessary and accumulate wealth that is generally deployed for exploitive ends. They do not view corporations as institutions whose human membership may pull the levers of corporate power with a careful consideration of the consequences for societal welfare. In fact, only slightly more than half of millennials (55 per cent) reported believing in even the possibility of business having a positive impact in our contemporary capitalist society. And this number is six percentage points lower than findings from a year earlier, indicating the possibility of a continuing downward trend of cynicism and disconnect.

Perhaps most striking in this survey is the disclosure that a full 49 per cent of working millennials stated an intention to quit their current jobs within the coming two years. As if that were not enough of a potential economic disruption, requiring the development of a well-considered policy response and accompanying corporate action, it was also revealed that a quarter of the same respondents reported actually having left an employer within the past two years. Only 28 per cent of millennials said they would remain with their employer for at least five years. Think about what this means for the future of work and the instability this trend will bring to an already historically unprecedented disruptive business environment.

And now, on top of all the challenges brought by the first two decades of the twenty-first century, the 2020 Great Pause introduced a new subgroup into this cohort: Generation C, the cohort coming into their own in the shadow of the COVID-19 pandemic. This group includes those who were finishing their degree programs, who recently graduated, or who were in their first post-graduation jobs as the pandemic lockdown took hold. These youngsters are uniquely vulnerable to the effects of a short-term catastrophe, as people in this group are most likely to see their careers derailed and finances crushed. Given the depressing lived reality of such a substantive share of our workforce, it is wholly reasonable to wonder if our contemporary work lives are inherently at odds with the drive for spiritual purpose. Can work today still be approached as something with significant spiritual potential?

The answer has to be yes. As noted in the discussion above, a deficit of trust seems to be at the heart of millennial discontent with capitalism and work. If they don't trust business leaders to concern themselves with principles other than greed and self-enrichment, if they don't trust corporations to use their power in a manner that exhibits concern with social welfare, then why would they commit to being loyal participants in such a fundamentally broken enterprise?

Millennials are not alone in observing that businesses have become consumers of trust rather than producers. Businesses today face complex problems in a fast-moving environment that requires the sort of sophisticated human interactions that put judgment and reaction at the foreground as well as trust, commitment, and a well-honed sense of purpose. They need employees who are seasoned and secure to optimally represent the organization, but don't offer the opportunity for a sufficient amount of folks to become so.

In sum, there is a deficit of trust that is unlikely to be reversed anytime soon. The largest demographic cohort in our workforce feel massively disconnected. They are increasingly, and justifiably, pessimistic about the possibility of our economic system delivering on its promise of social betterment. Something has to change – and soon – or the system will fall apart. If there is even to be a hope of getting things back on track, we need to demonstrate that work can, should, and needs to be a spiritual practice. We need a coherent spiritual strategy.

The Path Forward

This book is organized to systematically address the three pillars of a spiritual experience: meaning, connection, and wonder. We just explained why a spiritual experience involving meaning, connection, and wonder is so important today. The coming chapters will guide readers on how we can link our physical, mental, and emotional faculties in a practical way that will support better decision-making, encourage the development of new social ties, offer a novel lens for the way to see work, and open up a new method for cooperating.

Part I of the book is entitled "Meaning in Work." We will start by exploring three of the most historically influential approaches to finding meaning in work. Of the three, mindfulness poses a unique challenge as it represents the dominant contemporary paradigm for spirituality at work. And so, we will spend some time discussing how to undo the "mindful*mess*" that many of us find ourselves in.

The next chapter will lay out the case for why meaning is more likely to be found by doing spiritual work than by being spiritual. We will look at the power and limits of our reactive faculties, paying particular attention to the Jewish spiritual ideal that doing is necessarily prior to being.

From there, we will explain in detail how ordinary actions invite the sacred through an outward-focused spiritual framework. We will consider the Jewish concept of *mitzvah* and how a moment of *doing* can create a space for *being* while binding us to act as responsible members of a wider cooperative community.

Part II of the book is entitled "Connecting through Work." We will explore the tactic of approaching cooperation as a transformative encounter. Oftentimes, when management gurus talk about cooperation, what they really mean is self-sacrifice. Cooperation in this paradigm is contingent on us repressing ourselves. In contrast, the type of cooperation we will present as spiritually motivated is a transformational activity of co-creation.

Building on these ideas will lead us to a consideration of the political realm. Engendering transformational cooperation is rooted in a sense of responsibility for others – the "we." As many in the liberal West reject this political tradition in favor of a more exclusionary us-versus-them populism of the left or right, we will show how those disillusioned by recent political events can still find their power and lead transformational cooperative change designed to build something of meaning for us to pass down to future generations.

We will then shift our attention to the economic realm and propose a version of what might be called "connected capitalism." We will show how *mitzvahs* can repair capitalism and look closely at the spiritual work involved in offering financial services, radically transparent markets, and infrastructure for the common good.

Part III of the book is entitled "Wonder at Work." We will instruct on reigniting curiosity, the first step in seeking wonder, outlining how we can shift from feeling afraid to step outside of our familiar social bubbles to instead staying curious, open-minded, and engaged with those outside our in-groups. Critical here is rejecting the notion that verbal exchanges need to end with a winner or loser. We will also make the case for why the elusive feeling of wonder can be actualized in the context of spiritual work.

We will continue the prescriptions of how to enact wonder at work with what logically follows – forgiveness. If civil discussion between people who disagree with each other must shift – evolving from a near impossibility to a regular necessity – we must learn how to forgive those who have exploited their economic power or supported what we believe are immoral political stances. Contemporary psychology offers rationales for forgiveness that have an inward emphasis on personal wellness. But this is not a strategy for thinking about forgiveness in a substantive way. We can't forgive all transgressions. We need to forgive, but we need to do it in a skilled and thoughtful way.

The book will close on the optimistic note that wonder inspires and hope follows. Whether the question is what is best for my family or what is best for our industry, we no longer have access to a formula for bottom-line calculations because of the rate of change. But there is a solution: learn from ancient Jewish spiritual traditions. The spiritual arena is far more than inward bliss. Work is more than exploitation. Every action we take has the potential to transform. Collectively, the prescriptions for action described throughout this book make up a strategy for hope, concerned with engaging in work in ways that change us, the environment in which we work, and all those who come in contact with us. This spiritual work will allow us to find meaning, connection, and wonder in our everyday.

PART ONE

Meaning in Work

1
Mindful*mess*

Spiritual Work in the Recent Past

In the minds of many who are struggling to find meaning, connection, and wonder in their everyday, work – particularly in a capitalist context – is framed as an activity which is antithetical to spiritual expression. As we struggle with the question of how to bring the holiness our ancestors associated with sacred time and space into our contemporary lives, whether consciously or unconsciously, cooperative value-creating work is rarely centered as a possible solution.

Over the coming pages, I hope to change that perception. Appreciating the spiritual possibility of work has the potential to force a rethink of the question of how best to raise up the not insignificant part of our lives that has been holding us down. When engaged in spiritual work, we should be able to thrive amidst the chaos and disruption of our capitalist economy. But getting there requires a significant paradigm shift. We need to completely move away from the idea of work as managing people and things, and instead see it as cooperative partnerships of value creation. Being reactive and assertive can be spiritual, so long as the intentions are not to be controlling and exploitive. We need not be in a passive state to find spiritual peace. Ironically, the global pandemic of 2020 may have helped get us closer to this point as the work of grocery store clerks, delivery people, and factory workers were finally recognized as the critical source of social value creation they always were.

But before a new model rooted in the wisdom of ancient Judaism is presented, it's important to understand the existing paradigms. We need to assess both the strengths and weaknesses of past approaches to meaning in work to figure out what is missing. There have been a number of approaches that have been successful in linking work to spiritual goals in Western capitalist societies. These frameworks, to varying degrees, have given practitioners a motivating sense of something more than the ordinary.

What do they have in common? How widespread has their adoption been? Let's look at three of the most historically influential spiritual paths to meaning that have been embraced by significant numbers of twenty-first-century workers: a religious calling, secular workism, and mindfulness.

1. Work as a Religious "Calling"

During the Industrial Revolution, a work ethic was developed by adherents of the Protestant branch of Christianity that aimed to bring spiritual meaning to the workplace through the concept of a "calling." In the Christian Bible, the word "call" is used most often to refer to God's initiative to bring people to participate in the redemptive effort of a religious practice. By extension, God is seen as issuing a call for people to engage in particular types of work. As such, the "calling" construct can be understood as a somewhat technical term with specific application in the Christian faith. As it is understood by believers, God summons righteous people of faith, and they respond by taking religiously motivated action. In this instance, the believer is meant to contemplate what sort of particular job or type of work they are being called to do, commit to it fully, and see their calling as a source of meaning.

Sociologist Max Weber argues that this was a radical innovation, accelerating the introduction of modern capitalism. For while many other, even ancient, cultures may have recognized the value of routine activity, they did not elevate work to the same extent as the Protestants. What was portrayed as new in the introduction of the Protestant Work Ethic was the idea that the highest moral activity which a religious individual could undertake was to be devout in doing their everyday job.

Furthermore, the spiritual value of work was not contingent on its nature. Work as a calling meant that God wanted every individual to engage in the unique activities that they alone were sent to do. It does not matter whether it was the physical work of a laborer employing their hands or the intellectual work of a teacher who draws on their mind. The meaning emerged not from the specifics of the work, but from doing what God wanted the faithful individual to do.

Every calling was of the exact same moral worth from the perspective of divine judgment. As such, devout Protestants saw in their work a command of God to fulfill the particular duties imposed on them. They found deep meaning simply by remaining in their station. After all, they were answering their particular calling. God had indicated the appropriate place for them, and they were content to remain there for their entire lives.

The Protestant Work Ethic held people responsible for doing their best at these worldly stations rather than disengaging from the world in a quest for perfection. Although the ethic thus gave meaning to the workplace, researchers who study the history of spirituality and religion in this context observe that this move also emboldened those at the top of the hierarchical order to exercise autocratic rule and power. These were not efforts of co-creation. Those at the top of organizations were emboldened to exploit and control their devout workforce. Spiritual purpose was used as a management tool designed to minimize employee conflict and resistance to work. In other words, those who took their calling seriously were susceptible to exploitation by the powerful, not just God, who wanted to keep them at work and in line.

According to David W. Miller, director of the Princeton University Faith and Work Initiative, the next unique Christian push for meaning in work came in the first half of 1900s, when Americans saw the rise of the Social Gospel. Christians were encouraged to address both personal and societal change by entering the business realm and transforming it from the inside. Then in the latter half of the twentieth century, there was the rise of the Ministry of the Laity among Protestants, where laypeople were motivated to use their work in the everyday world to spread a religious message of meaning.

The Social Gospel emphasized how the ethical teachings of the Bible could help fix the emerging problems driven by the growth of capitalism. Leaders of the Social Gospel prioritized the biblical message of "love thy neighbor as thyself." They believed that their calling was to create systemic changes to oppressive political structures. And there were significant successes attributed to this movement. They supported legislation for an eight-hour workday, the abolition of child labor, and government regulation of business monopolies. The Social Gospel belief that religious faith must be committed to the transformation of social structures empowered workers with a higher sense of meaning in their everyday lives.

2. The Secular Ethic of Workism

We are currently witnessing what has been labeled by writer Derek Thompson in *The Atlantic* as "workism," defined as "the belief that work is not only necessary to economic production, but also the centerpiece of one's identity and life's purpose." As recently as forty years ago, those with the highest incomes took on fewer working hours than those in the middle of the income scale or at the bottom. Today the most prosperous members of the workforce are logging longer hours than both poorer men in the United States and rich men in similarly rich countries. They are finding that meaning only comes through work, and thus seek more, not less of it, even as they experience great success.

This shift to working more as one becomes more affluent and successful is in opposition to economic logic and economic history. The rich have always worked less than the poor, because the historic logic was that if you had the financial means to increase your leisure time, you would certainly take advantage of it. But this is not the case amongst those who find meaning in workism.

In fact, this new ethos was spreading across gender and age prior to the Great Pause of 2020. In a recent Pew Research report, 95 per cent of teens reported that finding meaning at work is more important as an adult ambition than having a family or being kind. We are thus seeing a secular return to the Protestant notion of work as a calling.

3. Mindfulness in the Workplace

In a complementary secular move, corporate giants like Google, Apple, McKinsey, and Nike, to name a few, have made great efforts to address the spiritual need for meaning in their workist employees by making mindfulness part of their corporate culture.

The Wisdom 2.0 conference attracts leaders from Facebook, Twitter, LinkedIn, and PayPal annually to talk about "mindful management" with thousands of well-heeled seekers. For the masses, Headspace offers mindfulness coaching delivered through apps, generating over $100 million in revenue a year. Even General Mills has now added meditation rooms to its buildings. Clearly, thinking about spiritual meaning at work is still considered to be of the utmost importance, even in our secular post-truth age of information.

The billion-dollar mindfulness industry has not so subtly changed the way a substantial amount of Westerners think not only about spiritual meaning in particular, but how we *think* in general. Yet, despite the growing "success" that is the cultural phenomenon of mindfulness, the question needs to be asked: Is mindfulness the most effective cognitive framework for finding meaning in all experiential contexts? Does the mindfulness toolkit work as well in, for example, corporate settings as it does on wellness retreats? And is this approach any more empowering than the Protestant Work Ethic? Or is it another tool of control with an upgraded feature of lowering the likelihood of burnout?

While there is an important place for mindfulness in mainstream Western culture, I will argue that an inward, passive, non-judgmental approach to uncovering meaning is insufficient for our current working needs. Making effective decisions in the fast-paced and always changing contemporary work environment does require drawing on spiritual faculties in addition to rational and calculative faculties, particularly as we need to improvise through a great deal of unknowns. And mindfulness, a spiritual system honed by those who idealized a monastic life, is not well-equipped to help us navigate cooperative endeavors such as modern work.

At its core, mindful meditation is about developing the ability to be present without judgment or reaction. But workers seeking meaning need to hone the ability to react, especially in exploitive and disruptive environments. We cannot afford to let our spiritual instincts be less productive than our other instincts. And even those of us at the top of our workplace hierarchies should want something more. For we can be Zen in the economic arena if other, "less enlightened" people are actively innovating and bringing us opportunities from which we can calmly select. But why not inspire the whole constellation to be spiritually reactive? Why not look for co-creative partners?

Can We Work with Passivity?

The difficulty in supporting any of these three approaches is that they fail to robustly offer a satisfactory path to the three pillars of a spiritual experience articulated in our introduction. If work is to inspire *meaning*, it needs to be understood as a practice of more than passive adherence. In other words, finding meaning at work has to be an active, not passive, exercise. Furthermore, if there is to be *connection*, spiritual work must encourage the development of new partnerships. And finally, if there is to be *wonder*, then spiritual work must change the worker and everyone in their environment. As such, spiritual work as we are defining it cannot be framed as a peaceful falling in line to hierarchical powers, be they human, divine, or even the oneness of being.

Each of the three historical paradigms for spiritual work proves insufficient for our purposes due to the underlying premise of passivity that informs all of them in a surprisingly similar way. The paradigms of spiritual meaning on offer here are not the promise of boundless potential. To the contrary – each of these systems asks the struggling seeker to embrace a very narrow sense of meaning, a controlling type of connection, and no lasting sense of wonder.

This is unfortunate, because the gap which spiritual work needs to fill is wide. A religious calling requires workers to accept the limitations of their station and trust in a divine plan. A workist calling insists that workers disregard their all-too human need for social connection and seek every manner of fulfillment solely through their vocation. Mindfulness tells workers to disregard their reactive instincts and just be where they are, even if where they are is exploitive. The message in each of these spiritual systems is a variance of the same: work, pray/aspire/breathe, and carry on. That is enough. But is it?

Those who find meaning in their calling and faith will continue to do so, and that is beautiful and admirable. My goal is not to proselytize for any faith tradition, but to find tools that can be widely applied. In the context of wide applicability, approaches rooted in passivity, in a "know your role" philosophy, are not likely to help the contemporary seeker raise up what is currently holding them down. These tools are not enough to transform ordinary work into a practice of excellence. They will not motivate the radical actions needed to reform our oppressive capitalist system into one of broad multifaceted value co-creation. Remember the twofold problem identified earlier: work is both more demanding and less rewarding than in generations past. We need another model to help us find meaning, connection, and wonder in work.

The Rise of Workplace Passivity

How did we get to this point? How did a spirituality of non-reaction and a paradigm of passivity come to dominate a work life that demands assertiveness? "Be patient and let things be" is a spiritual strategy. It is a cognitive framework that helps practitioners find meaning and purpose amidst the chaos and suffering of everyday existence. But what of a Jewish approach that might be labeled as "react and enact the world you desire"? It is no less a viable spiritual strategy for navigating life's everyday challenges than letting things be. However, accepting this strategy requires something of a paradigm shift. For it takes at its roots the first necessary, but unpopular, idea shared in the introduction: internalizing the notion that spirituality is so much more than a state of inward bliss.

Both of these strategies, passivity and reaction, have the potential to change the way we work, albeit in very different ways. Any spiritual strategy is of course better than none at all. But a starting point for using spiritual tools to acquire meaning and hopefully instigate social change as a consequence is an openness to reconceptualizing our understanding of the sacred.

Enacting meaning, connection, and wonder within our work will require us to link our physical, mental, emotional, and spiritual faculties. A spiritual lens can support better strategic decision-making and indicate the path toward a new way of thinking about work in a disruptive environment. Is one of the two spiritual strategies denoted above more pragmatically suited for living in an era typified by disruption, complexity, and ever-changing information?

With no promise of balance, we find ourselves in something of a "mindful*mess*." Our economic system increasingly seems to help entrench the few to exploit the many. The political arena is facing a rising tide of populist revolts and authoritarian responses. And our culture is allowing technology to infringe on every aspect of our being, with platforms designed to control and isolate us, as artificial intelligence is advanced to replace us. What could be a spiritual response to these enormous challenges?

In the early days of capitalism, Westerners adopted the perspective of a religious "calling" to find meaning. Now, many are turning to a secular form of Buddhist mindfulness for that same end. Some of the world's biggest firms have incorporated a version of mindful meditation into their corporate routines. Leaders within these firms hope that mindfulness will offer a way to transcend the increasing stress/depression and decreasing focus/motivation amongst their organizational members. And in many ways, the outcomes of these efforts are not all that different from what was concerning about the religious "calling." Namely, they are starting to look a lot like management tools designed to minimize employee conflict and resistance to work.

How widely has mindfulness penetrated American corporate culture? A recently conducted National Health interview survey of the US workforce found nearly one in six white-collar workers reported engaging in some form of mindfulness-based practice over the previous year. This is an astonishing number. It represents a twofold increase in corporate participation in mindfulness programs in the past decade alone.

Advocates of mindfulness in the workplace believe that the practice can address multiple workplace wellness needs, benefiting both employees and employers. But there is a critical, and increasingly questionable, assumption behind these now common assertions. Specifically, those boosting mindfulness as a corporate cure-all assume a positive direct relationship between the Buddhist sense of meaning or well-being and workplace productivity. While there is a demonstrable link between mindfulness and stress reduction for some people (but not all), this overemployed tool may offer nothing more than that.

As we will see below, the research findings are decidedly mixed. One recent critical study suggests that mindfulness meditation may, in fact, not be the best way to increase our motivation at work. If correct, this would be particularly disappointing for those who view spirituality as yet another lever of managerial control. And another, randomized controlled study of mindfulness training in the workplace found reduced work/life conflict and increased job satisfaction, but that's it. Which means that even if mindfulness does what it claims to do, that is not enough to make contemporary work spiritually fulfilling. Where is the meaning? The sense of connection? The feeling of wonder?

None of this is surprising, as mindful workplace techniques are cribbed from an ancient monastic tradition disinterested in the needs of householders. And by the way, this spiritual tradition idealized something other than the tranquil bliss that is marketed as the primary outcome of mindful meditation today – a detached state of alertness is not synonymous with how most of us define bliss. And so, we need to critically explore the current Western obsession with mindfulness. We need to ask whether we are demanding that this cognitive framework offer something it was not designed for. There is no doubt that new technologies which demand constant attention and increase anxiety are creating a mental health crisis for which mindful meditation offers a partial solution. But is this a useful path to meaning in contemporary work?

The mindfulness teaching of non-reaction does not increase motivation, inspire curiosity, lead to superior decision-making under uncertainty, help in calculating opportunity costs and trade-offs, support greater agility, direct apportion of risk, harness the capacity for innovation, or offer direction in the management of change.

In other words, we may feel "better" and less stressed while not making effective decisions. And more importantly, especially for those in the earlier stages of professional advancement, we find work utterly purposeless, often feeling lonely and finding denizens of our workspace to be lacking in empathy. Telling me to take an hour in a meditation room, delightful as that break may be, will not make me view work as uplifting. But inviting me in as a cooperative partner might.

The Many Meanings of Mindfulness

Let's take a step back. What are we talking about when we discuss a spiritual strategy of mindfulness? The mindfulness concept has been adopted in so many different, even oppositional, contexts that it is often hard to tell. To be honest, it is not always clear if there is much more than the most superficial of links between applications.

Mindfulness has become more of a brand than a coherent practice. The concept has been manipulated to serve the interests of a host of diverse agendas. Most notorious are the individuals who have come to exploit spiritual language from a position of questionable intent. It is therefore imperative to clarify what precisely is under consideration when we look at the possibility of mindfulness as a workplace tool for spirituality.

Outside of a rigorous Buddhist practice, mindfulness on its own does not offer the larger-scale transcendence that a spiritual strategy designed for the needs of ordinary life can. More importantly, mindfulness is not giving the largest working cohort the sense of connection that can build the type of reciprocal trust so desperately needed for modern endeavors to succeed in a manner that benefits our increasingly fragmented society. Mindfulness has become a billion-dollar industry with widespread corporate application, and yet, as the data has shown, millennials who are building their careers under the guidance of mindful HR are less satisfied at work than any generation before them.

We need to undo the mindful*mess* that has come to dominate contemporary discussions of spirituality in the workplace. We need to critically explore whether our cultural gatekeepers have convinced us to seek relief in a manner that is antithetical to making better strategic decisions, encouraging creative cooperative endeavors, and coping with our disruptive world. We don't want our negative feelings to be managed or momentarily subdued. We want to reform the system that holds us down.

Where Is the Buddhism?

Mindfulness originated as a Buddhist construct. While most contemporary mindfulness advocates are offering a secular approach detached from its religious roots (which comes with its own difficulties, as we will see shortly), we cannot hope to understand the benefits or limits of this tool without first recognizing that it was developed hundreds of years ago as a central piece of Buddhist mental training.

Classical Buddhist accounts of mindfulness highlight clear-minded attention to an awareness of what is perceived in the present. The secular heirs to Buddha's mindfulness believe that this strategy can help us find meaning, and thus make us happier at work. They generally do not feel the need to preach the Four Noble Truths – of suffering, its cause, its end, or the path that leads there. Instead, they find it sufficient to note the single truth that our workday is full of stressors that take a significant toll on our well-being. We have been socialized into believing that we cannot stop while we are on the clock. Learning secular mindfulness is presented as a life hack that tells our brain that it is OK to do nothing. Sometimes, the best response to a challenging situation is to focus on our breath until mental peace finds us.

Jon Kabat-Zinn, founding executive director of the Center for Mindfulness in Medicine, Health Care, and Society at the University of Massachusetts Medical School, and probably more responsible than anyone else in mainstreaming the secular version of mindfulness, describes mindfulness as an "umbrella term" for a collection of practices and personal values that enable one to live mindfully. He notes that the "terminology and emphasis have always changed over time as the Dharma entered new cultures, and this is happening once again in our era."

As a Buddhist practitioner himself, Kabat-Zinn recognized that there was a risk in removing mindfulness from its Buddhist context and giving it undue emphasis as the only important element in what is at essence a spiritual practice. However, he reflects that had his mindfulness-based stress reduction (MBSR) program employed traditional Buddhist language, it might have prevented these concepts from ever taking root in secular Western culture.

A Trait, a Path, or a Process?

The umbrella term of mindfulness has made its way into contemporary work culture via the field of psychology and the wellness industry. In experimental and clinical psychology, the term "mindfulness" tends to mean one of three things: it can be a mental trait; it can be a spiritual path conceived in health-promotion terms; or it can be a single cognitive process commonly trained across multiple activities. A growing number of researchers are making the argument that mindfulness is best thought of as a variety of cognitive processes.

Rather than trying to pin down the specific motivations or beliefs behind individual decisions to start looking at the world through the lens of mindfulness, it may be worthwhile to instead focus on where the mindful practitioner ends up from a cognitive perspective. In which case, it may be most helpful to understand mindfulness as a cognitive tool that inspires mental processes that may have different names but similar behavioral outcomes. For example, some folks view mindfulness as a personality trait strongly associated with being aware, flexible, and generally relaxed. Others see mindfulness less as a trait and more of a spiritual exercise designed to cultivate well-being and lower stress.

Whether mindfulness is a trait, path, or process, the critical distinguishing feature that allows it to stand out from other traits, paths, or processes is its emphasis on attention united with an awareness of that attention. Let's take a moment to be technical and unpack these seemingly ordinary terms. "Attention" means taking notice of something. "Awareness" is the conscious registration of how that something has stimulated our five physical senses and the subsequent activities of our mind.

Most of us are not very good at controlling our attention. Our ability to focus attention on an object tends to be brief. Once stimulated, it is usually a very short time before we experience a cognitive or emotional reaction to the thing that has drawn our attention. We perceive, focus for a moment or so if we're lucky, and then we judge. We judge whether the thing that has captured our attention is good or bad, beneficial or harmful, novel or mundane, and so on. Furthermore, we often base these reactive judgments on our past experiences. As such, when something draws our attention, it also begins a process where labels and judgments are imposed on whatever it is we are encountering.

The essence of mindfulness is not found simply in a focused attention. To be attentive is a necessary, but insufficient, condition of mindfulness. The uniqueness of mindfulness is being cognizant of our attentive state. We are paying attention. And we are aware that our mind is paying attention. Which means we are also paying attention to the process of judgments that may instinctively follow. And we observe our observing, without falling into the trap of being distracted by the processes that move us away from the focused attention.

If we try and simplify this idea, we can say that a further definition of this umbrella term is understanding mindfulness as attention to and awareness of present events and experience. Meaning emerges from this awareness. We are trying to retain our focus on the current stimulus that has drawn our attention, as it is. Mindfulness is a tool in support of not clouding our experience of in-the-moment perception with the biases of past experiences and other distracting instinctual responses. With this definition, the classic understanding of mindfulness is retained, but it is also ambiguous enough to allow for the breadth of ways in which the mindfulness idea has come to manifest in modern corporate culture.

Can We Find Ultimate Meaning without First Inferring It in Our Experiences?

Now that we have a better understanding of what mindfulness might be, we need to return to the original question: If spirituality is more than inward bliss, and more about connectivity, is secular mindfulness the best spiritual strategy for finding meaning at work? If what we want are partnership opportunities for co-creation, will peace and quiet do? Before we answer that question, let's consider an unattributed ancient Zen parable.

In this tale, our hero is a hard-working farmer. For decades he toiled in his field. Critical to his work was a horse he kept that helped him pull the plough through the soil to create furrows, or the cart to collect and transport his harvest to the market. All was well for this decent soul until one day when his horse ran away.

To his community, this was perceived as a tragedy. How would he be able to continue to manage his farm without a horse? Friends and neighbors came to comfort the farmer in light of such an unfortunate happening. All they could say was "What bad luck ..." to which the farmer replied "Maybe ..." and went to bed.

The next morning the farmer arose to a surprising outcome. As he left his house to begin his daily work routine, he discovered that the horse had returned to his field. Not only was his trusty steed back, he had brought with him a band of wild horses.

The neighbors who had come to comfort the farmer the previous evening saw this as a fortuitous turn of events. What good fortune has unfolded in the farmer's life! For now, the farmer would be able to continue to tend to his field. On top of that, his assets had increased substantively. And with this attitude the neighbors came to his field to congratulate him and express their joy at what was clearly a momentous break of good fortune. All the farmer said once again was "Maybe ..."

Well, the next day the farmer's son decided that he was going to try and tame these wild horses. He grabbed a saddle, placed it on the back of one of the horses, and tried to ride the dominant mare of the band. This horse was having none of it and immediately threw the lad hard to the ground, causing him to break his leg. The neighbors again came to offer their sympathy on the misfortune that had befallen the farmer's family. "Maybe ..." was the farmer's only response.

As it came to pass, a few days later the village in which the farm was located was targeted for selection by military drafters. Stern officers came searching house to house for able-bodied youths who would be recruited into the army and sent into battle. When this group came to the farm, they saw that the farmer's son was hobbled by a broken leg and so they let him be.

The neighbors could not believe the good fortune that this farmer and his family continued to enjoy. Ultimately, everything had been for the best, and they congratulated the farmer on how well things had turned out. "Maybe ..." said the farmer.

What is the best strategy for finding meaning, connection, and wonder at work? Is it found in the farmer's practice of non-judgment? There is certainly wisdom in this approach. As finite and fallible beings, we really don't know when there is an "end" to what we perceive as a connective or causal narrative. Given our bounded rationality, we cannot predict the ultimate outcomes of events we set in motion. The only thing we can be certain about is the limits of our certainty. The farmer found great peace in accepting the limits of his predictive ability. He accepted each day as it was, whether it brought good news or bad. He observed what unfolded without judgment, and went about his work.

Contemporary work demands that we be motivated, curious, and agile, while comfortable with uncertainty, trade-offs, and risk. This aligns somewhat with the perspective of the farmer, although not completely. And where it departs is critical to success in the modern work environment. We recognize that we are operating in a field of uncertainty, and the ability to get to a stance of "maybe" is certainly valuable. But we also need to aspire to reach beyond the maybe. We need to be curious enough to want to take risks, to make trade-offs, to react despite the reality of "maybe." Maybe is passive. It suggests things happen to us. Such a constricted perspective offers a very limited sense of meaning. Meaning is achieved through being active, not passive.

The cognitive orientation associated with reaction has the technical label of a "conceptual processing mode." In this orientation, which is the central cognitive paradigm in achieving our goals at work, it is thought and analysis that dominate our attention. Unlike the farmer in the Zen parable, we observe the events that happen to us during our workday and we also judge in order to discern meaning. We judge with frequency, we judge with haste, and we judge not only despite the uncertainty but precisely because of uncertainty.

Throughout our ordinary work encounters, we tap into a constant noisy stream of thoughts. Our mind is engaged in a rapid operational system of constant evaluation and interpretation. It is not enough to sit at work and perceive without judgment. The mindfulness of the farmer represents something quite different than what we do at work. For even when we may say "maybe," we still worry and dwell on the possibilities of what might be coming next.

The practice of non-judgment, the cognitive frame for mindfulness, involves what is termed "experiential processing." In this orientation, we are paying careful attention to the thought or emotion itself in a registering of the facts observed. Experiential processing means we are looking at the phenomena as it is, without any immediate attempts to derive meaning from it. My horse has run away. I breathe. I observe a feeling of concern for my future, but let it go. My horse has returned. I breathe. I observe a feeling of relief, but let it go. In experiential processing, common psychological content like the mental images we create with our imagination, the conversations we have with ourselves to try and make sense of a confusing situation, or even our impulses to act rooted in evolutionary instinct can be observed as part of the ongoing stream of consciousness.

This paradigm has sometimes been referred to as "decentering," as it involves attending to experiences within a wider context of awareness. The farmer just viewed his thoughts as thoughts. His neighbors, on the other hand, were constantly reacting to the events they were observing in the farmer's life. Each event was interpreted as bearing positive or negative implications for the farmer. His horse running away was a bout of bad luck. The subsequent return with a band of wild horses was a sudden turn of good fortune. They saw a narrative unfolding, while the farmer just took each moment as it came.

So why is the cognitive orientation of the farmer considered to be superior to that of his neighbors? Both the farmer and his neighbors were observing empirical events. They were both paying attention to the world around them. But the farmer had chosen to place a degree of mental distance or disengagement between the real events he was observing and his life's narrative. His inference of meaning from any of these events was limited.

In contrast, his neighbors were consumed by less grounded, less clear evaluations about the implications of these real events on the farmer's future and overall well-being. Advocates of mindfulness believe that the farmer's capacity to witness events, thoughts, and emotions as they play out with non-judgment positions him as better suited for dealing with the challenges of life. His neighbors will forever be burdened by the emotional rollercoaster of highs and lows as they constantly interpret their lived reality in a manner biased by memories, associations, and future projections. Thus, the real meaning emerges from staying above the fray of inference.

And so the questions remain: Does this type of cognitive framing work to make our lives more meaningful today? Can we be profoundly motivated, curious, and agile at work without embracing past associations or forecasts for the future? Is it even meaningful to talk about trade-offs or risk management without conceptual processing? And will these tools ultimately make us more docile in an exploitive economic arena?

Those who push for mindfulness as a spiritual work strategy insist that mindfulness is not antithetical to evaluation or judgment. They specify that in the state of alert attentiveness that characterizes mindfulness, evaluations, judgments, and associated memories can be closely attended to by a mind that is aware of what is happening moment to moment. But does this lead to better decision-making in a work context? Can one even imagine being so disconnected and distanced? And is that even desirable?

Evidence of Support from the Experts Is Limited

The short answer is No. If we are to be less than mindful for a moment, and impose a sense of judgment on some observable data, we are likely to conclude that the stated positive effects of mindful meditation are highly unreliable. What we know with certainty is that mindfulness can reduce stress, but no more so than simply sitting still does. But mindfulness also carries a risk of exacerbating depression, anxiety, and other negative emotions in certain people.

And while scientific and clinical research on mindfulness, meditation, and related constructs have dramatically increased in recent years, interpretation of these research results has been, to use a non-judgmental term, challenging. Researchers Richard Davidson from the University of Wisconsin–Madison and Alfred Kaszniak from the University of Arizona have enumerated an extensive list of difficulties. These include the challenges posed by intervention research designs in which true double-blinding is not possible; the nature of control and comparison conditions for research that includes mindfulness or other meditation-based interventions; issues in the adequate description of mindfulness and related trainings and interventions; the question of how mindfulness can be measured; questions regarding what can and cannot be inferred from self-report measures; and considerations regarding the structure of study design and data analyses.

But let's leave aside these technical difficulties in data interpretation. We can defer the methodological debates to the experts – because our concerns can be addressed more practically. Our goal is much simpler. We are seeking a tool that has the potential to support spiritual fulfillment in the context of our work lives. We are increasingly cynical about the possibility of our economic system delivering on its promise of social betterment, we don't trust those in power, and we need something to change. Can a mindfulness strategy be the driver of this much needed change? While this paradigm may work for a simple farmer of yore, it's not clear how it can be equally effective for a knowledge worker today. In fact, it seems designed to reinforce existing power structures.

This does not mean to imply that mindfulness is without its benefits in the workplace. For example, a mindfulness practice has been connected to an improvement in our ability to sustain our attention on a work task. It seems as if we can lower the likelihood of our mind wandering through a meditative practice. Mindfulness has also been demonstrated to allow us to better control our attention and support the economical use and allocation of our attentional resources. This too is a positive outcome. Our minds are among the most mysterious parts of ourselves, and any exercise that improves mental functioning should be explored. But how does better allocation of attentional resources make us happier at work? How does preventing our mind from wandering while working on a task bring meaning when we are being exploited?

To be fair, advocates for mindfulness have an answer, but it is somewhat unsatisfying. They argue that these qualities of attention are theorized to influence cognitive, emotional, and behavioral functioning. When we refine our capacity for attentiveness, we are also improving our mental ability to be flexible. When we are more flexible, we can better regulate our emotional responses to the events we observe, and can thus temper our behavior.

So we can concretely state that mindfulness appears to influence emotions via attention. From there, we can theorize that this in turn influences our selection of stimuli for observation, which then alters how the stimuli are evaluated and appraised, which ultimately shapes our emotional reactions. So, mindfulness may alter the life cycle of our emotional reactions, as well as the overall tone, meaning the positivity or negativity, of our emotional experiences.

In this manner, mindfulness can be seen as conferring superior self-regulation of behavior that shapes workplace functioning. In other words, if our work sucks then we won't be happier. But maybe we will be less quick to label is as "sucking." If we are being exploited, we won't find meaning. But maybe we will be more hesitant to decide that we are being "exploited." If we can't trust those around us, we won't feel connected, but maybe we'll change our criteria for trustworthiness and not rely on standards based in past experience. Is this really a good thing? To me, the answer is a resounding "NO!"

The research on mindfulness also suggests questionable findings about whether mindfulness detracts from our ability to set and pursue goals. Mindfulness implies a sense of non-striving and attention to present-moment events, which would appear to be at odds with the future orientation of goal setting. In 2018, researchers at the University of Minnesota enlisted hundreds of participants to try and answer that question by having a meditation coach instruct one group in mindfulness techniques while another group just let their minds wander. Both groups were then given a task to complete. The researchers found that the self-reported motivation levels to complete the task were lower in the group exposed to mindfulness than in the group that just sat around. They concluded that individuals focused on being present without judgment seem to have lower motivations to achieve certain goals than those who do not allocate time for meditation.

As a co-author of one of the studies, Andrew Hafenbrack, explains in a *Harvard Business Review* interview: "Meditators were less focused on the future and more relaxed, and thus less motivated, which should have dampened their performance. But some elements of their experiences were beneficial to it. In particular, meditation gave them a break from stress, obligations, and worries, which helped them concentrate on the next task better. When it came to performance, it seems that the negative effect of reduced motivation and the positive effect of increased task focus canceled each other out." On the other hand, and this twist should not be surprising, given the trend we have uncovered in this stream of research, mindfulness may support our pursuit of goals through improvement in – wait for it – attention.

It seems mindfulness practitioners show reduced work/life conflict, increased job satisfaction, and an increased ability to focus their attention. Those are certainly some nice outcomes. But they are of limited utility in equipping us to make better strategic decisions or cope better in our disruptive world. At its core, mindfulness is about passivity and looking inward. It does not improve motivation, inspire curiosity, support better decision-making, or calculate risk. And these are the traits that research in strategy has shown are most desperately needed in leaders today. Furthermore, it seems that mindfulness makes us more malleable for manipulation and exploitation. If someone were already suspicious about corporate intent, learning of a mindfulness wellness program would on the surface appear to be another tool of corporate control and worker manipulation. And today, work needs to be more than exploitation.

We cannot afford to let our spiritual instincts be less productive than our other instincts. Prior to the 2016 election, the Silent Thunder Order advised its readers that Zen philosophy requires them to be apolitical, arguing, "Those of us who hold it dear (Zen, not politics) do not want it besmirched with the mudslinging of realpolitik." I don't have the data to know how many Americans sat out that critical election because of this type of thinking, but even one would have been too many.

More recently, the Dalai Lama was asked to comment on the COVID-19 pandemic. He is one of the most inspiring figures on the planet, and his general message was a necessary and welcome reminder that it is natural to be filled with anxiety and fear in the face of an ongoing crisis. But what does this message offer in the way of guidance for those seeking a solution? The Dalai Lama shares: "I take great solace in the following wise advice to examine the problems before us: If there is something to be done – do it, without any need to worry; if there's nothing to be done, worrying about it further will not help." I believe that those of us in the West who do not identify as Buddhist may not find much value in this type of advice. It is not enough to be managed into silence and passivity.

Mindfulness is not a good spiritual path for the 99 per cent of us who need to make things happen for ourselves – the ones getting our hands dirty crafting deals and navigating the mudslinging. If mindfulness is far too limiting a spiritual paradigm for many of us, finding an alternate path becomes urgently necessary work. We need a new way of thinking about meaning, a more appropriate tactic for tackling our complicated times. And that approach to meaning can be found in a different ancient tradition.

2

Be Spiritual or Do Spiritual Work?

"Maybe" Means Saying "Yes" to Risk

Volkswagen is a firm that has vocally sought to bring mindfulness and non-judgment to its corporate culture. The company went beyond just offering meditation instruction and actually gave their employees specially designed smartphones that turned themselves off at 6:00 p.m. and came back on at 7:00 a.m. the next morning in order to help members of the organization in their quest to find inner peace.

Of course, as many of you will hopefully recall, Volkswagen is also the very same company that came up with another technologically innovative shut-off. They made the decision to install software in 11 million cars that would cheat on emissions tests, leading to what the *New York Times* labeled as one of the great corporate scandals of our age.

Cheating on emission tests enabled Volkswagen to sell their cars as offering better mileage and performance while saving the company money by negating the need for expensive pollution-control systems, all the while allowing Volkswagen to create and maintain the illusion of an ethical corporate persona. While the employees who made this decision likely had a better work/life balance than their peers at other automotive companies, this balance did not lead to superior long-term outcomes. Recent revelations demonstrate that the choice to cheat was made over a decade ago, and that senior members of Volkswagen's board of directors were made aware of the decision well before the public were informed, although ostensibly not after 6:00 p.m.

The Volkswagen scandal is not a story of whistleblowers. The company got caught. The mindfulness culture and better work/life balance did not lead to more ethical decisions, nor did it inspire a culture of ethical action or a sense of collective responsibility. Nobody in the organization was motivated to speak out on their own, or even to work from within to redirect the troubled culture. It is not at all apparent how a culture of mindfulness, even if it were done better, might have changed this outcome. We saw in the previous chapter an assessment of the claim that mindfulness may help support emotional regulation in the workplace. But would a better developed sense of non-judgment have led to more moral decision-making in the context of this scandal? It seems very unlikely to me … What was required were people with a more finely tuned and assertive sense of judgment, reaction, and responsibility – people who viewed themselves as partners in creating value not just for the company, but for all stakeholders.

The Volkswagen narrative is not unique. The global financial crisis is littered with examples of individuals ignoring risks in the pursuit of higher profits, while critical voices in favor of curbing risky behavior were either not in existence, or marginalized. Mindfulness does not help a worker assess risk or construct a persuasive narrative of a problematic culture as allegedly unconnected events start to unfold. Like the farmer in the Zen parable shared in the previous chapter, a framework of non-judgment simply encourages the practitioner to say "maybe" and passively let events out of their control take shape.

The behavior on display at Volkswagen, of workers seeking excessively risky opportunities in pursuit of personal gains when left to their own devices, and of boards of directors looking the other way in order to keep shareholders happy, is neither surprising nor novel. Classic economic theory suggests that we should, in fact, always expect workers to explicitly choose risky behavior if they perceive it to be in line with their personal interests.

A nuanced example of the complicated manner in which we assess risk can be found more recently in the open letter advocating for an anti-racist public health response to the 2020 demonstrations against systemic injustice in the midst of the COVID-19 pandemic. The publication of this letter led many conservative commentators to call out perceived hypocrisy in what they identify as ideological motivations. The signatories to the letter state that "we do not condemn these gatherings as risky for COVID-19 transmission. We support them as vital to the national public health and to the threatened health specifically of Black people in the United States." How is it that over 1,000 experts who advocated for policies prohibiting families from gathering for a funeral or visiting a dying loved one could now allow for tens of thousands to gather in protest as the pandemic continued?

In fact, this letter was evidence of the fact that public health experts think about the management of risk in the exact same manner as corporate executives and managers. Decision-makers tend to overestimate the good they and their institutions can do, while underestimating the harm they cause. So, when faced with a pandemic as the primary challenge, public health officials focused on possible "wins" for their intervention. If governments were to enact lockdowns on their advice, attention will be focused on "flattening the curve" as a metric of success. The acceptability of a risky alternative depends on the relation between the dangers and the opportunities reflected in the risk and some critical aspiration levels for the decision-maker. In this instance, the aspirations were a public health outcome superior to the projections. The ethical and social risks in this position (i.e., overall population health) were not as salient as reducing COVID infections.

So, how does this explain the shift in position of public health experts to contradict their earlier advice and support the protests? Sadly, the concerns raised by the Black Lives Matter movement are not new. The vast majority of Americans recognize that there is no denying the problematic ongoing reality of racism, particularly in policing. Thus, there is little cause for optimism on the part of public health experts in this instance, especially since they do not control the institution of policing. And so, given that broader society was turning to them for a signal on an issue of great social importance, and one which they do not have the tools to improve on, breaking the lockdown was seen as reasonable.

Integrating wellness, business, and social policy is a complex, multifaceted, long-term exercise. And a good chunk of it is work we will need to do for ourselves, as it is not within the power of policy-makers to create a less risky or volatile new world into which our society can emerge. Believing that the government can "fix" this and solve these problems will only exacerbate the long-term pain. Managing new levels of risk will be a key task, not only in shaping big-picture economic and societal health but also in tending to our personal well-being. And the path to achieving these ends will be through a holistic approach that integrates our rational/calculative faculties with our emotional and spiritual senses.

Which is exactly why it is so important to make risky behavior a spiritual task motivated by the higher goods of meaning, connection, and wonder, as opposed to greed and personal enrichment. It is not only the worker who benefits from a spiritual perspective but also our broader society. We all have a stake in Volkswagen, for example, doing the right thing; in public health officials offering sound medical guidance; in how our fellow citizens demand appropriate social reform; and in how powerful corporations enact change.

Moses and Buddha

The essential disagreement between advocates of mindfulness and the type of Jewish spirituality that forms the core of the model being developed in this book can be summarized as follows: In the search for meaning, do we focus on the limits of our reactive faculties, or on their power? Do we privilege passivity because so much is out of our control, especially in a contemporary work context, and because we believe that most of our efforts will end up being unproductive exercises in frustration anyway? Or do we boldly take action in the hope that it will bring about change?

Even more importantly, especially for those of us who are sympathetic to both paradigms, is the question of trade-offs. How much mental peace and, dare we say it, efficiency from non-reaction should we be prepared to give up in order to tap into the creative, albeit unpredictable, potential of spiritual action? Are there specific situations that demand we embrace more of one perspective over the other? Can we strike a balance?

To really gain an appreciation for the historic intellectual tension between these two competing views, let us now consider a pair of well-known spiritual tales crafted to inspire adherence to each of these respective paradigms. The first is from the Buddhist canon, while the second is a biblical narrative from Jewish historical mythology. Read these tales as thought experiments. Place yourself at the center of the narrative, and contemplate what you would do.

While there are many stories in each tradition with the same moral, the two parables below were selected because they share a thematic link, and thus can readily facilitate a fair and direct comparison. In each instance, the featured protagonist was tasked with attaining water to quench the thirst of someone in need. Yet each story provides a very different lesson about how we should respond to such demands, especially when made in an ever-changing external environment. When confronted with the need to make critical decisions and plan out a course of action, is it best to be passive in the face of uncertainty and forces perceived as being beyond our control? Or is it best to react and respond, even though the consequences of our actions may be unclear, inefficient, and not always optimal?

Let's start by recounting the often shared Zen story of Buddha walking along a stream with a few of his disciples. The group pauses and, deciding he's thirsty, Buddha asks the youngest in his entourage to go and get some fresh water from the stream, which he sets out to do. But as it happened, an ox cart was crossing through the stream at the time, kicking up dirt and muddying the water. Seeing that the water had become unfit for consumption, the youngster returns to Buddha and the rest of the group to let them know. Buddha smiles, and a half hour later, sends the same disciple back out to complete the task.

Buddha's eager pupil returns to the stream to find that the water is still muddy. Trekking once more to where Buddha has encamped, he offers the disappointing update. More time passes, and once again Buddha asks him to go back and fetch potable water. However, this time he finds the situation on the ground has changed.

The mud finally settled down to the floor of the stream, and the surface water is clean and clear. The disciple can now complete the task. And so, he fills a jug with fresh water and brings it to Buddha, who drinks and exclaims, "See what you did to make the water clean? You let it be, and the mud settled down on its own. Now you have clear water."

Buddha wanted to teach his disciples the power in embracing a type of thinking that was not yet natural to them: Respond, don't react. Be patient and let things be. Neither thirst nor agitation will speed up processes that we don't control, so we might as well let the feelings go as we wait for the world to resolve itself. Meaning emerges from knowing the limits of our powers.

Contrast this type of thinking with a well-known story from the Jewish tradition. After wandering the wilderness for forty years, the Israelites are on the verge of entering the Promised Land. Yet the mood is not joyous, but fearful. They have run out of water, and are lamenting as to why Moses would lead them out of Egypt to die miserably in the desert.

Moses races to the entrance of the Tent of Meeting to ask for divine guidance. God tells him to take his walking staff, gather the people, and speak to a sacred stone so that it will offer its water to all who thirst. Moses does as he's told, but with a twist. Instead of speaking, he uses his staff and smashes the stone twice. Water comes pouring out, allowing the Israelites to drink to their hearts' content.

Moses, a prophet revered by the three major monotheistic religions, wanted to model a cognitive framework significantly different from the type espoused by Buddha. He believed that there was no natural order or optimal path and we cannot simply wait for things to unfold on their own. Moses taught that we need to enact the results that we want through our creative efforts ... through our work. Moses also cared about his community, and we need to do the same. We need to be assertive, not passive, when faced with a challenge and when our community needs us to lead, even if the path of passivity will lead to its own resolution.

An astute reader might object to the surface reading of these stories, noting that the muddy water in the story of Buddha is a metaphor for our muddied minds. The real teaching is knowing how to pause our thoughts, even when we feel overwhelmed, even while at work, doing nothing but breathing until mental peace finds us. It is a cognitive strategy designed to mitigate the Buddhist truth of suffering. Meaning comes from this peace.

In a well-known Hasidic discourse delivered over one hundred years ago, Rabbi Shalom Dovber Schneersohn of Lubavitch explained that the story of Moses is also metaphorical. While some traditional scholars view Moses' actions as problematic, the fifth spiritual leader of Lubavitch casts his actions in a decidedly positive light. Basing his insight on the Kabbalistic text *Tikkunei Zohar*, Rabbi Shalom Dovber explained that the stone represents sacred wisdom. God wanted Moses to speak to the stone, symbolically letting wisdom come to those seeking it with clarity and ease. But Moses had a different spiritual plan – and he felt empowered to assert himself and directly challenge the divine plan. He believed that wisdom born of passivity would be of little value to the stiff-necked people under his care; if they were to encounter meaning in their lives, it would require both worldliness and the effort of work.

Smashing the stone in this biblical tale of reaction symbolized the idea that meaning starts off hidden, and is only revealed through work. The cognitive framework Moses wanted his people to embrace centers a spiritual imperative of uncovering the sacred within our ordinary surroundings. Moses' death before entering the Promised Land was a necessary consequence of this way of thinking, both in claiming a price on Moses and in forcing the Israelites to work harder to find meaning in their new, settled lives without Moses as a direct liaison to the divine. They had to figure out how, through effort that was spiritual and physical, to reveal meaning on their own.

Which of these two scenarios better mirrors the contemporary state of Western democratic capitalism in which we work? Is our current socio-political climate more like a disciples' stroll by a stream with a beloved mentor, or are we more like a fractured people lost and leaderless in the wilderness, uncertain about the viability of our natural resources and justifiably concerned that our terrifying future will be worse than our past?

There's another difference in these two paradigms that speaks loudly to the modern challenge of work. Buddha seems to be offering a style of leadership that may be described as micro-managing. Leaders today seeking to emulate him will want to manage, with compassion, the needs of their stakeholders. They would presume to know what can and cannot be changed, what their workers are feeling, and what actions are best to satisfy these feelings. It is a compassionate model, but still presumptive and hierarchical.

In contrast, Moses wanted to initiate a partnership. He wanted to encourage cooperation with what he described as his "stiff-necked people." Leaders looking to this paradigm would be less interested in tools of management, and more interested in techniques to encourage co-creation. He smashed the stone because implementing the divine plan was not his priority. He recognized that he and his people were in this together. If this was the more difficult path, so be it. From conflict will come meaning.

"Doing" versus "Being"

The substance of the point of departure between the differing spiritual paradigms of Buddha and Moses comes down to the question of whether the primary challenge for seekers of greater meaning is finding a way to *be* spiritual or to *do* spiritual things. In the first story shared above, Buddha was suggesting that the best way to get things done in a meaningful manner is by *being* in a spiritual state. The disciple had a task to complete. He needed to get clean water. But nothing he could do was going to get the water to be clear and drinkable any faster. The natural processes needed to run their course.

And so, Buddha's lesson was that meaning would emerge from knowing our small place in an interconnected world. It was best for the disciple to just *be*, to meditate with the group, and wait for the right time to arrive on its own accord, at which point the task could be completed and he could play his role. Agitation will not speed up processes that we are not in control of. Let go of these feelings and wait for the world to resolve itself.

Being mindful and present in each and every moment without judgment or agitation is an appealing cognitive strategy for coping with life's frustrations. In fact, it is a behavioral model that retains much of its power and resonance to this day, even among non-Buddhists. The muddy water metaphor is apt. There is much more dirt being kicked up in the digital age to pollute the streams of our consciousness than there may have been centuries ago.

As such, the cognitive tool taught by Buddha continues to prove to be timeless in its utility. Mindfulness meditation offers a path to pausing our thoughts when we feel overwhelmed. It is designed to mitigate the Buddhist truth of suffering, a view of life which many of us can sympathetically relate to. There is no disputing the fact that we'd all be better off if we incorporated mindful breathing into our toolkits for coping with the pressures of our disruptive times.

What is in dispute is whether or not our society is well served by the growing trend of advocating for a diluted approach to mindfulness as the only way to successfully bring the hunt for spiritual meaning to modern work settings. Passivity in the face of overwhelming chaos is one strategy. But it is not the only strategy.

For many in the West, spirituality has slowly, but noticeably, become increasingly absent from our working lives. There are, of course, demographic and behavioral factors that can explain this trend. As we as a society became less religious, made less time for our emotional needs, and let down our guard in defending an appropriate work/life balance, a new social reality emerged. And for a host of reasons, most of them either pragmatic or attributed to the entrepreneurial instincts of those interested in selling/monetizing mindfulness, companies that came around to recognizing the importance of spirituality in the workplace, with few exceptions, ended up embracing the paradigm of *being* spiritual through mindfulness and meditation.

This was a curious turn, as it is very clear that the vast majority of businesses today need their workers to embrace a cognitive mode that supports *doing*. We can only be successful in our work so long as we plan for the future, draw conclusions, interpret complex data, set and achieve goals, and focus on getting things done, mindfully or not. This is in opposition to the cognitive mode demanded by mindfulness.

Embracing mindfulness as a tool for meaning in work requires us to orient toward being and away from doing. But in the context of twenty-first-century work, this is a misdirection. We desperately need a spiritual framework that emphasizes reaction, or workers will continue to struggle in a manner similar to my friend at Google. They will want to embrace spiritual tools and resources to aid them in *doing*, while facing pushback arguing that the practice is around *being*.

The challenge inherent in reorienting a society-wide work culture that has decided to center passivity as its spiritual ideal is no small task. In the last chapter, we carefully and meticulously demonstrated why the rise of the mindful*mess* may be very problematic. But continued growth of the mindfulness industry, and its ability to successfully infiltrate the human resource department of economic powerhouses, seems to show that there is a very well-defined inverse relationship between adaptation and data around the effectiveness of these approaches. As evidence that corporate mindfulness programs are not having the desired effect becomes more concrete, the programs are becoming more entrenched and widespread.

Despite mindfulness advocates suggesting that there is nothing simpler than focusing on our breath, the broader paradigm represents a radically different mode of thought and action than is typical in how we approach work. *Being* involves attending to the present without striving, whereas *doing* involves cognitive operations that support the goal-oriented behavior often driving organizational life. The chasm between operating in a mental mode of being versus a mode of doing is massive.

All workers need to be able to find meaning in their everyday. However, in terms of the long road of personal growth and spiritual development, we are not arguing that it is a situation of either/or. While we have been framing the spiritual strategies of being and doing as oppositional, the fact is that there is a role for both approaches in each of these spiritual traditions.

As we already noted, a mindful state of being is a prerequisite for doing in the Buddhist tradition. The disciple in our tale still completed his task, through action undertaken by himself. He still brought the water to quench his master's thirst. But he was brought to an understanding of the limited potential of his actions first. He was shown that before he could *do*, he needed to *be*.

In the Jewish tradition, there is also an important role allocated for the passive state of spiritual being, even as creative reaction is favored as the more frequently employed state. However, the relationship between these two orientations is not the same as the clean linear relationship expressed in mindfulness. Quite the opposite, in fact.

The Sabbath as a Paradigm of Planned Passivity

One decidedly Jewish contribution to managing the inhuman aspects of contemporary work life that seems to be resonating is the notion of taking time off for a Sabbath. For example, in her book *24/6*, internet pioneer and Webby Award founder Tiffany Shlain argues that a necessary strategy for living in our 24/7 world is turning off all screens for twenty-four hours each week. Shlain believes that stepping away from our phones and computers in order to practice what she calls a "Technology Shabbat" can actually help us become more productive at work.

Rabbi Abraham Joshua Heschel, the soulful leader who marched with Martin Luther King Jr. in Selma, calls the Sabbath "a palace in time." Heschel movingly writes that if we want to experience spiritual peace, we must first

> lay down the profanity of clattering commerce, of being yoked to toil ... go away from the screech of dissonant days, from the nervousness and fury of acquisitiveness ... say farewell to manual work and learn to understand that the world has already been created and will survive ... Six days a week we wrestle with the world, wringing profit from the earth; on the Sabbath we especially care for the seed of eternity planted in the soul ... Six days a week we seek to dominate the world, on the seventh day we try to dominate the self.

As told in the Genesis story passed down through the generations, it is said that God's first instinct was to create. And in Judaism, the optimal state of being is found in imitating the divine. So the behavioral model that is offered in the very first words of the tradition's sacred text is a paradigm of doing, followed by a planned state of restive passivity six days later.

Stated in Hebrew, "*Bereishit*," the first word of the Torah, can be translated as "In the beginning." This choice of opening is meant to signal with clarity that the narrative about to be developed is foundational.

The second word tells us all that we need to know about origins: "[He] created." Our story begins with God creating heaven and earth; in other words, everything. But the results of this creation were described as *tohu*, loosely translated as chaotic. More specifically, *tohu*, explains famed Kabbalist Rabbi Isaac Luria, is a state of isolated ideals. A world of *tohu* is a world where no two things can work together.

Think about the implications. The Torah does not begin its narrative by stating, "In the beginning God was." It does not start with an assertion of being. That would come much later, as the Ten Commandments shared in a revelatory moment at Mount Sinai start with the declaration "I am God," an assertion of being. But at this point in the Torah, in its opening words, God is introduced in a story that starts with creation.

And unlike the divine creative efforts that will follow, the initial act of creating heaven and earth is not described as good. It is described as chaotic. God, in His initial act, creates everything. But there is no harmony in this everything. There is no order. And so the real work, the meaningful type that humans are to emulate, would now begin.

God asserts His will in an effort to end the state of universal isolation. His first corrective effort is to separate light from darkness. Once achieved, He looks at this work and decides that the task has achieved some good. And only after this judgment does He demarcate the first day of creation. (I am using the traditional gendered language just for the purpose of hewing to the original material; feel free to read in alternate pronouns.)

As the myth is shared in traditional sources, the sun and moon were not created by God until the fourth day. The light that was judged to be good and created on that first "day" (a curious term clearly not referring to a twenty-four-hour period, as we don't yet have planets, stars, or orbital rotations) was some sort of primordial light that was pulled from out of the chaos. It was an effort to make the world into something that can be worked with.

In fact, on that note, Rabbi Menachem Mendel of Rimanov suggests that this primordial light continues to shine for those engaged in spiritual work. It is invisible to those who don't themselves do the difficult work of spiritual creation because they are choosing to privilege the initial chaos of isolation.

Over a consecutive six-day period, God creates the world that we know, a world where we can work through the isolation and bring connection, with the final creative act being the formation of humanity in His image. Only on the seventh day did He enact a passive state by resting.

In the divine model that Jews are to learn from and emulate, passivity should only come as a respite after extended creative assertiveness. We rest after we work. The non-reactive state of spiritual being emerges following a lengthy period of creativity, reaction, and judgment leading to the conclusion that what was achieved can be labeled as "good work."

Rabbi David Hartman was an inspiring Jewish philosopher whose legacy included the founding of the Shalom Hartman Institute, a scholarly center still dedicated to developing a new understanding of classical Judaism that provides moral and spiritual direction for our confrontation with modernity. He framed the tension between assertiveness and passivity in Jewish spirituality as a dialectic. By this label, Rabbi Hartman was saying that in the search for meaning these oppositional forces need to be thought about in tandem. In order to fully comprehend the spiritual utility of passivity, we need to understand how this force works with its opposite state, reactivity.

In mindfulness, the difference between the two is resolved with the presumption that a passive state must always come before any assertion of reaction. In that spiritual strategy, we need to *first be* in order to *then do*. Which means that the real spiritual opportunity is only found in passivity, a state that is always logically prior. There is no way for reaction to itself be considered a spiritual act, only the continuation of a spiritual path that starts in a passive state.

In contrast, the Jewish approach to resolving the spiritual tension between passivity and assertiveness takes its cue from the biblical creation myth. According to Rabbi Joseph Soloveitchik, an early twentieth-century philosopher who was Head of the Yeshiva that is housed within Yeshiva University, what is required is an expanded awareness of the spiritual opportunities inherent in the secular work week. The biblical injunction found in Exodus 20:9, inspired by the creation story, stating that "six days you shall labor and do all your work," has far-reaching spiritual significance. If the creation story is not simply a cosmological event but a model to be imitated by human beings, and creation itself is not the exclusive right of God but shared with all of humanity, then spiritual work becomes the highest source of meaning.

As part of this spiritual tradition, we are passive on the Sabbath, the seventh day, when many Jews disconnect from the hyper-plugged-in contemporary world. But to earn the Sabbath, to build to a passive state, to get to the day of rest, we are first active for the duration of six working days. And so creative reaction becomes both the natural and the most frequently employed spiritual state in Judaism. We need to first work, react, and create in order to earn the right to step back, see the good, and then be passive.

But what joy there is to be found in regularly stepping back! Reb Zalman used to advise spiritual seekers to "Do *Shabbos* (the Yiddish term for Sabbath) first." He argued that everyone should embrace some form of Sabbath practice, as "Sabbaths are like periods inserted into an otherwise endless run-on sentence ... they remind us to take a weekly break from living in commodity time to re-anchor ourselves in what we might call organic time." Commodity time is delineated by the clock. A new day starts at midnight, and we accept it without feeling it. Organic time is starting a Sabbath on Friday night, as we see the sky darken, making the conscious choice to turn off the cycle of work and tune in to a natural rhythm until the sun sets again. And it should be experienced as more than a break from technology; it should be a time set aside to read, eat, sing, and joke with loved ones. A time to be, before we start doing once again.

The Good Is Found by Doing

Rabbi David Hartman further notes how in the Jewish tradition, if we take these ideas seriously, then we need to conclude that the realm of the sacred does not stand in abstract antithesis to the secular realm. Initiative can be labeled as holy – what we are calling spiritual work. Because, as we have been emphasizing, in this framework holiness is not achieved in a withdrawal from reality and responsibility. To the contrary, in Jewish spirituality the sacred is expressed in our interaction with the everyday. The work we do for six days is as meaningful and necessary as the rest we take on the seventh. This is the balance that keeps us human.

In sum, and in contrast to the three approaches we started the last chapter with, the Jewish vision for work is not one programmed into passivity or fear of self-expression. And whatever our religious orientation, including none at all, we can draw inspiration from the main message of the biblical creation model. The message, in brief, is that the spiritual individual cannot sit passively when there is meaningful work to be done. Or conversely, and perhaps more on point to the purpose of this book, engaging in active spiritual work is the optimal path to finding meaning. And while it is a cooperative enterprise, it is through a partnership of equals – not a hierarchical falling in line.

Equally important, it should be emphasized that in the framework I am proposing, the individual worker is empowered to decide for themselves what type of spiritual work is most pressing, most meaningful, and might best constitute good-faith work. We fill in those blanks for ourselves. And that act of blank-filling is itself good-faith work. The move from contemplation to action is as necessary as it is difficult.

Like Abraham, who argued with God over the destruction of Sodom, we reject the myth that suffering is the inevitable fate for some, even if it is God deciding that fate. Part of spiritual work is pushing back against established norms, resisting principles we find abhorrent, changing the world as it is, and unleashing the chaos that may come from toppling an established order.

For example, as Rabbi Hartman shares, one of the profound spiritual implications of technological progress is the increase in the scope of personal responsibility. The growth of social media, for example, means we can no longer claim ignorance of suffering. As we become more connected, it is not our primary responsibility to answer the calls of our employers. Instead, we must answer the calls of our conscience.

In the Zen parable shared earlier, it was taught that the good can be found in passivity. The primary lesson the disciple was to learn is that the greatest good is in overcoming the noble truth of suffering. Yes, the Master is thirsty. And yes, you have an obligation to help quench his thirst. But there is nothing to be done until the water settles on its own accord. So don't waste your time running back and forth. Don't waste your brainpower contemplating alternative courses of action. Just be still as the water stills.

But in Judaism, moral responsibility demands an action in response to the ever-repeated question of "What should I do?" Ethics is not an abstract contemplation of what is right or wrong – it's a call to action. This call cannot be answered by being mindful of your reflecting on the emotional response to experiencing this call. It is rooted in the duty to *act* with the utmost thoughtfulness. And most importantly, ethics demand that you act *now*. This urgent call to action coupled with the infinite responsibility toward reflection creates what the French philosopher Jacques Derrida calls the "impossibility" of the ethical moment. You want to act responsibly, you want more time to think things through, but you need to act now.

Former chief Rabbi of Britain Jonathan Sacks identifies this demand to take responsibility and act as what makes Judaism different from other spiritual traditions. Judaism is a spiritual system that centers human responsibility as the ultimate source of meaning. The good is found in doing, in answering the ethical call to action. From this call you can't hide. Judaism does not see human beings as powerless subjects to forces beyond our control who need to passively submit to higher powers. We believe that we are God's image, free as He is free, creative as He is creative.

Going back to our two parables, we noted that Moses took action, and paid a price for it. That price was that he was not going to live to lead the people into the Promised Land of Israel. He had made peace with this reality, as smashing the stone and tying the accumulation of wisdom to worldly effort was a worthwhile spiritual contribution to the development of his people.

But before his death, he offers one last passionate speech in which he explicates this paradigm of action over passivity. In this speech, often referred to as "The Song of Moses," he instructs the Israelites to not blame God when things go wrong. That is what Moses feels so passionately. As Rabbi Sacks states, God is not there to relieve us of responsibility. It is God who is calling us to responsibility.

Ethical decision-making is all about the complexity of answering the call to responsibility with decisive action. We react and accept all the consequences that may follow from asserting ourselves. We are inspired by the biblical model of Abraham, who as a child smashed his father's stone idols on the principle that he viewed them as emblematic of passivity, but as a consequence of this revelatory moment he then had to leave his father's house and the land he grew up in.

We are inspired by Moses, who would smash the water-bearing stone, who earlier had to flee the Egyptian palace of those who raised him, the only home he knew, after making the choice to take violent action against a perceived injustice. Witnessing an Egyptian slave master mercilessly beating a Hebrew slave, he reacts by killing the oppressor and burying the body in the sand.

Even though murder is morally problematic, and even though Moses exacerbates the situation by choosing to run away rather than face justice, this act is still seen as an important part of Moses' development. In the early stories about Moses – including his rescue from Pharaoh's decree that midwives kill all Hebrew boys, his being placed in a basket set adrift in the Nile, and his discovery by Pharaoh's daughter and adoption as if he were her own – he was passive. In this story, we finally see Moses assert himself, leaving the privileged confines of the palace, joining his people, and taking action.

Both Abraham and Moses argue with God frequently, and take action quickly in the face of injustice. They both show a deep concern for their fellow human beings, especially those who are suffering. And they both make mistakes. They both, for example, cause pain to their wives with their choices. Abraham hurts Sarah with his choice to have a child with Hagar and bring this second family into their shared home. Moses hurt Tzipora by leaving her and their children behind in Midian. But their moral errors are also rooted in the traits we praise. They tried to take the right action, recognizing that the good is found in doing, even while working with limited knowledge about the effects of their choices.

This is the spiritual paradigm we need in contemporary work – one that allows for mistakes, because innovations come from trial and error, as long as the intentions are good. This ideal is what Israeli philosopher Yoram Hazony describes in his book *The Philosophy of Hebrew Scripture* as "the ethics of the shepherd," an ethical model exemplified by Abraham, Moses, and David, but perhaps made most clear by Jacob:

> Jacob appears in the History of Israel as a founder of a people that will bear the name *Israel.* Israel is, in the understanding of the History, the founder of an entire nation of shepherds: an entire nation that will not accept the command of a king, or the command of a god, unless it can be shown to conform to the demands of the shepherd's ethics ... What in other cultures would have been sacrilege – the claim to have struggled with God himself and prevailed – is thus elevated into a national symbol and the crux of biblical belief: *the refusal of the shepherd to accept the order of the universe as it has been decreed, and the demand to know why it cannot be made to conform to the demands of his own outsider ethics.*

This "outsider ethics" encourages reaction, not passivity, because in a disruptive, fast-paced, ever-changing environment it's easy to be overwhelmed. And it is one that empowers individuals to draw on their own faculties, and not expect them to fall in line to old hierarchies.

As was noted in the introduction, and which bears repeating here, we need to internalize the notions that spirituality is more than inward bliss because spiritual pursuits are efforts to attach one's self to an actualized purpose; that ethics is more than selflessness because the creative actions of meaningful work are ethical, even as they differ from what we generally regard as the sphere of the moral, manifesting in skills and traits like an entrepreneurial instinct or an innovative mind; and that work is more than passive adherence, more than falling in line to higher powers – be they human or divine – but is creating new value and disrupting old power structures.

The idea that an ability to calculate risk or engage in creative scenario planning should constitute a moral good is especially important in light of recent research in psychology revealing that the decision to engage in behavior with potentially significant harmful consequences is often the result of our asymmetrical perceptions of the harm–benefit relationship. As new details emerge in the story we opened this chapter with, the Volkswagen scandal, this certainly seems to be the case. It appears that the motivation to engage in deceptive practices was due to an underappreciation of the severity of the consequences. In other words, it appears as if many of these workers simply embraced the mindfulness perspective of "maybe."

Why are the potential ethical and social harms of business activities so consistently underconsidered? Research over the years has demonstrated that in the pursuit of profit-generating activities, workers tend to ignore possible events that in their assessments are unlikely, even if the magnitude of consequences are severe. Most workers have functional training, but they are not trained to think about ethical and social risks in a sophisticated manner. As such, if they employ sophisticated quantitative modeling tools to assess financial risk, yet lack the tools (or the willingness to apply them) to understand ethical risks, then even workers trained in assessing financial risk will tend to underestimate ethical risks and associated social harm.

On top of the fact that the possibility of ethical and social harm will generally be underanalyzed, our perception tends to be asymmetrical. The possibilities for gain are of primary significance in assessing the attractiveness of alternatives. So when the possibility for profit exists, workers will even underconsider the ethical risks that have been identified. In the instance of Volkswagen, it was the desire to dominate the US market, coupled with an inability to contend with emissions regulations, which led Volkswagen engineers to roll the dice. Now, an advocate for mindfulness would argue that a mindful worker would be aware that their perceptions are asymmetrical ... but would that realization have been enough to radically change the dominant behavior?

The acceptability of a risky alternative depends on the relation between the dangers and the opportunities reflected in the risk, and some critical aspiration levels for the decision-maker. Usually, the aspirations relate to financial performance. As such, ethical and social risks are most often ignored or underappreciated. There is a further tendency for managerial evaluations of alternatives to focus on a few key aspects of a problem, as argued by the late James March, formerly of Stanford University, and New York University's Zur Shapira. They found that most managers limit the scope of their assessment to the variables which they are most comfortable dealing with.

Once again, given the fact that most workers are trained in functional disciplines and have limited exposure to ethical analysis, the tendency to focus on a narrow set of issues does not bode well for a robust risk analysis. Or in the case of public health officials trying to offer society-wide guidance for navigating a pandemic, they are experts with functional training that allows them to employ sophisticated quantitative modeling tools to assess the epidemiological risk. However, they lack the tools (or the willingness to apply them) to understand ethical risks and social harm, pleased as they are by their sophisticated modeling.

Furthermore, managerial forecasts of anticipated future outcomes of their innovating activities are often rooted in scenarios of success rather than past results and therefore have a tendency to be overly optimistic. All of these behaviors seem to be quite immune to modification via nothing more than a mindfulness practice absent a broader spiritual system. These behaviors could certainly continue even if an individual were to recognize the "maybe," not dwell on past results or experiences, avoid judgment, and go with the flow.

What might have made a difference at Volkswagen is good corporate governance, where, for example, the board of directors, acting in the interests of the shareholders, might have reined in the overt and aggressive risky tendencies of management who were overtaken by unreasonably rosy forecasts. But this would have required judgment and reaction. Attention to the unfolding behaviors of managerial decision-makers without judgment would not make much of a positive difference, even if the managers themselves were aware of their behavior and aware of their awareness that this may be risky. Mindfulness encourages passivity and thus didn't encourage anyone to step up. They were committed to being, not doing. And despite the mantra that public health should be above politics, policy-makers won't be able to eliminate risk. As such, there will be times when we will need to rely on our own spiritual and ethical faculties. I'm thinking of the advice offered by the late poet and Jewish Buddhist Allen Ginsburg: Be bold and careful. Only then, will we find our way to a world where wellness, business, and social policy can thrive.

The Futility of a Practice without Purpose

It should be emphasized once again, however, that the weaknesses faced by the mindful practitioner are not built into the Buddhist religious system. As Ron Purser, a professor of management at San Francisco State University, and David Loy, a Zen teacher, write in the *Huffington Post*: "Rather than applying mindfulness as a means to awaken individuals and organizations from the unwholesome roots of greed, ill will and delusion, it is usually being refashioned into a banal, therapeutic, self-help technique that can actually reinforce those roots." In other words, the Buddhist tradition would have encouraged its practitioners to free themselves from these systems of oppression and live a very different life.

Writer Glenn Wallis, who seeks to stem the "swell of western Buddhaphilia," observes in his blog: "The mighty 'Mindfulness' juggernaut continues to roll joyously throughout the wounded world of late-capitalism. And why shouldn't it? The Mindfulness Industry is claiming territory once held by the great occupying force of assorted self-help gurus, shrinks, health-care workers, hypnotists, preachers, Theosophists, the church, the synagogue, actual gurus, yogis, meditation teachers, and even – gasp! – Buddhists themselves. Who, after all, can compete with an industry that claims to offer a veritable fountain of bounty, an elixir to life's ills?"

But as we have already began to show, there is a way to think about work that can support the development of the traits we need to thrive in every sense. In our disruptive economy, value is created by work that changes the worker, changes the environment in which that person works, and changes all those who come in contact with the worker through their meaningful activities.

This is markedly different from a Protestant or a workist calling, or a call to be mindful; as we demonstrated earlier, all three are focused on the singular individual and the limits of their station. Spiritual work in the Jewish lens takes a different approach. We can look to Abraham and Moses and other biblical figures who discovered meaning by throwing themselves head on into complexity and ambiguity, who made explicitly moral choices, who took action, and then dealt with the fallout.

3

Mitzvah in the Workplace

With the last chapter, we began to systematically map out our pro-
posal for a more multifaceted spiritual system that can help us reshape economic organizing and bring a sense of meaning to those
involved in the cooperative efforts of value creation. This system goes
further into the potential of spiritual motivations than simply telling us to remain in our divinely ordained life stations. This system
doesn't expect innovative people to accept without judgment the
things that on the surface may appear to be beyond the reach of
their actions. This system is for those who know and appreciate that
workers today don't want to be managed, even benevolently. They
want to be partners in co-creation. This is a spiritual system that will
encourage practitioners to exercise more judgment, more reaction,
and more cooperation as they work. It is our only hope for rebuilding
capitalism as a worthwhile system of economic organizing after the
Great Pause and in response to the call for a racial justice reckoning.

This paradigm for spiritual work encourages us to aspire to create an economic landscape where all businesses, without exception,
are incentivized to operate under the principle that they have a demonstrably positive impact on society. Business responses during the
COVID-19 pandemic demonstrated the very best and worst of capitalist instincts. Some businesses immediately repurposed their operations toward a more impactful end. For example, Choura Events

was supposed to be building stages for the Coachella Music Festival. When the crisis hit, the tacit knowledge within this company, developed in the context of building tents for Coachella, was utilized for a social good as the company quickly pivoted to building hospital tents.

And the truth is, this should be the norm even in non-crisis situations. This should be what we mean when we talk about the need for businesses to be agile. Imagine what kind of capitalism could be enacted if business leaders and workers of every stripe began to generate meaningful trust with those who they come into contact with. All we need to do is get beyond the framing that our strategic options are limited to binary choices. Embracing capitalism does not mean that we have to celebrate greed to assure material success, or altruism to be a de facto not-for-profit. Being spiritual at work does not mean we have to embrace either the ascetic spiritual practice of monks or the mindful*mess* of a spiritual bypass. The options for an assertive spirituality in cooperative value creation are literally infinite.

This move toward measuring success in terms of the broad value (economic and social) that is created could very well be the radical reformation that could save capitalism from being relegated as a failed ideology, one which ultimately contributed to more societal harm than good. To prevent that outcome, we need to see the value of an ancient spiritual paradigm crafted to inspire the sought-after feelings of meaning, connection, and wonder at work, while being fully cognizant that creating a space for this is no small task. We should not be naïve about the outcomes we are pursuing.

Our goals are nothing less than the extremely ambitious desire to reform an institution that is as powerful and entrenched as it is broken. And we hope to do this not through a revolutionary rebellion but through the incremental efforts of individual workers opening up to a different type of meaning. The Polish Hasidic luminary Rabbi Simcha Bunim, who continues to inspire more than two hundred years after his death despite having no written works, was said to have taught the idea that Jewish law forbids us from deceiving our neighbors; however, the righteous seekers who want to go beyond the mere letter of the law need to work hard on not deceiving ourselves.

How a *Mitzvah* Creates the Space for Meaning

In 1995, when a fire burned his company's factory to the ground in Lawrence, Massachusetts, Aaron Feuerstein, the CEO of Malden Mills, made the very big, very controversial, and very expensive decision to rebuild locally. In interviews, Feuerstein used the language of *mitzvah* to explain how his spiritual identity caused him to view the world differently than other business people might. From a purely financial perspective, there was strong pressure to rebuild overseas and save a ton of money. But Feuerstein believed he had a unique mission with his work, which was to take meaningful corporate action that would better his local community. Sure, the company needed to make money; but the primary responsibility under his leadership was to prioritize the meaningful relationships they had built over the years with local workers and their families. That's where the spiritual work had to be done.

This is a beautiful and often-cited story of how a powerful executive took the opportunity to do a *mitzvah* (a term which I will define shortly) instead of indulging in greed. But, as we said from the start, we are not going to be naïve in our considerations. Because the truth is, this is a one-of-a-kind story. It is continuously brought up by apologists to illustrate the positive possibilities of capitalism, even though it is more than twenty-five years old. It is one of the go-to stories when folks want to talk about meaningful work because there really aren't that many others.

The inability to fully employ our spiritual faculties in the search for meaning at work is problematic for the future of capitalism. Some might say that capitalism as we know it today does not deserve to have a future. While there are some encouraging signs that the exploitive capitalism which privileges shareholder wealth maximization above all else has run its course, meaningful changes to how we organize our economic interactions are not happening fast enough. In fact, the tensions between those who seek to further entrench the short-term, shareholder-focused type of capitalism that dominates our markets and those working for even the possibility of a more ethical approach that puts people and multifaceted value first are becoming more pronounced.

I'm going to borrow from Rabbi Art Green, founding dean of the rabbinical program at Hebrew College in Boston, the definition of "spirituality" as the cultivation of a life in the ordinary world bearing the holiness once associated with sacred space and time. But, as is emphasized throughout this book, I want to add that the cultivation of this life can create a sense of meaning, connection, and wonder in work.

Rabbi Green explains that in Hasidic tradition a *mitzvah* is read as "a place of encounter … it is an act in which we open ourselves … a moment, a place or a deed of awareness and response." In the Jewish tradition, an action taken in support of this end is what we mean by the term *mitzvah*, a moment of *doing* that creates a space of *being* with the sacred.

Reb Zalman points out that while *mitzvah* was once translated as "commandment," in "a democratic society the word commandment has lost its power. The old understanding of being commanded was … of an authority beaming down upon us from above. Today any sense of commandment must come from within."

A *mitzvah* is an action we take in order to open up a space where we can create a meaningful moment with other people. My friend Rabbi Tzvi Freeman notes that the word *mitzvah* is related to the Aramaic word *tzavta*, meaning to attach or join. *Tzavta* can mean companionship or personal attachment. In this sense, a *mitzvah* creates a relationship and essential bond.

In the last chapter, I shared tales of biblical heroes like Abraham and Moses choosing reaction over passivity, and in so doing offered a model for initiating creative change driven by spiritual purpose. But, as I noted at the end of the discussion, unbridled reactivity is dangerous. For reaction to be a spiritual trait, there must be something to reign in our assertiveness and help mitigate the potential negative consequences that emerge from error and miscalculation. This is the *mitzvah*.

Rabbi Mordecai Kaplan, founder of Reconstructionist Judaism, explained that a *mitzvah* obligates us to participate as part of a community. It creates a space for the sacred by binding us to other people. This in turn creates feelings of connection, accountability, and responsibility. A *mitzvah* helps us access our agency and sense of possibility for the future. Assertiveness is preferable to passivity, but we assert ourselves knowing that we are primarily accountable to our community. Acting in selfishness is not spiritual. Meaningful spiritual work must always build social connections. What we create with a *mitzvah* is the outcome of cooperation.

Rabbi Mordechai Yosef Leiner, founder of the Izhbitza-Radzyn Hasidic dynasty, uncovers a profound insight in his contrast between the "wisdom" and the "understanding" that come through enacting the meaningful work of a *mitzvah*. As he explains, the necessary wisdom before performing a *mitzvah* is knowing the moral rule or principle that we are about to apply within the confines of a very narrow set of circumstances. From this type of thinking, individuals can come to deduce the moral traits their society expects of them. For example, in the case of Malden Mills cited earlier, the wisdom of the *mitzvah* which Aaron Feuerstein sought to enact was "don't oppress the working class or create extra hardship on the needy." From this principle Feuerstein was able to conclude that the appropriate behavior would be to rebuild the destroyed factory locally in order to retain the jobs so many local workers depended on.

But the understanding that emerges from meaningful acts of spiritual work, according to Rabbi Mordechai Yosef, creates a deep and instinctive feeling for where we create our personal boundaries in assertiveness, and makes sure these boundaries are not overextended. The internalization of the deep responsibility we must feel toward others is a necessary precondition of unleashing our reactive instincts. In other words, if our actions are truly meaningful, over time they become natural.

However, we first need to hone our instincts. We need to determine, through experience, appropriate internal boundaries. These are set by assessing the impact of our deliberate and principled action. Wisdom informs the principles. Understanding allows us to internalize them and turn them into something more. In Feuerstein's case, his personal understanding led to the decision to go beyond the principled responsibility to not oppress, and into the proactive choice of paying these workers even while the factory was being rebuilt and they were idle. He understood that the principle of non-oppression in his life would lead to an internalized commitment to being trustworthy and building a community.

With work we can be empowered to act against existing power structures because, like Abraham and Moses, we can trust our instincts. Perhaps the clearest example of this is in the speculative Talmudic discussion of the questions asked by the Heavenly Court after death, which was mentioned earlier. Through this frame, the goal of a spiritual perspective is to help workers create a story of transformation with the seemingly simple acts of their good-faith business activities. This theme is repeated throughout the Talmud, with the sages going so far as to state that the guide to sainthood is to be found in the study of the tractates on damages – not the lofty esoteric discussions of deep mysticism, but the practical exploration of good-faith business interactions and meaningful work.

Why? Because the most important work we do is work that transforms both ourselves and those around us through everyday activities, making behaviors that once came from rules into a natural and intuitive reaction. Being wise enough to adopt the trait of honesty, for example, is fine and good. But internalizing this honesty, and finding a way to assert our honesty so that we come up with new products that transform our industry into one that creates meaningful social value, changes our colleagues so that they embrace an ethical approach as well, and alters our customers whose lives are significantly enhanced by our innovation – that is a higher good. Moses Pava, professor of business ethics at Yeshiva University, argues that Jewish business ethics differs from secular approaches in that it acknowledges the centrality of the community and holds out the promise that men and women (living in community) can transform themselves. That is the spiritual work of a *mitzvah*.

Tapping into the Mystical

A critical part of finding meaning in the spiritual experience sometimes involves going beyond the sphere of the rational. For many of us, we turn to mythology to feed this need. While there may be rational and pragmatic reasons to act in good faith and radical transparency, there is also a mystical branch of Jewish spirituality inspired by Lurianic Kabbalah that may be worth drawing on even in our secular explorations.

In the mystical view, the essence of a *mitzvah* is a moral action that serves both a reparative function of healing the cosmos and a connective function of binding the participating parties in a sacred space. How do ordinary actions invite the sacred? In mystical terminology, everything in existence is an artifact of a divine spark. The creation myth that is shared in the Kabbalistic tradition attempts to fill in the gap between when God created heaven and earth and the subsequent creative activities that took place over the next six days.

As noted earlier, the initial creation was described as *tohu*, chaotic. This chaos caused the divine sparks (we will explain what these are in the next paragraph) to scatter, described by the Lubavitcher Rebbe Menachem Mendel Schneerson as something like taking a book and throwing all its words and letters into the air. The job of humanity is to rescue and liberate these sparks so that we end up with a harmonious and meaningful world. We do this by putting the pieces of the puzzle back together in such a way that everything starts to make sense, thus giving things value and meaning.

At the heart of the Lurianic cosmological myth is the notion that the physical world was born of a primal divine conscious thought. Rabbi Tzvi Freeman likes to tell the story of creation in the Lurianic tradition as beginning with a primal, singular, deliberate ray of conscious thought holding all that was ever to be: time, space, wisdom, beauty, wonder, and creativity. However, this initial creative thought was chaotic, and thus too intense to contain itself. Each idea it conceived of left no room for anything other than itself. The idea of wisdom left no space for the idea of understanding. The idea of kindness left no space for the idea of judgment.

Subsequently, this thought exploded in a frenzied rebuke to initial attempts at cosmic order, scattering the fragments of these ideals throughout our world. In Kabbalistic mythology, these shattered fragments are described as sparks trapped within a shell. The sparks are the ultimate meaning of thing, while the shells are the noise and dissonance that shrouds those sparks in our world as a consequence of the violent shattering.

To engage in spiritual work is to see past the shell, discover the spark of meaning within, and reconnect the spark to its place in the grand original vision. I want to use the narrative of sparks and *mitzvahs* to reimagine work constructs like the creation of value. By making connections between seemingly disparate parts of our world, we are capable of creating new value through our meaningful work. As we connect these fragments in ways that make sense to us, that are consistent with our own sense of the good and honors our reactive instincts, we are also acting in a way that honors our ties and responsibilities to all those around us. And so, we are using our secular work to achieve the lofty spiritual challenge of reassembling a broken world.

Meaning Comes by Finding New Partners

At the core of spiritual work in the Jewish tradition is an argument that demands a rethinking of the pursuit of firm-centric profit maximization and exploitive practices at the expense of meaningful social and personal development. At the end of the day, the actions of *mitzvahs* and releasing the sparks are designed to bring about new cooperative relationships. Viewing work as an endeavor of co-creation links what may start out as our individual pursuits of meaning to the formation of new connections. Thus, spiritual seekers end up working together, increasing the effectiveness of efforts to craft innovative products and processes of multifaceted value even in a competitive environment of disruption and uncertainty.

One source of difficulty faced by workers today, and why many struggle to find meaning within work, is that most prescriptive business advice (even in mindful approaches) seems to direct attention to the role current stakeholders can play in helping us achieve our goals. We are told to consider the needs of our existing shareholders, customers, suppliers, co-workers, and so on. But the hunt for spiritual meaning should turn our attention to that which is in a state of potential: future customers, prospective colleagues, unrealized innovations, new alliances, and the ever-present hope of expanding our community.

Empowering our reactive faculties means being prepared for the uncertainty that will inevitably follow our efforts to initiate change, no matter how well thought out our plans may be. Error is not a dirty word. It is an expected outcome. But catastrophe emerges when we are unprepared for the new realities that materialize in the world we have wrought. It is always possible that our spiritually minded efforts will set off a chain of events that may bring about a worse tomorrow. One of the purposes of work, then, is to find the currently unknown individuals who will have the skills to fix our unanticipated mistakes.

Future cooperative partners are equally, if not more, strategically important to the long-term success of our assertive efforts as current partners. The pool of people we work with should not be limited to current strategic alliances. A critical challenge is figuring out how to expand our network by thinking about what skills, traits, or assets we might need to assure that the wrongs of the moment are set right down the road. For example, many companies in the auto industry are building relationships with new partners that have skills in building vehicle charging stations or developing the infrastructure to support a ride-sharing service in order to prepare for a potential future dominated by self-driving, electric-powered autonomous vehicles. Thinking about this leads to uncovering new levels of meaning.

Our outreach efforts must somehow succeed in bringing those at the edges of our wider community into a close relationship with us. It is a task of meaning and purpose because we use the feeling of uncertainty, which in other paradigms may lead us to look inward, to instead extend outward. Because of the absolute uncertainty over the future and what may be the skills, resources, or partnerships that we will need to draw on at a later date, our work lives are dependent on gathering strangers and forging unexpected connections. Aston Martin, famous for luxury sports cars, partnered with Triton to build a very different form of transport: a luxury three-person submarine. IKEA, the Swedish build-it-yourself furniture company, acquired Task-Rabbit, a company that sends tool-wielding freelance workers to rescue customers befuddled by build-it-yourself furniture kits. As IKEA's CEO explained, "In a fast-changing retail environment, we continuously strive to develop new and improved products and services to make our customers' lives a little bit easier. Entering the on-demand, sharing economy enables us to support that."

Potential partners include fellow workers currently engaging in efforts that may be extraordinarily useful for our future working needs. The best way for us to one day be able to engage these currently unknown stakeholders is through a committed mission to releasing the sparks, doing the *mitzvah*, taking on the spiritual quest to look for the hidden, potential relationships that we are uniquely poised to actualize. And so we find meaning as we make these new connections, repairing our fragmented and broken society in the process.

Unleash Trustworthiness

Researchers in business management have long argued that we need to develop trusting relationships with all of those with whom we interact during the course of our work. The presence of trust allows these numerous but interdependent relationships to function smoothly and realize the strategic objectives behind their creation. So I am offering nothing new when I say that building trust within our relationships is important. What is novel, however, in what I am advocating, what is truly radical, is suggesting that the spiritual work is to be seen as trustworthy even by those with whom we do not yet have a relationship. This is a significant leap from the current norm of privileging trusting relationships with those who are already within our network.

What is the significant conceptual difference? Being seen as trustworthy by those who we currently work with is pragmatic. It is a smoothing mechanism to allow the existing relationship to operate with minimal stress. In contrast, seeking to be seen as trustworthy by those who we have yet to meet is how we will reshape capitalism. It will allow us to engage in long-term meaningful work in a turbulent and unpredictable environment. It is what will convince those parties not currently known to us but who may hold resources that we will require down the road to sustain our positioning and encourage them to join our stakeholder mix. Trustworthiness is the trait required to develop a sustainable path to superior performance in turbulent industries.

Building on Columbia University's professor Charles Sabel's definition of trust as the mutual confidence that no party to an exchange will exploit another's vulnerabilities, leading management scholar Jay Barney has defined trustworthiness as the attribute of being worthy of the trust of others in not exploiting any adverse selection, moral hazard, hold-up, or other exchange vulnerability. The sort of strong-type trustworthiness necessary for spiritual work reflects the values, principles, and standards that we will bring to an economic exchange. Those values, principles, and standards will reflect our history, culture, and personal values.

In the business world trustworthiness is only viewed as valuable to the extent that it proves to be a source of a competitive advantage for a company. Furthermore, trustworthiness is believed to facilitate this amoral advantage because it lowers transaction costs. In other words, under conventional business thinking, as long as the cost of developing and maintaining trustworthiness, plus the cost of discovering trustworthy exchange partners, was less than the cost of relying on or erecting social or economic governance devices, it was a worthwhile trait. Why? Because those firms which had the advantage of being in a strong-form trust relationship enjoyed a cost advantage over those in a semi-strong trust relationship. Crudely put, it is cheaper to do business between trustworthy parties.

The type of meaningful work I hope to develop here needs to depart from this reductionist view of trust in two important ways. First, the dominant view argues that the only reason to develop trust with current stakeholders is to achieve some sort of competitive edge due to cost savings. I have long argued that work motivated primarily by efficiency will never be meaningful. Our focus should be on acting with meaning and purpose to attract potential future partners with whom we can enjoy a transformative relationship – that is, folks who are committed like we are to enacting a more hopeful future.

Second, most researchers in business have argued for the importance of mutual trust. The cost savings only emerge if both parties trust each other. But in this framework of spiritual assertiveness and reaction, I am conceptualizing something different. For my purposes, it is sufficient and necessary only that we act with spiritual purpose and become trustworthy. While trustworthiness on the part of a partner will always be viewed as a welcome attribute, it is not a necessary condition in order for us to find meaning in work.

In fact, this message was brought home clearly in the early phases of the COVID-19 crisis. The lack of trustworthy CEOs clearly had an impact on our ability to make good decisions during the crisis. For example, Lloyd Blankfein, former CEO of Goldman Sachs, tweeted what might otherwise have been an interesting conversation starter. He observed that "crushing the economy, jobs and morale is also a health issue." While phrased inelegantly, I believe his point is that the extreme community-based public health measures implemented to "flatten the curve" and mitigate the impact of the COVID-19 virus, such as the lockdown and stay at home orders, has led to catastrophic effects on our society's economic well-being, which in turn will have significant adverse health and welfare consequences as well. He was mercilessly pilloried and silenced by the Twitterverse whose users interpreted this statement as a wish to see vulnerable workers return to potentially lethal workplaces as members of the business elite like himself would see their wealth increase while remaining safe.

Most of us were far more sympathetic to the doctors who were pushing the singular message of "shut it down." Doctors, based on their training and experience, found factors like overrun hospitals, limited resources for treatment, and the highly contagious nature of the virus most salient, and made their call. But for business leaders, different variables were salient in their decision-making, particularly around the economic devastation that was unfolding. They were wondering what the world would look like when we emerged from this crisis.

But in times of crisis, the moral character of those advocating for specific positions becomes more relevant. And here is where the trust deficit most acutely took its toll. A good chunk of the population don't trust business leaders to concern themselves with principles other than greed. So why would we listen to economists or CEOs during a crisis, especially to those like Blankfein whose moral position during the last financial crisis was "long-term greedy"?

Who is more likely to appeal to us – the selfless doctors working tirelessly to save lives at great personal risk or the seemingly selfish

CEOs laying off their vulnerable employees? The health-care workers who are a part of almost all of our daily lives or the aloof senior executives who rarely interact with us?

We needed business leaders to be part of the difficult conversations that were being had even in the early days of the pandemic. Being seen as trustworthy by those whom we have yet to meet is the radical path through which business leaders might re-earn a seat at the table as we try and manage the crisis. It is our best hope for emerging from this crisis well-prepared for the next.

We need to lead and shape the world that we want. We need not be passive and wait for other trustworthy parties to enter our orbit. Instead, we internalize the trait of trustworthiness, then go out into the world and perform the *mitzvahs* that allow us to build connections.

How is the concept of trust developed in ancient Jewish sources? Is it as reductionist a construct as it appears to be in business research? Remember, trust in management is simply the mutual confidence that no party to an exchange will exploit another's vulnerabilities. But the word for trust in biblical Hebrew is *bitachon*. This word implies more than a confidence that we will not be exploited or taken advantage of. In fact, it means that we can rely on each other.

The root of the word, *batach*, means to lean or rest on someone or something. While traditionally this reliance was on God, in our modern age it might be more meaningful to place this reliance on people. In fact, in modern Hebrew *bitachon* refers to security. When we lean into a relationship, it's not simply so that we won't exploit vulnerabilities, but so that we can have faith that each of the parties in this relationship will be there for each other in a meaningful way. It allows each party to assert themselves in a hopeful and optimistic manner. Consistent with the philosophy of reaction we have been developing, *bitachon* is a creative act. It allows us to state that this new relationship is going to work because we want it to work, because we are creating the space to ensure that it works.

In an op-ed for *The Times*, Rabbi Jonathan Sacks talks in detail about the importance of trust in the work environment. He notes that the difficult work begins by thinking deeply about the values we hold, insisting that no institution can be sustained without trust. Rabbi Sacks shares practical anecdotes of how commercial enterprises fail when trust falters. One is a conversation with a retired CEO who watched with horror from the sidelines as his successor took a salary of ten times as much as he had taken, and then systematically destroyed whatever trust there was in the company. Another lamented that in the past the first thing he would do before making a deal would be to establish the character of the counterparty, but now lawyers play that role.

Where are the efforts to find meaning in work, to pursue a higher purpose? Rabbi Sacks worries that in our modern era most of us have given up on the search for meaning. We have lost the distinction between the value of things and the price of things. He argues that when it comes to flagrant self-interest, markets combine the maximum temptation with the maximum opportunity. Markets need morals, and morals are not made by markets.

Connective Community

The next strategic trait required for meaningful spiritual work is one that focuses on a capability to minimize the social distance between us and our potential work partners. As will be discussed in detail in the next part of the book, our success depends on building connections to the widest array of people, growing, strengthening, and entering into new communities. Researchers at the University of Virginia's Darden School of Management have identified communities as rooted in geography, identity, or interaction. "Geography" refers to close geographic proximity; "identity" refers to a group whose members share a sense of belonging built on a shared set of beliefs, values, or experiences; and "interaction" refers to a set of social relationships based on regular interactions.

We want to not only increase and improve on the connections we have to those we currently work with but also to set the space for potential stakeholders who are not yet clearly in our orbit to know that they will be welcomed. We might discover these new communities through efforts to enhance our relationships to those who share our geographical locale by the work we do. We might find new partners as we proudly assert the diverse elements of our multifaceted identity, bringing our complete selves into our work. Or we might find new relationships by ensuring that everyone we interact with, no matter what the context, is treated with dignity.

Taking this approach one step further, it is also likely that we would seek to increase geographic proximity in order to gain closer relationships with relatively distant or potential stakeholders. Apple's strategy of opening brick-and-mortar stores in order to have a physical place for its employees to meet and interact with customers can be viewed as a contemporary business example of rethinking geography and interactivity. The Apple Store was not created as a place for people to buy products. Apple uses the space to increase geographic and interactive proximity with its customers, to help these current and potential stakeholders feel an ownership experience and therefore to build trust and loyalty to the company. In other words, the creation of the Apple Store was driven by concerns with meaning, values, and legitimacy, not classic business-level concerns about a place to sell goods.

Interestingly, it was shared with me that the individual who designed the Apple Store's hiring process puts on a party as the setting to conduct interviews. He does this because it is precisely a noisy, chaotic, and social environment that successful employees will need to thrive in. One-on-one interviews would not offer accurate indicators of competency. Similarly, questions about selling tactics are also beside the point. The job of an Apple Store employee is to build relationships through actual face-to-face encounters and ultimately to manage the party.

Reaction Strengthens Some Relationships
while Weakening Others

But, on the flip side, making one set of customers happy invariably means making other customers, suppliers, employees, and alliance partners unhappy. The risks of a reactive strategy is that we cannot please all of the people all of the time. One advantage of passivity is that it is less likely to offend. Whatever our stance, when we assert ourselves in an effort to bring about meaningful change we are just as likely to alienate folks who have power and influence as we are to endear ourselves.

There is no clean way to actively deal with conflicts rooted in values. Meaning and purpose trump all in a world where contrasting ideological positions are a fact of life. Modernism privileges the discourse of science and rationality as the grand narrative by which to evaluate all knowledge. But a rational modernist would need to grant that nothing in the most recent tools and advances made by the scientific method offer a clear path for workers at any of the companies whose recent poor decisions serve as useful case studies in this book.

We live in very chaotic times, where ethical decisions need to be made in real time and in an ambiguous public space. Choosing passivity instead of reaction, turning inward to our attentive faculties, won't lead to better outcomes in these scenarios. Refining our capacity for attentiveness, improving our mental ability to be flexible, and better regulating our emotional responses to events in a manner like those described by advocates of mindfulness, on their own, are insufficient tools for solving our large-scale contemporary dilemmas.

We need to internalize the traits that will allow us to present as trustworthy. If we are successful, then we will be given the space to make mistakes without damaging our reputations as spiritual workers. Many of the rationalist models of decision-making assume a predictability and homogeneity that just doesn't exist anymore. Workers, business leaders, and policy-makers need to be able to experiment, and we need the space to sometimes make the wrong decisions as we figure things out. As a consequence, we need to show that we are always acting in good faith. Then, members of our broader society can trust us as decision-makers who put our personal sense of responsibility at the forefront of decision-making. But this can't happen if we privilege non-judgment and non-reaction. "Maybe" doesn't support urgent action. "Maybe" defers responsibility to someone else. Reaction shoulders the burden of responsibility personally, while also opening up the space for error.

Let's look at a recent challenge faced by Starbucks. Remember when Starbucks outlets nationwide shut down for a day of sensitivity training because a store manager in Philadelphia called police to remove two African American men accused of waiting for a third party to arrive before ordering? Then a year later, the company found itself in trouble once again after a barista in Arizona asked a group of police officers to leave the store or move out of the sightline of a customer who complained of not feeling safe. What links these two events, beyond the predictable volley of partisan outrage, is a more important lesson about the complexity of taking what we perceive to be meaningful action in response to the difficult ethical challenges that face businesses in our era.

Starbucks has now been (rightfully) attacked for privileging the powerful at the expense of the powerless and vice versa. The ethical issues it, and other companies, continue to face on a daily basis are highly complex, volatile, and risky. It is clear from the training videos posted online that the sensitivity sessions were not going to impart situation-specific guidance for its workers. Instead, the onus falls on the staff to make some very difficult decisions that involve managing the constant collision of competing norms.

The challenges experienced by workers at Starbucks as they navigated their personal quests for meaning amidst the ethical quandaries they were facing throughout their workday are not atypical. And this reality hammers in a critical point: finding meaning at work is not an abstract contemplation of what is right or wrong – it is an urgent call to action. In other words, meaning at work does not materialize through meditation or isolated contemplation of principles. It emerges by taking the actions which duty demands. We just aren't always prepared for the consequences of the actions we take.

The barista in Arizona was faced with a very complex predicament that called for decisive action. They were confronted by a customer complaint around the feeling of safety, which represents one of the critical elements of the Starbucks' experience. Yet implicated in creating an unsafe experience was an individual the barista knew was non-threatening, not just because of their professional affiliation but through personal connection. They wanted to act responsibly and therefore considered the sensitivity training they went through. But they also needed to act quickly. This was particularly difficult given the conflict between opposing conceptions of meaning and connection, the personal and the professional. They may have even considered implications for the store's bottom line. But there are limits to what we can know in our decision-making process.

We have incomplete information about the consequences of our choices and a limited understanding of alternatives. The barista drew on the training they had received. The videos they had seen showed African Americans being harassed by police in public spaces. The implication was clear – police could be a hindrance to the feelings of safety experienced by certain customers of color when in the Starbucks' space. The well-intentioned barista could not have foreseen the risk to Starbucks' corporate reputation when they asked the police to move in the name of customer safety. Suddenly, the outcome of their lauded sensitivity training, a day that cost $12 million in lost profits, had led to an unattractive pay-off.

Solving these problems will require workers to draw on their reactive spiritual faculties in addition to their rational faculties. They will need to take a chance on unleashing spiritual sparks and following their instincts without necessarily knowing how to convince others of the appropriateness of their assertive responses. Were it otherwise, one might argue that Starbucks should simply encourage its staff to engage in a quick calculus of which position would satisfy the greatest number of profitable customers. But this was the failed logic that led to the Philadelphia controversy, forcing Starbucks to articulate a policy that states its facilities are not just for paying customers, as many paying customers were horrified at the humiliating treatment of the not-yet-paying.

And it's not just Starbucks. On a pre-holiday Saturday afternoon in December 2019, the Hallmark Channel aired six commercials for the wedding planning company Zola. Two of the ads featured straight weddings, while the other four centered on the experiences of same-sex couples. Within minutes, the online social conservative activist group One Million Moms mobilized, pressuring Hallmark to pull the ads featuring same-sex couples under the logic of "protecting" children.

Curiously, Hallmark gave in, despite the fact that same-sex weddings are very much a part of the current fabric of American life – as legal and wholesome as opposite-sex weddings. They announced they would not air the ads again. And so, moments after that, all still on this same Saturday afternoon, the #BoycottHallmark hashtag began trending. Zola's banned commercials were now being widely shared on numerous social platforms, and an even more vocal contingency of Hallmark's stakeholders were speaking up.

By Monday, Hallmark executives had changed their minds. CEO Mike Perry released a statement on how the company had been "agonizing" over the decision to pull the ads, mindful of "the hurt it has unintentionally caused," admitting that it was "the wrong decision." Like Starbucks, Hallmark thought there was an easy calculation to be made here. The Christian moms' group was noisy, fast-moving, and far-reaching. Hallmark thought it wise to quickly make this critical customer base happy and move on.

The Hallmark decision-makers should have reflected on their company's values and principles and made the decision that aligned with their search for meaning in work. They should have taken the time to consider the social and emotional effects of airing, and then pulling, the ads showing gay weddings but not straight weddings. They should have analyzed the wants and needs of all of their stakeholders, not just those reacting in the immediate moment. The Hallmark execs naïvely thought they could make this scandal go away before it became too scandalous. But there are ethical implications behind every business move. And there is no clear way to make everyone happy.

Consider how the CEO of Whole Foods reacted in the early stages of the COVID-19 pandemic. CEO John Mackey sent an email stating, "Team Members who have a medical emergency or death in their immediate family can receive donated Personal Time Off (PTO) hours, not only from Team Members in their own location, but also from Team Members across the country." The policy of donating and sharing PTO hours was instituted by Whole Foods in the 1980s as a way for the then-small grocery chain to move around sick leave that would otherwise go unused. At that time, this policy was actually a socially conscious move to build community and help people out. But Amazon purchased Whole Foods in 2017 for $13.7 billion. Amazon's CEO Jeff Bezos is the richest person in the world, with a total net worth of $160 billion at the time of writing, likely more as you read this. What was ethical for the CEO of a struggling chain to ask of its employees in the 1980s is decidedly unethical for a multi-billion-dollar behemoth to hold on to as policy today. As former Whole Foods employee Matthew Hunt told the *Washington Examiner:* "You've got the richest man in the world asking people who are living paycheck to paycheck to donate to each other. That's absolute bullshit. With the amount Jeff Bezos makes in one day, he could shut stores down and pay employees to stay safe."

Meaning Leads to Connection

Recognizing that assertiveness and reaction are sacred activities, and more useful in the context of meaningful work than passivity, is step one. But there is another piece to this spiritual paradigm, one which ultimately helps mitigate the fallout from our imperfect reactions and the negative consequences they sometimes bring with them. This other piece, the second step in our spiritual model, is connection. It involves recognizing that all spiritual action binds us to other people. It means being conscious of the fact that we do not take action within a social vacuum, but are part of a deep constellation of beings.

We've spoken a lot thus far about the first component of the spiritual experience: meaning. We've talked about how passivity does not allow us to manifest meaning, but wrestling with ethics and answering the call to action does. But the second piece is connection – not to some supernatural force or energy, but to other people. Every action undertaken by Abraham and Moses was done with the intention of bringing them closer to their community.

In the last chapter we talked about the *tohu*, the chaos that came with the initial creation of heaven and earth. Rabbi Sholom Dovber Schneersohn explains in a hundred-year-old Hasidic discourse that the souls of the doomed citizens of Sodom originated from the realm of *tohu* because their primary trait, the characteristic shared by all of its citizens, was isolationism. The divine act of creation and the sacredness of spiritual work is to support connection. We are a collective. Work must be an act that brings different people together in cooperative and mutually beneficial endeavors. There is no meaning without connection. And that is the true underlying principal of reactive, creative spiritual work.

Rabbi Abraham Joshua Heschel explains that "human being is never sheer being; it is always involved in meaning." He understands the search for meaning to be behind all creative efforts, for it is a necessity of our very being. Rabbi Heschel's theology does not allow for the possibility of finding meaning in passivity. We are each here for a purpose, and for him the question is "how to live a life that would deserve and evoke an eternal Amen." Heschel uses language much stronger than what I have been using here when assessing the tension between being and doing. He describes passivity as an offensive evasiveness, and he certainly lived his life in a manner that was very consistent with his principles as a leading activist in the civil rights movement. And so he states a truth that applies to spiritual work: it can't be meaningful to us unless it is of value to someone else. The next phase of our explorations will focus on what must follow from a search for meaning – connecting through work.

PART TWO

Connecting through Work

4

Transformational Cooperation

Do, but with Others

The first part of this book made the case for discovering meaning in work through an assertive, reactive, and co-creative paradigm of spiritual doing. I argued that meaning, ethics, and purpose in our everyday will only be realized through action, not passive reflection. But at the same time, we need to recognize that there are risks inherent to this approach. Taking a stance of "doing" means we heighten the potential for setting into motion unexpected consequences – the spirituality of Moses is not one of compassionate micro-management guided by a higher voice, but risky cooperation with empowered and opinionated individual people.

This risk, of course, does not mean that we should evade our responsibility to honor our creative instincts, answer the call to act, and initiate change through our work. Besides, as discussed earlier, a passive stance of "maybe" also involves innumerable risks – perhaps made abundantly clear in the mix of uncertain responses to the 2020 global pandemic. So instead of backing down from the challenge of action and the uncertainty it sets free, we need to recognize that spiritual work is a robust, multifaceted construct of doing *with others*.

We take action, but never in isolation. We react, create, and work within a social environment. Thus, with every action we take, there is a responsibility to connect both with those who are impacted by our actions, and those who could impact the effectiveness of our actions, for good or bad, with their own subsequent reactions. We co-create with current partners, while always being open to finding new alliances down the road.

When we start to engage in the *mitzvah* of work – or in more mystical terms, when we set out to release the sparks of meaning hidden in our everyday exchanges – we need to be cognizant of the hope that our efforts will lead us into new social relationships. There is no question that what we do will affect how others can be. But the hope is that the manner in which we have our effect will encourage transformation, cooperation, and co-creation, not retaliation.

We need to plan and account for the fact that a search for meaning, and the reactive efforts this hunt requires, will inevitably lead to greater interpersonal connection. And in the optimal scenarios, these sometimes surprising new relationships that emerge as a consequence of our doing will help mitigate potential missteps.

Engaging in the act of doing with others, hand in hand as partners, makes us better equipped for the uncertain future that we are shaping with our reactions. Our new friends and allies will work with us to ensure the changes we initiate will be for the better. And the reverse is also true: disconnected actions will lead to unpredictable reactions from those who we alienate.

For those of us whose current working lives are bringing us down because of a lack of meaningful social connections, where the actions of those who can affect us are more consistently alienating as opposed to inviting, there is a solution. We need to use our spiritual faculties to raise up our currently uninspiring encounters with others. We need to allow ourselves to be transformed through the cooperative enterprise of work.

Retreating from the social realm of proactive cooperation into a state of non-judgmental observations will only exacerbate the problems faced by workers in this disruptive age, especially if we perceive the actions to be alienating or harmful. Change is a constant. It is best for our social order if those leading the change are driven by a sense of meaningful, connective spiritual work and not greed or selfishness.

For example, in the early days of the COVID-19 global public health crisis, it was revealed that US Senator Richard Burr, who chairs the Senate Intelligence Committee, sold $1.6 million in stock in one day, including hospitality industry holdings, after receiving a private brief-ing that warned about COVID-19, while assuring the public that all would be fine. Similarly, Senator Kelly Loeffler unloaded millions in stocks after receiving a private briefing and invested in a remote-work company, while tweeting that the economy was strong, Americans had nothing to worry about, and suggesting that Democrats were sowing fear for political purposes. Leaders whose immediate reaction after receiving a classified briefing about a crisis is to profit rather than prepare a response that benefits their constituencies are not lead-ers at all. How can we convince those who believe that the traits of self-interest and greed will continue to dominate in any future work environment to have hope and confidence that refocused efforts can lead to increased connection?

Well, as a starting point, we should emphasize that spiritual work in the Jewish tradition rejects privileging the pursuit of firm-centric profit maximization as a legitimate corporate objective. While greed often seems to be celebrated by the current elite of our capitalist sys-tem, it need not be the defining characteristic of successful business endeavors moving forward. We can reform capitalism from within so that our economic exchanges are still creative and innovative without embracing the harmful assumptions that have led to such alienation in our workforce.

Of course, hoping that a future version of capitalism rejects share-holder wealth maximization as its primary objective does not mean to suggest that efforts to make money are in conflict with spiritual work. Clearly, any coherent approach to modern work within a capitalist system will still be based on celebrating the outcome of creating new value, which includes economic value. And within the Jewish tradition those who discover a way to release new value are encouraged to claim a fair share of their efforts.

But a spiritually inspired approach will center social welfare development. It will recognize that we need to take care of each other, not just because this is a moral good in itself, but because spiritual bonding and an increased sense of social responsibility are both necessary consequences of creative assertiveness. It means that profits become a welcome outcome of spiritual work, but are never expressed as the focused objective of any endeavor.

The Cooperative Friend

Recalling the gloomy data about millennials shared in the introduction, quantifying their dissatisfaction with our social institutions and media, near-absolute distrust of business leaders and the corporations they helm, and likely desire to switch jobs before enough time has passed to establish deep and long-lasting connections, where should we begin this next part of our exploration? What is the most logical, but at the same the most effective, first step we can take in deliberately building connections through our meaningful spiritual work? What can we do to support the success of our action-oriented *mitzvah* philosophy? The answer is as simple as it is profound: finding what ancient Judaism refers to as a *chaver*, the spiritually cooperative friend.

There is broad recognition that if capitalism is to be repaired or salvaged so that it can last another generation, we as a society simply must find ways to work together. History has shown that under the right conditions, in the right circumstances, and with the right people, meaningful cooperation can take place in even the most trying of circumstances. But the capacity to cooperate is not a universal trait. In many instances, cooperative endeavors fall apart as quickly as they form. Yet cooperation is critical to political, economic, and social success.

The common refrain is that only through the sacrifice of personal benefits for the common good can we work together to achieve what we are unable to achieve alone. But a narrative of personal sacrifice in isolation from a larger sense of meaning and purpose is not particularly compelling to workers today. Being acknowledged as a "team player" who is asked to enact passivity for the sake of the larger group is a lot like the feeling after winning a participation award ... it's something ... but not all of it's good.

In fact, as the *Wall Street Journal* has recently reported, even a proactive "good team player" can be harmful to themselves and their organization. There is a growing recognition of the risk of burning out when seeking to accommodate every co-worker's request or saying yes to too many meetings. The research shows that the trend toward collaboration has turned some personal qualities that might be strengths in other settings into weaknesses at work. A desire to help, a need to feel in control, or even a wish to be seen as an expert can cause people to say yes to non-essential work. Thus, even being a team player who is not on the bench can be not only inefficient but also downright destructive.

So, how do we encourage better cooperation in work? It's a question asked by researchers in fields as diverse as psychology, sociology, neuroscience, and anthropology, but with disappointing answers. Even cutting-edge research shows that it is nearly impossible to support reliable cooperation. That's why it becomes a spiritual challenge. The quest for meaning must lead to new and better connection. In many ways, passivity is a much easier spiritual path than assertiveness and reaction. But it's not meeting the practical needs of workers today, and it's not shaping our culture in a way that inspires much hope for the future.

Approaching cooperation as a potentially transformative encounter, and not simply as a sacrifice of personal benefit (as it is often conceived), helps workers thrive amidst complexity, disruption, and information. It allows participants to generate, not just consume, trust. It manifests in creative situations where everyone involved is actually needed to achieve an end, where we are more than simply cogs in a machine, and come out of the creative process meaningfully transformed.

Where to start? Find a friend.

Friendship as a Meaningful Work Resource

Writing that last sentence was difficult. Even as I look at it now, a foreboding sense of eye-rolling accompanies it. Some of us are probably skeptical about what sort of novel application can come from rethinking friendship. But to the doubters, a plea to not abandon this journey we are on together just yet. Because friendship may just be the rarest, most valuable, and inimitable resource that exists to aid us in successfully accomplishing our work objectives in a spiritually fulfilling manner.

Looking at the ancient Hebrew word for "friend" yields all sorts of interesting insights into why an exploration into spiritual work would veer toward discussions of friendship. The term itself is "*chaver.*" In ancient Hebrew, all words are formed by a three- or four-letter root word. In this case, the *shoresh* or root means "to link." Another word constructed from the same root is "*chibur,*" which means "connection." This little bit of etymology gives us a window into how ancient Hebrew speakers made sense out of their world. We see from the construction of these terms that to the ancient Jewish spiritual seeker, the most natural place to look for connection in work would be in finding a friend.

Over the centuries, Jewish sages have put a lot of thought into the role friendship plays in having a meaningful and productive life. For example, Yehoshua ben Prachiah offers some oddly worded advice on the topic in Pirkei Avot (1:2), an ancient compilation of Jewish ethical teachings, which has captured the attention of numerous commentators throughout the ages. He is quoted as telling us to "acquire" for ourselves a friend. The Hebrew term he employs is "*keneh*," which means "to buy." The obvious question is: Why does ben Prachiah choose the instrumental language of commerce to describe the initiation of a friendship, instead of moral or relational language?

Human beings constantly engage in a dance of influence, playing to different motivations as we try to entice others to cooperate with us, or accede to the influence efforts of others. There are at least three distinct motivations: a moral motivation tied to our internal system of values; a relational motivation to establish or maintain a satisfying relationship with another based on either reciprocity or modeling; and an economic motivation to enrich ourselves or avoid loss. These three motivations are not mutually exclusive, but are present at all times in all individuals to some extent, depending on the situation.

Knowing the underlying motivation behind friendship and cooperation is critical to getting to a place where cooperation can be transformational. For example, one unique characteristic of moral motivations is that we accept an offer to cooperate based solely on our internal assessment of how well the situation aligns with our internal system of values.

In other words, I am cooperating with you because I believe that doing so accurately reflects my personal values. As such, I'm likely to adopt an evaluative perspective toward our ongoing relationship. This means that although my ongoing support is fundamental to the success of our cooperative partnership, it will only work so long as the situation at hand remains in line with my moral values.

In contrast, relational motivations are based on the need for identification through social relationships. This means that I choose to cooperate with you primarily because I want and expect to establish or maintain a satisfying relationship with you, usually based on reciprocity.

So when you are thinking about repairing our relationship after cooperation has broken down, you need to remember that in this context, it was the relationship itself which had the most significant value to me. This is very different than the moral motivation discussed above.

Being relationally motivated means that, more than anything else, I want to ensure that our relationship will grow stronger. As a consequence, my perceived obligations to you will override other aspects of my personal moral value system. It's why otherwise principled people can get co-opted into doing bad things for the greater good of building or maintaining a relationship. For example, think of the case (without labeling him as principled) of disgraced lawyer Michael Cohen, who acted as Donald Trump's fixer in the corporate world. He testified at his trial that he was so taken by Trump's cult of personality that he was prepared to do anything to get close to him.

Awareness of how we influence others to cooperate with us and what their motivations are for choosing to accept our invitation to work together is critical to developing a framework that centers connection in spiritual work. Understanding how we engage in this exchange of influence, with insight into the motivations we bring to certain social contexts as well as the influencer motivations we are most receptive to, will allow for more seamless cooperation in our professional and personal lives.

With this knowledge, let's get back to Yehoshua ben Prachiah's advice, and try to parse out which of the motivations he is alluding to.

According to Rabbi Judah Loew, better known as the Maharal of Prague, the reason why it is accurate language to say "acquire a friend" is because a friend is actually an acquisition. That is to say, the nature of friendship is one of mutual benefit, and so a friend can be viewed as an asset. Indeed, many thinkers have emphasized the instrumental language to infer that if friends must be bought, so be it. Friendship is a valuable asset, and using whatever means are at our disposal in order to acquire meaningful friends, including financial resources, is strategically worthwhile.

Some of us might bristle at this view. But is that not what we mean when we talk of social capital? We might be troubled by bringing this sense of instrumentality to friendship. But as we explained earlier, motivations are fluid and contemporaneous. Just because a friendship is initiated by an appeal to our instrumental motivations does not exclude the possibility that over time the friendship might endure because both parties choose to stay in the relationship for moral or relational reasons. Furthermore, being drawn in by instrumental benefits doesn't rule out having these other motivations at the same time.

Some commentators have said that the instrumentality is meant to motivate individuals into putting the same care, consideration, and commitment into the acquisition of a friend as the acquisition of any other significant asset.

In fact, recent research coming out of Harvard Business School discovered that avoiding talented and productive people who engage in behavior that is harmful to an organization (employees who engage in egregious company policy violations, such as sexual harassment, workplace violence, or fraud) can save companies even more money than finding and retaining superstars. The researchers compared the cost of a toxic worker with the value of a superstar, which they define as a worker who is so productive that a firm would have to hire additional people or pay current employees more just to achieve the same output. They calculated that avoiding a toxic employee can save a company more than twice as much as bringing on a star performer.

Now, if avoiding working with someone who exhibits anti-social behavior is recognized as being of such high import, clearly the reverse would also be true. Namely, finding those folks that we can consider as possible trustworthy friends to work alongside us must be as valuable as finding workers whose skills are measured exclusively by non-social metrics.

We know that elite cultures are those that exhibit highly connected work environments, where there exists meaningful relationship across the organizational hierarchy, from the senior executives to front-line employees. Where folks envision a future of working together, bonding socially and professionally, for the good of the company. Where the relationship is more than short term and transactional.

Furthermore, the instrumental language reminds the seeker that this is an exchange, which means there will be costs and trade-offs. This type of thinking is useful at the frontend, prior to entering into a friendship. Once the friendship has been established, and once both parties are committed for moral or relational reasons, we then may be blinded to these costs.

In cognitive research, cooperation is defined as involving any action where one individual incurs a cost in order to benefit others. Critically, cooperative acts are not always selfless; sometimes we help others at a cost to obtain rewards in the future. For this reason, some researchers distinguish between altruistic cooperation, where future rewards are ignored, and strategic cooperation, where future rewards motivate the cooperative act.

Rabbi Yonah ben Abraham Gerondi, author of *The Gates of Repentance*, a work that many Jews turn to for inspiration during the High Holidays, sees friends as useful assets in three primary ways. First, we tend to learn more from our friends than our teachers. As such, bringing a social element to those we need to cooperate with will undoubtedly improve the efficiency of our on-the-job skill acquisition. Second, as I alluded earlier, given the risks of reaction, friends can be counted on to offer criticism when we are on the wrong path. We are less likely to listen to somebody we just view as a co-worker and, quite frankly, they are less likely to take an interest in our well-being. So blurring the lines between the personal and the professional is important for meaningful feedback. Third, friends are important sources of positive advice and guidance. On this last point, he quotes the advice of the wise King Solomon who wrote in Mishlei (15:22), widely known as The Book of Proverbs: "Plans are foiled for lack of counsel, but they are established through many advisers."

This type of approach is consistent with the spiritual strategy of reaction we have been developing throughout the book. Even friendship needs to be born of assertive conscious choices, not passive acceptance. In the context of work, friends are valuable resources. Social capital is as important as financial capital. And if we believe that to be true, then acquiring friends for the purpose of having more folks to create value with is not shameful; it is a moral good in our capitalist environment.

Now, for those who are still unsure as to why we are choosing to use the language of friendship, it should be noted that cutting-edge research seems to demonstrate that the decision to engage in pro-social behavior stems primarily from intuition. Which is to say that when we cooperate, in general, it's not because we engaged in a deep analysis of the situation and came to the rational conclusion that the activity is worthwhile. It's actually because of feelings.

According to these findings, it makes little sense for us to cooperate in scenarios that are anonymous or one-off. We offer our cooperation when there is the possibility of building longer-term relationships with real human beings who have names and faces. Furthermore, it appears as if cooperation stems from error-prone intuitions, whereas self-interest stems from more corrective deliberation. And finally, boosting reliance on intuition as opposed to rational deliberation should mean increased cooperation, as rational deliberation only reduces cooperation in social dilemmas, but never increases it. This contradicts the traditional belief that cooperation primarily stems from the deliberate restraint of our selfish impulses. Our unique capacity for self-reflection, as it turns out, does not make us more cooperative than other animals.

But more importantly for our purposes, is there a model of spiritual friendship that can inform our working relationships? Are there specific traits or behaviors that can encourage the people we come in contact with through work to be more cooperative, creative, and committed to achieving the same purpose and ends as we are?

To use the terminology that has populated this discussion thus far, *chaver* can also be understood as the state of being a friend. Once the relationship has been initiated, we are friends even by simply being. Is there a term born of the same root word that signifies a strategy of doing?

The *Chavrusa* Methodology for Creative Work

The term we are looking for is "*chavrusa*," a technically Aramaic word from the Hebrew word *chaver* that literally means "friendship," but is in fact an ancient Jewish methodology of approaching cooperative intellectual endeavors. What I am proposing is that spiritual friendships can teach us how to engage in spiritual work. I will argue that the *chavrusa* model can be employed as a useful methodology for encouraging transformational cooperation in the contemporary work environment.

What is the *chavrusa* model of interacting? At its simplest level, it is a long-term, cooperative, intellectual endeavor between a pair of peers featuring both a social and practical component. In the Talmud, Rabbi Yossi bar Chanina says that scholars who sit alone to study the Torah become stupid. In contrast, the *chavrusa* relationship is said to make participants in the exchange "smarter" because it is designed to force reaction. Passivity is not a possibility here.

As classically conceived, it is a partnership effort to derive meaning from the study of a difficult text, while building a social bond in the process. But the paradigm can be applied in any work context, as it emphasizes that collaboration needs to be reactive, assertive, even confrontational, while also driven by friendship.

Key to the *chavrusa* exchange is communication and clarity, but these are achieved through challenge and intellectual innovation. It is not by accident that Rabbi Chama ben Chanina used the metaphor of a knife to describe the relationship. He explains that just as a blade can only be sharpened on the side of another, so our acuity can only be improved in the *chavrusa* relationship.

The intensity of this exchange can be sensed in the description Rabbi Yochanan offers of his *chavrusa* with Reish Lakish. He explained that whenever he would offer an assertion within this joint endeavor, his partner would come up with no less than twenty-four difficulties and objections. In turn, Rabbi Yochanan would have to come up with twenty-four unique solutions. And through this laborious process, clarity would emerge.

Let's break down the essential features of the *chavrusa* paradigm. First, it is authentically cooperative. That is to say, if one party were active and the other passive, the experience would be a lecture, not a *chavrusa*. It is of fundamental importance that both parties honor the need to be reactive. And this reactive state is a constant. It's not just the speaker who is in an assertive state. The counterparty needs to be engaged in active listening, where they listen in a way that is quite different to what we are used to.

The not-yet speaking party is still participating in and contributing to the endeavor in a critical way. This type of listening is quite foreign to many of us. We assume that we master the skill of assimilating external stimuli into our consciousness as children, often equating hearing with listening. But the act of listening involves participating in the experience in a more sophisticated manner.

The expectation is that both parties are in a constant state of engagement with the intellectual material. The analysis and interpretation is a collaborative endeavor driven by both the individual who is speaking and the listener who is processing the ideas of the speaker. The listener is always ready to challenge the speaker, not out of hostility but out of trust and respect for the work necessary to achieve the optimal outcome of understanding, progress, and friendship.

While this model is practiced as a method for analyzing Talmudic texts, there is no reason why we shouldn't be expanding it to all work contexts. Substitute the text with the work project, and we have a powerful paradigm for friendship and cooperation in work. All work projects should be approached as fully collaborative, transformative, spiritual cooperative efforts.

This means that all participants should engage in interpreting the challenge of how to create value in an open, trusting, and reactive environment. Each individual should make sure to listen with the same intensity as they speak, and challenge all other participants as appropriate, knowing they are bonded by a shared pursuit of deep understanding. Strategic discussions should be continuous, building on each insight, and risk-taking should be encouraged. Novel challenges require novel solutions. Through this process, innovation is most likely to emerge and the consensus eventually created will undoubtedly lead to the best possible outcome.

This is what we mean by the idea of transformational cooperation. Within a *chavrusa* exchange, the stage is set to facilitate surprise, friendly opposition, and truly radical interpretations. Put on display will be both the power and the limits of each individual's reactive faculties. In a *chavrusa*, we are actively pushed to do, not just be. By committing to an assertive and reactive relationship, where each participant is challenged and confronted rather than allowed or encouraged to remain passive, the experience changes us. And the outcome of our work will likely change the environment in which we operate. It is thus transformational.

Talent Wants to Be Pushed

And so the next questions are: How do we find these friends? What specifically can we do to encourage the type of transformative cooperation discussed here? To best answer these questions, it is perhaps necessary to learn via experience. It's fine to explore traditional sources on the *chavrusa* method, but I think we have gleaned all we can on the topic from textual sources. So I set out to make connections and have conversations, recognizing that it can be helpful to learn directly from someone who is successfully doing the difficult spiritual work of creating the space to connect.

Michael Solomon is the author of *Game Changer: How to Be 10x in the Talent Economy* and the co-founder of 10x Management, widely heralded as the first tech talent agency. He is also the co-founder of Brick Wall Management that has represented rock stars like John Mayer and Vanessa Carlton among others. Michael agrees that talented workers today want to be viewed as partners in co-creation, not pawns to be managed. In fact, he views this as the defining paradigm shift in contemporary capitalism. While others refer to our era as the "surveillance economy," he believes we are living through the "talent economy":

> The biggest change within the talent economy is a reframing of how these professionals see themselves. For the 10xers of the world that's primarily because they are so in demand and created so much value that they were afforded the ability to call their own shots to a degree and they're still learning this. They are not completely ego maniacal or as ego driven as musicians can be at their worst. They do not get the level of public adulation that musicians do, but they see the value they have created for billions of people and recognize they are talent and should be treated as such.

What I like about Michael's statement is the notion that workers who can create value need to be considered "talent." We historically reserve that term for artists. But anyone who brings their skills and talents to a co-creative enterprise should be viewed as "talent." Which is another way of saying that all skilled workers, broadly defined, should be afforded the same respect, flexibility, and space to be assertive that we offer rock stars.

Michael went on to explain that there is also a generational shift in play. Millennials grew up being the stars of their own stories on social media. They are used to seeing themselves as important and unique. Furthermore, many members of this generational cohort shape their expectations on what they see the so-called 10xers (superstar hires who bring outsized value to the firms they work for) are doing. They see the flexible type of work relationships that are typically offered by start-ups. So they come to the negotiating table with an understanding that contemporary working relationships need to be symbiotic and mutually beneficial. And because the West has enjoyed a prosperous economy over the last few years, these millennials have been in a position to demand changes in the way workers are treated and compensated.

What the 10x talent, and in fact the entirety of the younger working class, are demanding is a culture that is very much in line with the *chavrusa* approach outlined in this chapter. Michael clarified that the type of work culture most attractive to this cohort is one where everybody, up and down the hierarchy, is willing to take responsibility for what they do. Whether the outcomes are good or bad, those who take the risks of action own the consequences. Furthermore, a desirable work culture is one where all organizational members are truly interested in receiving feedback. A culture that values learning operates on the principle that when someone's work is in need of improvement, they will be provided with blunt but constructive feedback so that these individuals are given the opportunity to grow and to change.

According to Michael:

A 10xer is someone who is really good at what they do and never wants to stop learning or growing and finding out how they can do things better. A 10xer is constantly on the path of self-discovery and self-improvement. When you create a culture where everybody is on that path together, including the manager, where the feedback comes from all around you, where everybody is committed to that type of growth, you get away from the defensiveness, you break down the blame game and almost destroy the corrosive and corrupted political environment that so many companies have. Instead, you create an environment where everybody is working and growing together. This is how you create teamwork and foster a sense of community and understanding.

As I have said throughout this book, feeling like you are being managed is antithetical to meaningful and connective work. Work cultures that are likely to thrive today are those that create authentic feelings of partnership and co-creation. And as we saw in the *chavrusa* method, partnerships still push each other, still offer feedback, and still expect continuous improvement. But the pushing and the feedback are not unidirectional. They don't exclusively run from the top down.

Michael observes an interesting outgrowth of this trend, which he views as another generational shift: "When you imagine the old world, you think of the boss saying 'Have this on my desk by 3:00! I need it on my desk by 3:00!' That was a way people did business. It was an acceptable approach and the employees responded to it. Because the world has changed so much, the people who are still operating that way are having a tough time managing people who don't function within that paradigm. So one of the things that needs to happen immediately is that style of management being phased out fairly significantly." His observation that we are witnessing a generational shift is a fascinating insight. I have spoken to dozens of senior business executives who loathe managing the millennials working for them because they view millennials as lazy and entitled. But Michael has a different take on the phenomenon. He believes that for 10xers and this new generation of workers, success is a holistic concept not limited to what might be going on at work. If a senior executive is not interested in or not able to understand what is going on in their employees' lives, then they might view missing a deadline as laziness. But a senior executive who views work through a spiritual lens, who recognizes the importance of connection, will want to know what is going on in their workers' lives. They will want to manage in the loosest sense, privileging co-creation and cooperation. They will want to work with employees knowing, in Michael's words, "where they are and who they are." With this approach, you are most likely to get the best out of your team. In a cooperative endeavor of spiritual work, every party will give their all.

To be clear, taking a personal interest in the lives of your co-workers and abandoning the management style of "3:00 or else!" does not mean you become passive and non-judgmental. There's a huge difference between approaching power in work through a motivation to build relationships and being a sucker. Leaders can be kind and still hold folks accountable for what they do and what they say they are going to do. Human-centered management presumes accountability. As Michael explains, "If somebody can't do what they say they are going to do, then they need to go. They are in the wrong job. They are not going to succeed. They are not going to advance. They are not going to learn. Kind and empathetic is not the same as soft and unaccountable."

Setting the Stage for Transformational Cooperation

We have thus far discussed why those seeking meaning and connection at work should start by striving for spiritual friendship. We explored the lessons we can learn from the ancient *chavrusa* model of cooperative friendship, and how it could be applied in a work context. But the notion of transformational cooperation, and the idea that there was a generalizable methodology to enacting it, only became concrete for me after I experienced it first-hand.

It was after an experience that not only met all of the conditions we have outlined thus far but also brought them to bear in a contemporary, non-religious setting. Living it outside of the Jewish study hall let me know that this was a topic worth developing in support of spiritual work. So to best illustrate this type of spiritually motivated cooperation, we will now shift gears and turn to another arena where it seems to manifest most naturally at the present time.

I spoke to Michael Solomon because the field of technology seems to be embracing a cultural shift that is working in line with the spiritual approach we have been developing. But another field of work that seems to understand transformative cooperation is the industry of the creative arts and cultural entrepreneurship. In the coming chapters, we will be encountering the insights of a number of artist entrepreneurs. But for now, on the topic of the *chavrusa* method in work, I want to present as a paradigmatic example the achievement of award-winning puppeteer Ronnie Burkett.

Ronnie started exploring the art of puppetry at the age of seven. He began touring his shows throughout his home province in his early teens. He continued to hone his craft for another decade and a half before forming his Theatre of Marionettes in 1986. After years of hard work, the well-deserved accolades began rolling in. Ronnie received the 2009 Siminovitch Prize in Theatre, the Herbert Whittaker Drama Bench Award for Outstanding Contribution to Canadian Theatre, a Village Voice OBIE Award, and four Citations of Excellence from the American Center of the Union Internationale de la Marionnette. In 2019, Burkett was named an officer of the Order of Canada for his contribution to the art industry in Canada as one of the country's best known dramatic puppeteers. He is also an incredibly kind, generous, and engaging human being, a paradigm of someone you would want to collaborate with for spiritual work.

In the spring of 2019, Ronnie premiered his latest interactive work, *Forget Me Not*, at a local arts festival called Luminato. When audience members arrived at the show, we were guided into a cavernous warehouse-like space. There were benches, chairs, and a host of other random charming items for us to plant ourselves on. There was also a giant spool of lights threaded from the ceiling, cascading down like a Christmas tree. The tickets were sold without any details shared on the unusual nature of the performance. We were there because we trusted

Ronnie. And over the opening few minutes, it would become apparent that the show was to be performed by, not simply for, the audience.

In addition to being profoundly moving, this show turned out to be a masterclass in transformational cooperation. We, the audience, would bring the music to life, as we put records crafted by Ronnie's partner, John Alcorn, on to a turntable and dropped the needle to keep the sound flowing. We would use flashlights to spotlight the action and illuminate the puppets during critical moments of plot development. But most significantly, we discovered that each of us was to be handed a puppet by Ronnie himself and actually participate in developing the narrative. There was no way to hide or shirk this responsibility. We were the audience and the technicians ... and we were the supporting cast. The show's success was contingent on getting nearly one hundred strangers to cooperate and create something magical.

The risks involved in this approach were tremendous, ranging from the possibility of individuals damaging or stealing these very expensive puppets to making the choice to not participate. In an age of distraction, cynicism, and tribalism, Ronnie somehow managed on each night of this show's run to get one hundred people from all walks of life, the majority of whom were evidently not creative types, to embrace a type of child-like wonder that allows us to drop our defenses, be open to connection, and commit fully for two hours to this transformational cooperative experience.

The spectacle was unlike anything I'd ever experienced before – watching executives, lawyers, and doctors play out scenes with puppets, intimately interacting with complete strangers who had left their egos outside the theater, each of us in the room responsible for everyone else's experience. After the run was completed, I connected with Ronnie in his studio to find out how he managed to engender this type of cooperation, and what we can learn from him that can be applied in our project of spiritual work. I needed him to explain to me how he achieved this seemingly impossible feat. And also, a little bit, I just wanted to be his friend.

After giving me a tour of his workshop and patiently waiting for me to finish ogling his puppets, we jumped right into it. "What was interesting," Ronnie shared, "was the giving out of the hand puppets. Because I make eye contact with everyone. People aren't used to receiving and making eye contact. We're so behind our screen that we've become anonymous. It's so interesting to declare one's self. Like saying 'I disagree with you, but keep talking to me.'"

Ronnie instantly brought to the fore a critical point I had missed. Thus far in the chapter, I failed to identify eye contact as salient in our discussion of the *chavrusa* method. Since I was a child educated in the *yeshiva* system, I have regularly engaged in this face-to-face method of cooperative learning, but always taking the necessary physical closeness of the participants for granted and never recognizing the unique supporting role played by locking eyes whenever we looked up from the text.

Psychologist Dr. Christian Jarrett writes how researchers have found that direct eye contact holds our attention, making us less aware of what else is going on around us. Meeting someone's gaze almost immediately engages a raft of brain processes, as we make sense of the fact that we are dealing with the mind of another person who is currently looking at us. In fact, meeting the direct gaze of another also interferes with our ability to hold and use information in our mind over short periods of time. It starts messing with our imagination and weakens our ability to suppress irrelevant information. As well as sending our brains into social overdrive, research shows that eye contact also shapes our perception of the other person who meets our gaze. We in the West tend to perceive people who make more eye contact as more intelligent, conscientious, and sincere. As a result, we become more inclined to believe what they say.

Ronnie's deliberate ritual in how he handed out the puppets to participants gives us insight into the central importance of making eye contact with our potential partners from the outset of a project if we hope to instigate transformational cooperation. It also lets us know that spiritual work is unlikely to be remote work, at least not in the beginning. Although, research has also shown that eye contact mediated by a video screen still has a significant psychological effect.

The second part of his observation, the invitation to declare one's self as present even during an exchange of disagreement, confirms another piece of the *chavrusa* methodology. I discussed in our prior exploration the need to willfully open up and be challenged by those we interact with. The notion of consciously encouraging disagreement, seeing it as a positive force in a conversational exchange, seems to have fallen out of favor in modern times. This is a trend which needs to be reversed.

Ronnie went on to explain that audience members who might normally shy away from this type of intimacy tend to go along with him because they understand that his goal is not to embarrass them. And that the trust is a two-way street. It has taken him a lot of time to first learn to trust the audience. Then he shared the added invitation: "Let them attach to me. They can feel safe. But feeling safe doesn't mean you aren't expected to be active."

This is an amazing line. Feeling safe in his presence does not mean that we are freed from the expectation of being active. Our culture has begun to associate safety with passivity. We are only truly safe because we withdraw. Feeling safe in our current wellness culture is to let things be, to soften, to look inward. A "safe space" in woke culture is a place intended to be free of conflict, criticism, or potentially threatening actions, ideas, or conversations. Somewhere to hide and disappear. This is an idea that we have come to reject over the last few chapters, as we built a case for our philosophy of reaction. Creativity demands conflict and discomfort, and is not antithetical to safety. We can trust that our cooperative partners have our best interests at heart even as we are challenged to push ourselves and do something novel. Safety is not an excuse to just be.

As philosopher Liz Swan concludes, safe spaces let us hide in our comfortable, little existence, which is dangerous because they prevent us from growing and changing when faced with adversity, creating new neural networks and adapting. And the ability to do just those things is what has kept us alive as a species. The fittest in the competition for survival are those that can adapt in order to face challenges and overcome them.

Van Jones, former adviser to President Barack Obama, describes as "horrible" the increasing legitimization on Western university campuses of the view that students need to feel safe, ideologically and emotionally, at all times. Speaking at the University of Chicago on February 24, 2017, he admonished university administrators for protecting students from hearing things they don't like. Jones argues instead that they should be working to give students the tools to be strong and deal with adversity. He warns that those playing this game "are creating a kind of liberalism that the minute it crosses the street into the real world is not just useless but obnoxious and dangerous. I want you to be offended every single day on this campus. I want you to be deeply aggrieved and offended and upset and then to learn how to speak back."

Amidst the noise of invasive social media platforms and the dissonance of increasingly normalized political incivility, our ability in the West to have meaningful social conversations appears to be at a generational low. As a consequence, the dysfunction in the socio-political arena that was already present gets exacerbated as we become ill-equipped to effectively participate in critical democratic exchanges.

We have lost the ability to keep a healthy social conversation going across ideological divides. Conversation is in a state of decline, supplanted by online diatribes. This is concerning, because despite what the gatekeepers of social media may say about the benefits of these dominant platforms, when honest folks lose the ability to understand and respect intellectual differences, they are unlikely to be able to make sense of a complicated world.

Meaningful conversations across ideological lines can no longer take place on campus, cable news, or social media, venues that prefer a cult of victimhood, confirmation bias, and deplatforming – but they can take place in theaters and concert halls. These conversations can't be led by our established cultural or political elite – but they can be led by artists who explore dissonance in all its forms.

In the past year, several major art institutions have announced plans to either eliminate or dramatically lower admissions fees. Among them are Los Angeles's Museum of Contemporary Art, the Art Gallery of Ontario, and Boston's Massachusetts College of Art and Design, which debuted the MassArt Museum in February 2020 with free admission.

The timing of these initiatives is fortuitous. Moral progress is driven by imagination – hearing and telling stories that increase our sensitivity – not winning rational arguments. As a culture, we have historically put our trust in the imaginative expressions of artists to offer leadership in the task of extending societal sympathies. Art offers paths of transcendence and hope, a filling of the gaps in moral progress that allows our political class to follow. Making these spaces more accessible should be a social imperative.

What Ronnie said goes beyond these critiques because he emphasizes that the rooms he controls *are* safe spaces. He does take the time to signal emotional support. He does not seek to upset his audience. But within the confines of his safe space all participants are required to take action. And what he said next on the topic of how he creates a safe space really opened my eyes. As we will see, his thinking validates the thesis we developed in the last chapter.

Even today, people still associate the theater and galleries with spaces that invite the possibility of temporarily stepping outside of ourselves. We are programmed to be ready for the weird sounds, unusual colors, and strange ideas that we are likely to encounter in these types of spaces. We need to urgently build on this current social reality while it holds, because, in contrast, this is no longer true when we enter a university lecture hall or political town hall, where the dominant expectation is to have our biases confirmed, not challenged.

Throughout history we have turned to artists to be our social guides for a reason. Artists talk about hard work, community, reserving judgment, innovating, and healing in articulate and non-polemical ways – not talking points. There is a romantic instinct in the commitment to living an artistic life, and this instinct allows the artist to access feelings that are beyond the reach of calculative logic. Artists look for integration, and can assimilate a multiplicity of viewpoints more naturally than others. The type of art being discussed here celebrates the deep possibilities of our humanness.

When pushed to isolate the true defining trait that allows him to set the stage for transformational cooperation, Ronnie uses the language of friendship:

> An audience can tell if the performer wants them there ... Everyone is imprinting on the incident ... Your frame of reference is going to attach to my work in a way that maybe I didn't think about ... But for two hours each night these people are my best friends ... They've come to take a risk. Nobody wants this to fail ... I'm going to love them for two hours, and I'm not going to stalk them after. I know they leave. I know nobody will be waiting at the stage door to take me for dinner. I know all the rules ... But the most important rule is I will allow myself to fall in love with these people for two hours.

Imagine what working life could be like if we started speaking that way. Not mockingly or manipulatively, but authentically. If we internalized the psychological reality that cooperation is intuitive. It is born of an instinct rooted in feelings and relational motivations, not a logical calculus. Perhaps then more of us would be comfortable using the language of friendship in a professional context. More of us would then be better equipped to make our work spiritual, exemplified by meaning and connection.

There will always be those who are uncomfortable with this approach. For example, Princeton University philosophy professor

Alexander Nehamas argues that friendship cannot be conceived as a moral good because in his paradigm morality is supposed to be impartial and universal. To be moral is to treat everyone in the exact same way. But friendship is partial and preferential. We treat our friends differently from the way we treat everyone else. Furthermore, friendly action needs to be done exclusively out of friendship. Nehamas shares the example of visiting someone in the hospital because (a) we feel an obligation to do so, (b) we want to get something out of the visit, or (c) simply because we are friends. Only the latter approach qualifies.

What we have called the relational motivation is the only one that, in Nehamas's system, deserves the language of friendship. This is an overly limiting view that rejects spiritual work as an essential moral good, ignores the psychological reality that we can have all three motivations at once, and discards the pragmatic benefit of widening the possible definitions of friendship in order to positively redirect efforts to heal our disrupted social order. In that pragmatic spirit, Ronnie recognizes the various insinuations of friendship and adds the helpful idea of boundaries and rules.

So would he call his work spiritual? Yes. But ...

> The spiritual component is hard to discuss ... there is a lot of communing in the work because when you are trying to animate the inanimate, I only do a certain amount. I wiggle, I jiggle, I give them voice, I give them my focus, I give them words to say, but at some point, you have to give them the breath. Your focus and your breath is what makes it alive. So between you and between me this thing is suddenly imbued with life. I still don't understand it but I know ways to make it happen. I witness when it happens, and know when it doesn't. That's spiritual. We allow these vessels to become alive in some way.

There is much wisdom in this idea of how a cooperative partner contributes to a transformational spiritual experience simply by giving breath to the inanimate. I am reminded of Rabbi Menachem Mendel of Rimanov's similarly themed teaching when describing his unique, and somewhat controversial, take on what exactly transpired during the Revelation at Mount Sinai. In his view, the Israelites did not hear God belt out the Ten Commandments. Instead, God only pronounced the first letter, the *aleph*, of the first commandment, which begins with "*Anochi*" (I am). This is an amazing reading of the event, as the Hebrew *aleph* is nothing more than an exhalation. It implies that God breathed into the people the breath of inspiration that is the living spiritual tradition.

The Jewish moral imagination was stimulated by God, but left to evolve in the minds and actions of everyday people doing spiritual work. In many ways, my thinking on Jewish theology has been heavily influenced by this eighteenth-century Polish Hasidic master, who emphasized that this is the nature of the cooperative partnership, which allows us to do the heavy lifting of spiritual work. Anyone who has seen Ronnie perform has witnessed the incredible heavy lifting he does with his "wiggles" and "jiggles." I can get breathless just watching his exertion. But he notes that without the spiritual breath granted by the audience, his creative efforts do not come to life.

And as I have discussed repeatedly throughout this book, trust is inseparable from any type of spiritual work that hopes to lead to meaning and connection, and the connection that emerges must be rooted in authenticity. Everyone on the team must actually be needed. And they need to feel needed:

> It comes down to trust ... when we were planning the show, my stage manager said that we needed to get trackers for the puppets. I said we can't do that. She said we're going to lose some otherwise. And we probably will. Over the course of the show's run a few people probably will steal. BUT I have to trust that most people won't. So when I said I'm going to hand the marionette to someone to hold while I go do this scene, everyone went "Huh?!? You can't!" I have to. "What if they drop it?" They won't. I trust them. Because if I was in the audience and

someone handed me a Ronnie Burkett puppet I would do everything
in my power to not drop the fucking thing. That level of authentic trust
in the room comes from the understanding that their full participation
is really needed. A lot of times when we do collective stuff now, we don't
really want the entire collective involved ... somebody always takes the
lead. Somebody makes the decision. From trust comes the spirituality.
I've been in immersive shows where I was uncomfortable because they
didn't need me. I'm hyper aware that the audience know that they are
necessary. And that's the spiritual component – *you are all needed.*

With this chapter, I proposed a method for enacting connection
with spiritual work. Through a mix of ancient sources and modern
manifestations, I have tried to break down the specific actions we can
take to achieve this end:

1 **Use the language of friendship:** In the introduction, I identified
   the need to view work as more than passive adherence to the
   powerful. Here, I am going much further. Spiritual work should
   be a catalyst for friendship. Reject thinking that problematizes
   this approach or seeks to minimize the number of people we get
   to call friends. If we take transformational cooperation seriously,
   then anyone we cooperate with needs to become a friend. This
   means, as Ronnie shared, that we must set rules for such interactions, and adhere to them. Because respecting boundaries is part
   of what friends do for each other.
2 **Communicate with all our being:** This book offers not only the
   argument for an approach to making our reactive efforts spiritual
   but also some of the mechanics of doing so. Critical to this effort
   is learning to engage all of our faculties when we are active in
   order to invite cooperation. Meaning and connection are intertwined. Communication is how we manage our connections. We
   need to use eye contact to declare ourselves to our cooperative
   partner. We must speak honestly and transparently. And we must

listen actively, with the same intention and intensity as when we are speaking.

3 **Engender safety:** I spoke earlier of the need to become trustworthy, so that individuals not currently on our radar may be enticed to enter into a cooperative relationship with us when the time is right. What we are signaling is safety. That's why we do not shy away from the language of friendship and communicate with all our being. But safety is not the contemporary safe space that frees us from challenge or discomfort. It is precisely the opposite. The feeling of safety affords each party the right to challenge, to create discomfort, to require action for the purpose of realizing the value that will emerge from the cooperative relationship.

4 **Everyone is needed:** Transformative cooperation cannot be faked. We know when we are authentically needed. Just like we also know that when we are benched as good "team players" we are not maximizing our transformative powers. We know when a friendship is meaningful or hollow. We can tell when we are being listened to, and when we are conversing with someone who is just waiting to speak. In our working lives, we know the difference between endless meetings of reporting, versus useful meetings of action. Spiritual work means we engage with a purpose. If there is no purpose, we do not engage.

Ronnie talked about how to cooperate within a room of a few hundred, for a limited duration of two hours. How do we go bigger? How do we engage in spiritual work that seeks a society-wide impact? How do we do this over the long term? That is what we will explore next.

5

All "WE"s, Always

Life Is but a Dream

There is a fantastical story shared in the Talmud that can serve as an insightful postscript to our discussion of the *chavrusa* method for work. It leads us into an exploration of what must logically follow, which is the possibility of spiritual work whose impact is designed to last longer than us.

The tale centers on the alleged experience of Choni ha-M'agel, a sage living in the first century BCE, whose surname refers to the methodology behind his mythical talent for changing the weather. It was said that Choni would draw a circle in the sand (his name literally means circle drawer), stand in the middle of said circle, and threaten the heavens with the assertion that he would not leave that particular spot until an appropriate amount of rain had begun to fall.

As a scholar, Choni was completely committed to the pursuit of meaning through his intellectual endeavors. So much so, that we are told he had spent his entire life troubled by the question of how to decode the intended message of a particularly oblique passage in Psalm 126:1. The psalm was composed as a celebratory song commemorating the moment when Jews were finally able to return to Jerusalem after a seventy-year exile instigated by the Babylonian siege of Jerusalem. When Jerusalem fell around 588 BCE, the First Jewish Temple was destroyed. In 539 BCE, the Persians took control of Babylonia. A year later, Cyrus the Great, founder of the first Persian Empire, made a decree allowing the Jews to return to Jerusalem.

But it would take another twenty years before the Jewish presence was significant and the foundations for the Second Temple were able to be laid. When this momentous occasion was reached, the triumphant line which so perplexed Choni was written. It states that when God finally brought back those who were returning to Zion, "we were like dreamers." Choni was utterly dumbstruck by this choice of language. Why would any rational person describe a seventy-year period as dreamlike? After all, earlier in the psalms, seventy years is identified as the length of an average lifespan. Why would the descendants of the exiled Jewish people choose to minimize the entirety of a person's life, particularly those who never got to see the First Temple, by considering the time that has passed as feeling like nothing more than a dream?

Choni would get his answer to these questions, but it would require the experience of a journey first. And so, one day Choni was traveling along a road. He stopped to observe a local man hard at work planting what would turn out to be a carob tree. Interestingly, the Hebrew word for carob, *charuv*, has the same root letters as friend, *chaver*, albeit in a different sequence. The Hebrew spelling of carob is חרוב while the spelling of friend is חבר. The three root letters are the same: בחר (the ו found in חרוב is a vowel and not a root letter). This is certainly not an accidental deployment of a literary device meant to foreshadow the themes of critical import to the tale. At any rate, Choni is intrigued by this effort, and asked the planter how long it would take for this tree to bear fruit. He is told that it would be seventy years, which is, once again, a non-incidental response.

Choni was understandably intrigued by this fortuitous turn of events. He then decided to ask the planter if it was his hope to still be alive seventy years down the road. After all, it would be the only way that he would be able to enjoy the literal fruits of this effort. But the planter was realistic. He was not fooling himself into thinking his life span would be anything out of the ordinary.

Instead, he calmly explained to Choni that he had already been blessed. He had found, and enjoyed, fully grown carob trees on his familial property during his lifetime. The trees that had granted him this pleasure had been planted by those who came before him. His grandparents at one time engaged in an act of generosity for their future descendants. And so, in a similar spirit, this planter was now fulfilling his own responsibility to the future. He was doing the work that only the children of his children would profit from.

For those of us reading the story, through this encounter between Choni and the planter we can understand why the psalmist described the work of a lifetime as nothing more than a dream. We have just met such a dreamer. Here was someone whose hard work would not yield any discernible value within the limited span of his own lifetime. It was not even the intention of the work to bring immediate benefit.

The man planting the carob tree was working for a dream – the dream that one day his grandchildren would eat the carobs from the tree planted by their grandfather a lifetime before. A lack of present value does not mean that the work undertaken is without real value. To the contrary, just as we are the beneficiaries of work that was done by others for our benefit, we need to embrace our responsibility to do the same for future generations. Work for the future is of critical and lasting importance. It is another facet of spiritual work.

But Choni still didn't get it. Remember, this was an individual who drew circles, stood stubbornly within them, and demanded rain from the heavens – and had his ultimatums answered. He was the opposite of a dreamer. And so to learn the lesson that we just gleaned, Choni would have to dream. He sat down to have a meal, weathered by this confusing exchange, and fell asleep. A rocky formation enclosed him and he slept for seventy years. When he awoke, he saw the grandson of the planter joyfully harvesting the carobs. The dream of the grandfather had been realized. His spiritual work had led to a materially beneficial outcome for his grandson.

Now, some of us reading this tale might wonder at this point why the story needs to turn into a Jewish Rip Van Winkle. Couldn't Choni get the full moral of this story simply from the conversational exchange he had with the future-oriented planter? Rabbi Hyim Shafner, spiritual leader of the Kesher Israel Synagogue in Washington, DC, says no. He explains that Choni's question couldn't be answered by meditating on the planter's outlook or thinking through the costs and benefits of this approach to work. To fully understand this idea, it had to be experiential.

We all have our strengths and weaknesses. For Choni, wisdom could only be enhanced by doing. He needed to pass a lifetime dreaming because of his child-like approach to life. The child in Choni could not understand how it was possible for a whole people to live in a state of exile for seventy years and keep an unrealized dream alive their entire lives. Who would want to live so unfulfilled? Choni could not see the long term.

The story ends with Choni heading toward the academy after awakening to engage in learning. The Talmudic authors had one more lesson to teach us. As Choni entered the hallway, he heard scholars referencing his name as an authority in settling disputes. But when he announced to them who he was, that he had returned to continue his intellectual work, nobody believed him. Despite his best efforts to prove his identity and share his miraculous tale, he ended up alone.

Choni could not find intellectual companionship with those of the present generation. The cooperative friendships that sustained him prior to his lifetime of sleep were no longer available to him. And so he prayed: "*O'chavrusa O'misusa.*" He shouted to the heavens, "Give me a *chavrusa* or give me death."

Through this journey, Choni came to understand the importance of long-term cooperative endeavors. He saw that a critical element of spiritual work was doing our part for the future. And he realized something even more profound – that his part in the narrative of being and doing was done. He had planted the seeds of learning in his lifetime. Being recognized as an authority while alive was one thing, but he had the unique privilege, unlike the carob planter, to see for himself that his work bore intellectual fruit. And being recognized as an authority by future generations represented a higher level of achievement.

But now, nobody new would partner with him. The next generation was doing their work. They were meant to build on his efforts, but not build with him. In this world, Choni had no friend with whom to engage in cooperative spiritual work. And he knew that independent intellectual effort would only make him dumb. If he did not have a spiritual friendship with which to engage in cooperative activities, then there was no meaningful work left for him. Any further learning would be a practice without a purpose. So Choni prayed one last time. Only his prayers were not for communal relief from drought but for personal relief from uselessness. And as had always been his experience, Choni's prayers were answered. He died.

At a Crossroad

How do we cooperate on a larger social stage? How do we bring trust and friendship to the political arena, doing spiritual work that will hopefully impact future generations? If meaning and connection are so intimately tied, then we must turn our attention to the great work which needs to be done in our divisive political climate.

As neo-liberalism fades in the West, can we expect transformational cooperation to take place under populist, nationalist, or socialist regimes? Management researchers have come to realize that the increase in catastrophic environmental events suggests that business and government will need to work together to ensure that markets and communities are as resilient as possible. This was made very clear during the COVID-19 public health crisis. Businesses were asked to step up and become partners with government, to help assure social order. Some steps were small, like grocers who opened up an hour early and dedicated the shopping time exclusively to the elderly and immuno-compromised, to allow them to find a degree of safety and stability amidst the chaos and panic buying. Other steps were more significant, as when luxury goods conglomerate LVMH, the parent company of Christian Dior and Givenchy, decided to use all of the production facilities of its perfumes and cosmetics brands to produce large quantities of hydroalcoholic gel – hand sanitizer – and provide it for free to help French health authorities.

Business scholarship continues to privilege the language of economics. As such, we are unlikely to see extensive discussions of spiritual work, although maybe this book will change that. But using economic terms, the argument is being made that the distinction between rule makers and game players is difficult to maintain when changes in our natural or public health environment becomes a destructive economic force. And so, progressive voices from within the business community have come to acknowledge that despite their interests in limiting its size and reach, governments nonetheless have a moral mission.

This is why news of profiteering by government officials during a crisis is so demoralizing. The protection and empowerment of citizens is a higher-order good which makes the freedom to create prosperity possible. More and more business people are coming around to viewing government as an enabler of, not a constraint on, their corporate purpose. But that means government officials need to live up to the higher expectations that come with the job, and many are failing. Nonetheless, given the myriad social, ethical, and environmental challenges we are currently facing, the emerging prescription is that it may be best for businesses to view government as a partner in enabling and supporting markets rather than as a regulator that needs to be managed.

For those of us who are not only comfortable with spiritual language but recognize it as a necessity, a critical facet of this spiritual paradigm is viewing the political arena as an opportunity to seek an ever-expanding "we" as opposed to a divisive "us versus them." Spiritual solidarity can still be built in our contemporary political moment. But if we continue with an "us/them" mentality, why would spiritually minded individuals even bother to get involved in the political realm? And if we don't get involved in politics, we are leaving the work of shaping society for the next generation to those who are primarily motivated by a lust for power or interested in self-enrichment. This would be a massive abdication of our cross-generational responsibilities.

The possibility for long-term cooperation in the public space cannot be conceived of without support from the political environment. But for many in the West, liberalism is increasingly viewed as a failing form of social organizing. As author Mark Lilla observes, when it comes to inspiring future democratic citizens, "the old model [of liberalism], with a few tweaks, is worth following." Lilla criticizes depoliticizing forces that undermine the democratic "we" on which solidarity can be built, duty instilled, and action inspired.

Tactics for engendering transformational cooperation are founded in a sense of responsibility for others – the "we." This responsibility extends beyond our inner circle and present time frame. And so, with this chapter we will build on the last by exploring the potential for finding spiritual connection and transformational cooperative partnerships in light of rising interest in populism, nationalism, and socialism.

As a greater number of individuals in the once liberal West reject this political tradition in favor of a more exclusionary us-versus-them populism of the left or right, we will show how those disillusioned by recent political events can find their power within social institutions and lead transformational cooperative change. And once again, it is best to have a conversation with someone who is working hard to accomplish these things in the real world. Someone who is doing the work they know may not be fully appreciated now, but is driven by a responsibility for the future.

Connecting through Hope or Fear?

In the aftermath of the 2018 massacre at the Tree of Life synagogue in the Pittsburgh suburb of Squirrel Hill, organized North American Jewry called on the community to participate in a display of solidarity which they were calling "Show Up For Shabbat." They asked that we Jews make a concerted effort to attend a synagogue that weekend even if it was not our regular habit to do so. Yet, as a Sabbath-observing Jew, I needed to be someplace else that Friday night. As I wrote for *Tablet* at the time, my synagogue for the evening was Toronto's historic Roy Thomson Hall, where author and political commentator David Frum debated populist strategist Steve Bannon on whether the future belonged to populist or liberal politics.

David Frum is one of the smartest people I have ever been in a room with. And on that night, his words did not disappoint, even though by the organizer's flawed methodology the debate was deemed to end in a draw. Frum expressed a desire to speak to three categories of people. First, the few undecided folks subject to the error that the deceptions of populism may offer them something. He acknowledged that the genuinely undecided may be few in number but were nonetheless a critically important demographic. Frum let them know that populist politicians offered them nothing, did not care about them, and did not respect them. What they offered was anger and fear. As we have noted in this work, anger and fear are not the traits that will initiate or change cooperative endeavors.

Second, Frum wanted to address folks like me and the clear majority of those gathered who see populism as an obvious and explicit threat and have come together to loudly resist. He recognized our worry and fear, but saw as his mission the need to reignite our faith. He noted that history is rife with challenges to democracy brought on by those who sought to build themselves up through the act of tearing others down. But, using the language of cross-generational work and responsibility, Frum noted, "We are here to show that we are what our parents and our grandparents were, and the challenges and threats they met and overcame – we can do the same."

And third, he wanted to speak to the folks who saw populism for what it was and had nonetheless made the choice to support it. In a line that nearly brought me to tears, Frum boldly stated to those who defended Trump and his ilk that while the past five years had been good to them financially, it was coming to an end. And he warned of what could follow in the aftermath: "You will lose, you will lose. You have been winning – it has been five good years for those people – but you will lose. And when you lose, your children will be ashamed of you, and they will disavow you, and the future will not belong to you. And it starts tonight."

I needed to bear witness to those words. For his prediction is the flip side of the Choni story. Choni awoke to see the planter's grand-child happily harvesting the fruit planted a life time earlier. He saw the sages quote his work with respect, even as they didn't recognize him. But what if Choni had instead woken up to see that the planter's grandson was cursing the barren earth his grandfather had ruined? What if he entered the academy unrecognized to overhear them mocking the foolish rulings of the thankfully departed Choni?

This is what Frum was warning the audience about. This is the fu-ture possibility he foresaw. And the spiritual work Frum was engaging in that night was designed to influence those on the wrong path to reset their course. Taking on the language of a Hebrew prophet, he had come to admonish the people before it was too late, while giving hope and strength to those fighting the good fight.

The essential appeal of populism, as Frum explained, is in the angry and fearful move to make a segment of the population the "other," thus protecting the in-group from reflecting on the com-plexity of their social existence. The divisive voice of populism speaks to those who see themselves as virtuous precisely because it offers a false sheen of morality on immoral behavior. This spirit of illiberal-ism, as Bannon would happily point out, was infiltrating both the left and right. We experienced this upon arriving at the venue to hear these speakers. We were forced to endure a perp walk through a gauntlet of protesters. Most painful for us was the fact that many of those shouting at us were our leftist colleagues from local universities. To them, we were what media folks or Clinton supporters might have been at a Trump rally, an irredeemable "other."

The left-wing populism of my colleagues forced me to choose between my identity and agency as a Jewish person and grandchild of Holocaust survivors and my belief in the power of debate. I needed to be in that particular room on this particular night for the cathartic release of seeing a fellow Jew look someone as powerful and dangerous as Bannon directly in the eyes, reference the upcoming eightieth anniversary of Kristallnacht and affirm a liberal morality. Perhaps we take it for granted now, but Jews have not always had this power in the face of illiberal threats.

But ultimately, because of the words exchanged and the ideas shared, the evening gave me hope. I touched base with Frum a year later to reflect back on these events, and to see how his thinking had moved forward. I thought it very necessary to include his voice in this project, for much like Ronnie, I see him as a public figure committed to the long haul of building connection through spiritual work. For while others continue to attack Frum for positions he articulated in the past, I have great respect for anyone smart enough to change their mind.

The Challenges Shared by Present-Day Capitalism and Conservatism

One of the reasons I reached out to David Frum is because I see our respective fights as overlapping. Capitalism and conservatism in the West seem to be suffering from a similar malaise. So my starting question was how do we revitalize the institutions that we still believe in, but which have been badly damaged by a powerful elite taken by greed and self-interest? In response, Frum observed, "Revitalization begins with reform. Tell people that 'capitalism' means stagnant living standards, college debt, unaffordable childcare, impending environmental catastrophe – and of course they seek an alternative. Voters are not ideological beings. They want success. Elites are judged according to their ability to deliver that success. As Theodore Roosevelt said more than a century ago, 'reform is the antidote to revolution.'"

What remains unclear to me, however, is whether incremental reforms are sufficient at this juncture given the magnitude of the crisis. Reforming capitalism would mean introducing changes within the existing structure. And indeed, the argument of spiritual work is that change can be brought about from working within the system. While our end goal is a radical change of the status quo and an upheaval of the existing power structures, we hope to bring this reality into being through constructive discussions and confrontations, not violence.

But I think Frum is making a more important point, one closely tied to the theme of this chapter, which is that if we are building for the long term, we need to be patient. If we believe there is good in our present world, then the spiritual work is in revitalizing those institutions that have historically supported our creation of these goods. Capitalism is more than its faults, more than the unpleasant outcomes brought on by a selfish class. And elites are not by definition a negative force in the social order. Abraham ended up an elite. Moses ended up an elite. Power in itself is neutral. We need to judge the moral behaviors of those that wield it. We need to make sure they are committed to the spiritual work of expanding connection.

But getting back to the debate, some of the strongest points Bannon offered came through his critique of modern capitalism and the damning failure of the elites. Bannon saw a direct line of causality between the work challenges being discussed in this book and the reason why formerly liberal folks were now turning to populism. Bannon argued that the moment for reform had passed, and that populism would be our political future. The only question he saw as meaningful was whether the dominant form would be the "populist nationalism" of the right or the "populist socialism" of the left.

In a fascinating rhetorical move, Bannon decided to go back to the global financial crisis of 2008. He saw decisions made in that context as the defining socio-economic event heralding the fall of liberalism. Specifically, he credits the political moment when Ben Bernanke, chair of the Federal Reserve, and Hank Paulson, secretary of the treasury, advised the President of the United States to authorize a $1-trillion cash infusion into the American financial system to prevent it from collapsing. Bannon observed that "nobody's ever brought the United States to its knees like that day. Who did that? The financial, the corporate, the permanent, political class. What was their solution? To create money and bail themselves out."

Bannon scares the hell out of me. But nothing in the above quoted statement of his is substantively wrong. In fact, when asked to reflect on their actions a decade later while speaking during a forum at the Brookings Institution in Washington, DC, Bernanke and Paulson made no apologies. While recognizing why their actions were problematic, and may have led to the anger which Bannon would tap into, they still argued that they did the best they could with their power during incredibly trying circumstances: "We stepped in before the banks had collapsed and we did some things to fix the financial system which are very hard to explain because they are objectionable things," Paulson said. "In the United States of America there's a fundamental sense of fairness that the American people have ... You don't want to reward the arsonist." Yet that's exactly what they did.

I had written a paper at the time of the financial crisis asserting that the faith that public policy-makers had resolved the major economic issues associated with business cycles and volatility, combined with the private sector's faith in hyper-rational modern finance and unregulated markets, created an environment conducive to the growth of greed. The arrogant faith in the new financial order led to a lack of attention to governance and ethics despite the famous ethical failures which were littered throughout the business press. While it is often said that success breeds success, long bull markets and excess liquidity breed overconfidence and an overcommitment to revenue-generating activities as opposed to control activities. In this environment of weak governance, unethical behavior flourishes.

Frum's response to Bannon during the debate was pointed and strong. He calmly asserted that "the failures of a good system are not a reason to turn to an evil one. We have to renew and repair." It is consistent with the message he shared during our conversation. But Bannon pushed back, emphasizing that his agenda promoted "economic nationalism" that would deliver better outcomes to average people. He explicitly linked politics to economics, and the economic well-being of average folks to removing power from our current elites.

So as a follow-up to the first question in my conversation with Frum, I asked him where he saw the link between the efforts to renew and repair our system of political organizing and the efforts to renew and repair our system of economic organizing. To what extent were the tasks related to fixing capitalism that we were engaged in distinct from the tasks related to repairing conservatism or the Republican Party that he was engaged in? And to what extent were these two missions – repairing capitalism and conservatism – related? He responded, "The economic and the political are not so easily distinguished. One of the most severe problems in the US is the heavy burden of health care, driven above all by successful rent-seeking in the health-care industry. The problem presents as economic, but its cause is state capture. To address it, the grip of special interests must be pried open – and if that work succeeds, the result will be both economic and political reform." Which is a sophisticated way to draw our attention back to the fundamental problem of greed. As I explained in earlier chapters, "greed" is antithetical to spiritual work, but it is still unfortunately seen by many in our hyper-capitalist society as a virtuous trait.

It bears repeating that in the Jewish tradition, economic activity and the acquisition of wealth can be viewed as virtuous undertakings depending on the source and the purpose of the activity. Greed is a vice because it hampers the positive possibilities of economic exchange. It occurs when individuals seek an economic return of greater value than what the input should reasonably earn and in so doing imposes costs upon others. The other individual is harmed in this process because the other's ability to claim fair value is oppressed. In the context of the firm operating in society, greed is encountered when a firm attempts to avoid paying the full costs for its behavior (what economists call externalities). The pursuit of economic rents can therefore be virtuous provided that the economic actors respect the notion of mutually beneficial exchange as the ethical core of economic activity.

In Frum's example, health care in the United States poses a unique challenge intersecting social, economic, and political concerns. The enormous burden of covering personal health-care costs, a near impossibility for many working Americans, is presented as a straightforward economic difficulty. But in reality, the reason health care has become so unaffordable has a lot more to do with the political corruption than with supply-and-demand concerns. These unethical maneuvers have allowed numerous players in the health-care industry to use their influence to skew regulatory decisions in their favor, thus artificially driving up (meaning not market-driven) health-care costs. These "special interests" are another class of elites, not finance professionals or career politicians, but hospital CEOs, pharmaceutical executives, and, well, some financial professionals in the health insurance industry.

As Frum has stated elsewhere, resistance to solving the health-care problem on the Republican side of the equation has been couched in the false narrative that health-care costs have been driven upward by bad consumer choices, and thus could be restrained by better choices. If consumers shouldered more of the cost of medical care themselves, the story goes, they would think twice before calling the doctor and take better care of themselves. But, as he notes, Americans do bear more and more of their own insurance costs these days even as American health outcomes have deteriorated. And he concludes, "The future of health-care cost-cutting in America is top-down cost-cutting, not bottom-up. It's the providers who will have to be squeezed, not the consumers."

My discussion with Frum occurred prior to the COVID-19 crisis. Then, the conclusion was that even a problem as monumentally challenging as health care in the US could be tackled through reform not revolution. It could be done by increasing our skepticism in regards to the claims of the medical industry, pushing back where appropriate, but not necessarily unseating these elites. Post-crisis, this takes on new urgency. Andrew Sullivan suggests that "out of AIDS came marriage equality, a permanent shift in the relationship between gays and society. Out of this plague, let us erect in its memory another living monument in honor of the dead: health care for all."

We will talk a lot about what types of reform will be necessary to revitalize capitalism in the next chapter. But for now, let's sit with the idea that even the type of reactive spiritual work we are developing in this book can be done without a revolution.

Shaping a Different Future

In the debate with Bannon, Frum said, very powerfully, "The future belongs to my side of the argument, because the future only belongs to those who care about it. The future does not belong to those who immolate the future in order to achieve a temporary advantage."

In our conversation, I asked him about the future. How do we forgive, move forward, and build a shared society with the not insignificant share of the population who were, and even are, prepared to do anything for a temporary advantage? Why would we cooperate with those who are not interested in being transformed? Why would we partner with those who have shown a disinterest in answering the call of responsibility to future generations? He responded:

> I chose the word "immolate" carefully in the quotation you kindly remember. It's striking to me that the new authoritarian populism is everywhere united by its repudiation of the fact of climate change. This repudiation owes something to authoritarian populists' contempt for scientific knowledge. But it surely also derives from their electoral base among the old. If you are my age, I was born in 1960, warnings about troubles to come in the 2040s and 2050s can be dismissed; trouble in the year 2100 seems unfathomably remote. Even if the warnings are prophetic, I won't be here to suffer the consequences. My children will see the 2050s, however, and my grandchildren will see 2100. I should care not for myself but for the sake of people I should love more than myself.
>
> The new authoritarian populism is noisy in its contempt for and even resentment of the young. The outpouring of abuse against the climate campaigner Greta Thunberg is steeped in this resentment. How dare this mere child presume to know better than her elders! And indeed, for all her exaggerations – so she does.

Here is an echo of Choni. Too many people have no interest in doing the work of dreamers. If he were to undertake Choni's journey today, how many carob planters would he encounter? But perhaps more interestingly, as Frum has pointed out, in our upside-down world, it is the children who are looking toward the future. If those of us who have lived longer lives are choosing to ignore our responsibilities, then unfortunately it is the children that must step up for themselves.

Children seem to be significantly more comfortable seeing the links in their world than we adults are in ours. The "us-versus-them" distinction is not really well developed in childhood, and the simple view of the world offered by children can often be of great inspiration to really challenging tasks. A few years ago I paid a visit to my children's Jewish day school in order to give a presentation on business. For the presentation, I thought I'd talk about the essential story of business: that it is an exchange between parties stimulated by a scarcity of resources, and that the optimal system to organize these exchanges needs to be rooted in a spirit of fairness and cooperation. I sat down with this group of five- and six-year-olds and explained to them what economic scarcity was, and what it meant for their day-to-day lives. We then played a classic incentive game in order to begin to learn about strategies for cooperation.

In this game, participants are divided into pairs or groups of three. One participant is given a fixed amount of a product. In this instance, and given the group, it was licorice (when done with adults it tends to be money). The participant tasked with the initial disbursement is told that they can divide the product amongst the group however they see fit, with one important caveat: it is the other participants in the group who will determine if the allocation is fair. If the other group members, those on the passive receiving end, agree to the allocation as enacted, then everyone gets to keep their allotted portion of licorice. If the passive members deem the distribution to be unfair, they can refuse to accept what was offered to them, and the entire allotment is confiscated.

Usually when an incentive game of this sort is run with business students, the individual in control tends to privilege a disbursement that yields them an extra benefit. So, if the number of goods to be disbursed was odd, the allocator would generally take the extra unit for themselves. And most of the time, the decision to do so when there is an odd number and the difference in allotment between the different group members is simply one unit would be perceived by the passive members as fair and acceptable.

I expected these kids to behave the same way. Yet when I ran the game with these children that afternoon, the distributor, whoever it was, gave away any odd amounts to the other group members in each and every instance. At no time that afternoon did a child tasked with the responsibility of distribution privilege themselves.

Intrigued, I started to ask the children to tell me their story. I wanted to understand the narrative they were constructing around this primitive business exchange. And what emerged was not a narrative of altruism. Altruism is a willful choice to put aside considerations of the self and work toward the betterment of others. These children did not view themselves as nobly hurting themselves to help someone else. No one in the room was able to conceive of an alternative approach to this incentive game because they all wanted to follow the rules, and the instructions were to be *fair*. Remember, the essential elements of meaningful work outlined earlier? Reduce distance between social relationships, expand community, and increase trustworthiness. They did all of these things intuitively.

But for us older folks socialized in our bad habits, what can we do? How do we enact this type of connected capitalism? Frum continued his response to my question about the future:

> You ask what we can do: It's important that any reform coalitions take very seriously the problems of the young, not only to build support among the young but also because concern for the young is an ethical imperative. The United States will spend a trillion and a half dollars this year on Social Security and Medicare, programs for the over sixty-five. It begrudges nickels for maternal nutrition, for early education, for childcare – and refuses altogether to act on next-generation issues like climate and plastic in the oceans. That alone should indicate how much it is doing wrong.

Populism thrives on division. It is "for the people," but "the people" are a very narrowly defined in-group. The project of expanding sympathies, expanding the "we," is inherently a spiritual project, even when undertaken primarily with political or economic language. Is spirituality important to your project of political renewal? In his closing statement of the debate, Frum asked "for a little bit of an act of faith" from the audience, which is language Frum doesn't often use. So I asked him to speak directly on the topic of spiritual work:

> I'm a bad person of whom to ask this question, because contrary to the modern preference for "spiritual but not religious," I myself am "religious but not spiritual." I believe that one God created not only our planet and solar system, but every planet and every solar system: a hundred billion of them in our galaxy and then how many more in all the other billions of galaxies too. A whole universe is praying to him, and I imagine that God answering back: "I created consciousness and intelligence FOR A REASON. Use the brains I gave you!" Faith in God should teach us to have faith in the ultimate benevolence of the universe – and faith in the fellow creatures with which we share that universe. But the problems of our politics, we are going to have to solve for ourselves. God wants us to pray because praying is a valuable and useful activity in itself. But don't expect help from God. It's on us.

There is a contemporary joke that actually captures the essential challenge in spiritual work as Frum laid out quite succinctly. The joke tells of a world where some irresponsible business practices and lack of concern for the natural environment has initiated a process leading ultimately to the meltdown of the polar icecaps. In short, the world has three weeks before all inhabitable land will be submerged by the oceans. Amidst the panic, Jews gather to hear the words of a revered rabbi. After concluding afternoon prayers, the rabbi turns to the assembled throng and announces, "Jews! We have three weeks to learn how to live under water."

What is the purpose of spiritual work? What kind of narratives should we as a society expect to emerge from connective creative activities? These are not easy questions, and as we have shown, if we are to tell good and compelling stories of our good-faith work activities, stories that we would be proud of sharing at the end of our days, then we need to start by giving up on many of the simplifying dichotomies that we generally rely on to make sense of the world. Just as the rabbi in the introductory parable was encouraging his flock to disassociate "Jew" from "land-dweller," the challenge of overcoming many of our long-held biases in regards to what is normal or possible is a critical first step in reaching our goals.

As radical as the notion of giving up on certain dichotomies may sound, it's not impossible. Most of us only started to embrace these dichotomies later in our lives as we started to get lazy in our thinking. Rabbi Jonathan Sacks explains that what gives us our strength is our ability to cooperate as well as compete, which he grounds in the difference between a contract and a covenant. In a contract, individuals pursuing their own interests come together to make an exchange for mutual benefit. But a covenant is different. Think of marriage, where two people come together in a bond of loyalty and trust, to share their lives, by pledging their faithfulness to one another to do together what neither can achieve alone. A contract is about interests, but a covenant is about identity. It's about you and me coming together to form an "us."

The difference is huge. The social contract creates a state. But the social covenant creates a society. A society is about all the things that bind us together as a collective group bound to the common good, without transactions of wealth or power. In a society, we help our neighbors not because they pay us to, or because the state forces us to, but because we seek to expand the "we."

To summarize the key takeaway ideas from this chapter, spiritual work is future oriented. The transformation may occur before we enjoy the results of our efforts. Meaningful connection comes from expanding, not constricting, the "we." The former is hopeful, the latter is fearful. The question of reform or revolution remains open, but if we are building for the long-term, we need to be patient.

If we believe there is good in our present world, then the spiritual work is in revitalizing those institutions that have historically supported our creation of these goods. Capitalism is more than its faults, more than the unpleasant outcomes brought on by a selfish class. Elites are not by definition a negative force in the social order. And sometimes we should work for our kids, sometimes we should work with our kids, and sometimes we should let our kids do the work.

But the bottom line is that we still need to answer Bannon's argument for why the crisis of capitalism is a crisis of politics proactively. Because he's right in the diagnosis of the problem. The "Party at Davos," as he calls the segment of our scientific, managerial, engineering, financial, and cultural elites who gather at the World Economic Forum, bailed themselves out after the 2008 crisis, and evidence is mounting that they will do the same in response to the 2020 crisis.

They have left a financial wasteland, and they have decoupled from the middle class and the working class throughout the world. But economic nationalism is not the only way to reform capitalism. We do need to, as Bannon put it, "give the little guy a piece of action, and break up this crony capitalism of big corporations and big government." But we need to bring to the fore the capitalist instincts of my daughter's primary school class ... one that treats everybody fairly. We need a connected capitalism.

6

Connected Capitalism

When Everything Is Work, No One Is Connected

The truth is, we face challenges of connection because the work life that has become normal is exponentially different than what was experienced in generations past. It was radically different at the start of the twenty-first century, and the change that began then was accelerated tenfold after the Great Pause. What we do while at work, how and where we do our work, even the norms behind the overarching capitalist system under which we work, have undergone profound changes within the past few decades, few years, and few months.

For workers, one significant implication is that increasing numbers of us do not need to "go" to work. Thanks to advances in digital communicative technologies, in many instances our work can take place wherever we are. This means it is no longer uncommon to find ourselves at work while in the comfort of our own homes.

The ability to work from home has long been romanticized as the ultimate manifestation of personal freedom in work. Historically, this was an opportunity granted to a privileged and elite select few. The vast majority of workers in the past could only dream of the associated perks: waking up at leisure, avoiding a stressful commute, punching the clock from within the warm familiar comfort of our living space, and enjoying the superior productivity that would logically follow.

Now, thanks to the technological innovations that have made digital communication widely prevalent and cheap, more and more regular folks are able to work remotely. And during the lockdown phase of the COVID-19 pandemic, the ability to keep working from home proved to be very valuable to those able to access it.

And yet this revolution in where we do our work was not driven by workers. In fact, the shift to remote work has primarily been employer-driven. We can attribute this cultural shift to two types of corporate interest. On one side, there were large multinational corporations that started to positively conceive of the possibility of a home-based workforce. On the other, there were firms without much of a physical presence that wanted to grow quickly and cheaply through exploiting contingent workers.

Thus, the vision was driven by a consensus amongst both large-scale traditional employers and the new generation of start-ups to aspire for higher levels of economic efficiency at the expense of worker concern and well-being. Remote workers save the corporate giants with a large employee workforce significant sums of money by lowering the need for expensive office space in urban city centers. They also help support those companies that do not have traditional employees but contract out their work and want to expand their impact exponentially.

Just how widespread was the trend toward remote work prior to the COVID-19 crisis that temporarily forced the majority of the population to work from home? A 2018 survey found that 70 per cent of global professionals worked remotely at least one day a week. More significantly, over half of this group (53 per cent) worked away from the office for at least three days of every week. Meanwhile, a Gallup poll found that the number of American employees working remotely rose to 43 per cent in 2016 from 39 per cent four years earlier.

So the question must be asked: At least superficially, is it not reasonable to view the trend toward a greater proportion of work getting accomplished out of office as a classic win-win scenario for all involved? Workers get more freedom and leisure time. Corporations get to save money while getting greater productivity out of their employees. How can one not view this structural shift as anything but positive? In theory, given the associated benefits around reduced travel time, less invasive supervision, and more comfort and leisure while working, we should be finding higher levels of professional satisfaction within the work-from-home demographic. Is this the case? What does the data have to say about the psychological health of the newly liberated working class?

Having been unbound from the shackles of offices and desks, are we thriving in the freedom of our flexible and familiar environments? Has social technology improved both productivity and work/life balance? Unfortunately, results from recent surveys seem to indicate that this is not the case. Working from home has not created the labor utopia some expected.

In fact, over 20 per cent of remote workers have expressed feelings of loneliness and social isolation as their main on-the-job difficulty. Having no reason to leave our homes is not great for the psyche of social animals like human beings. Even things that were once idealized as near-utopian possibilities for how to spend a workday are presenting unanticipated challenges as they materialize into our technologically progressive but spiritually stunted reality.

Now, to be fair and as we noted, the ability to work remotely proved to be a blessing during the COVID-19 global pandemic. As countries were forced to encourage social distancing measures, many industries adapted quickly, finding ways to shift the majority of their operations to a remote format. And experts like Harvard Business School's Prithwiraj Choudhury believe that the experience of the crisis will have long-lasting implications, as many companies will start viewing remote work as a strategic necessity. However, he also warns that working remotely is only effective if companies restructure their organizational processes for how communication, socialization, and coordination happen. For example, remote work demands not only communicating synchronously on Skype or Zoom, but asynchronously, where individuals are not face to face on a screen. Furthermore, remote work demands well-established processes where people are socializing and no one is feeling isolated.

Because the flip side is that as a result of these technologies it has become rather unclear if any of us today ever truly *leave* work. Our wireless devices are either constantly on our person or within arm's reach. If work comes calling, the tools of our labor are always at the ready. And the expectation is that we be as ready as our machines. We need to incorporate the idea of "Shabbat" and the necessity of rest, as we discussed in chapter 2, into work.

The increased mobile connectivity is allowing work to seep into all aspects of our lives. This blurs the once-clear boundaries between when we are on work and when we are off work. Always being available to perform work-related tasks leads to increased stress, as reported by almost 50 per cent of folks who are frequently responding to work emails when no longer "on the clock." In many ways, it can feel like everything has become work.

Even those of us who may have a comfortable physical space to go to for work end up caught in a swirling sea of meaningless meetings, endless messages, and digital overload. We have experienced economic, political, technological, and environmental disruptions which all affect how we go about our work. As a consequence, many of us are constantly anxious, burned out, overworked, and feeling empty. Taken together, these experiences contribute to a growing sense that we are connected to our work by a digital tether, but disconnected from a bigger life of community, purpose, and fulfillment.

This is exacerbated by the fact that "work" was once a synonym for "career," while now it is often closer to "gig." Workers were once deeply committed to their vocations. And the commitment was mutual. There was a time when workers enjoyed the privilege of expecting a reciprocal long-term relationship with their employers that was built on trust and loyalty. This is no longer the case.

We have also seen a significant reduction in the number of public companies operating in the United States, accompanied by a massive growth in the size of the players that remain. Each of the ten largest employers in North America have an organizational membership in the hundreds of thousands. The biggest of them, Walmart, employs millions, albeit tenuously. Walmart is notorious for its low wages and terrible working conditions, including forced and unpaid overtime.

The second largest employer on the list, Amazon, is no better. Working conditions at Amazon's warehouses include the expectation that pickers handle four hundred items per hour, which translates into picking an item every seven seconds. In order to maintain that rate, workers cannot take bathroom breaks and face termination for not completing their assigned tasks.

At the same time, the boundaries of large firms are more expansive than ever, with the reach of many multinationals extending into almost every facet of our lives. This increase in scale, however, is not necessarily tied to the numbers of workers at these companies. In fact, one of the most profound changes the digital economy has brought to the competitive landscape is the fact that a large physical presence is no longer a prerequisite for amassing enough power to have an enormous cultural impact. Social media titans like Facebook and Twitter don't crack the list. When Instagram was acquired by Facebook for $1 billion, the company only had thirteen employees (it now has over 400, which is still a small cohort for a product that serves 112.5 million users).

Why the West Is Falling Out of Love with Capitalism

Capitalism has become a dirty word in many circles. And deservedly so. More young Americans than ever feel better about socialism (51 per cent) than capitalism (45 per cent), representing a twelve-point decline in young adults' positive views of capitalism over the past two years. Our economic system of organizing has led to punishing social fragmentation and environmental collapse. You know things are really bad when former secretary of the treasury Hank Paulson needed to take to the *New York Times* to write an op-ed entitled "How to Get Americans to Love Capitalism Again." As capitalism is increasingly coming under question, companies can no longer get away with an amoral stance on their purpose. And to be fair, not all do.

The massive ideological gap between these two world views was put on clear display over three sections in a single edition of the *Globe and Mail*, Canada's leading newspaper, on December 19, 2019. The front-page headline announced in all caps that "SNC-LAVALIN PLEADS GUILTY TO FRAUD." SNC is Canada's largest engineering/construction firm as measured by revenue. The company was accused of bribing Libyan dictator Muammar Gaddafi's son with yachts and prostitutes in order to secure lucrative local contracts for the firm.

Once caught, the company engaged in extensive political lobbying in order to avoid prosecution, causing a secondary scandal around the charge of improper influence attempts as the Prime Minister's Office appeared to go to bat on SNC's behalf. It seemed as if at every turn, SNC acted in opposition to good corporate citizenship, becoming the poster child for the capitalist excesses of greed and self-interest.

Yet the headline, targeting the newspaper's general audience, might give hope that the company was finally facing justice. A company pleading guilty to fraud would suggest that the worst instincts of capitalists can be reined in, and that even financially powerful and politically connected corporate behemoths can be held to task. On the surface, this headline had the potential to be a welcome bit of good news, signaling the start of SNC finally being held accountable for years of corporate misdeeds.

Except, those who were to flip to the first page of the paper's "Report on Business" section would find something of a different spin.

In this section the headline was geared toward a business audience, and thus succinctly shared the details most salient to capitalist elites: "SNC shares jump as legal saga ends."

Someone who only read the main section of the paper might have thought that the $280 million fine, which was imposed as a consequence of the company's guilty plea to fraud, was a substantive penalty that would impact SNC's bottom line. They might have been led to believe that this seemingly substantive sum would act as an effective deterrent to further unethical corporate conduct. But business readers were told that the market capitalization of SNC had jumped by $800 million on the news. Analysts were exuberant with this outcome, as many of them had expected fines in excess of $500 million, or even worse penalties. The conclusion to SNC's legal troubles was actually a burst of good news not for those hoping to see changes in our corrupt economic system, but for the *company* and its shareholders.

How could one make sense of these contradictory messages? Is this justice, as the main headline suggested, or an encouraging signal to return to business as usual? The answer to this question was to be found in the *Globe and Mail*'s editorial on the topic. The editorial team pontificated, "While it's fair to argue that SNC-Lavalin got off lightly, the bottom line is that the justice system appears to have done its job ... the shareholders and employees of a major Canadian company, who did nothing wrong, have been spared any more fallout."

Think about that final comment: investors who chose to park their money in a firm that for over a decade was engaging in illegal activities in order to boost its bottom line are described as having done nothing wrong. The ostensibly moderate editorial board, reflecting what they believed to be a moderate view, were asking how it would be just for shareholders in SNC to lose money just because the stewards acting on their behalf made some bad choices. More specifically, while it was OK for these shareholders to profit as a result of the company's crooked deals, it's now not OK for them to lose money as they are just innocent dupes? This problematic line of reasoning highlights the disconnect that is leading many in the West to be disenfranchised with shareholder-first capitalism.

Why have there not been more tales of *mitzvah* seekers throughout the 1990s, the 2000s, or the 2010s? In fact, in the decade after those workers in Lawrence, MA, got to keep their factory jobs, over 6 million of their peers were put out of work as more American factories closed down and sent the jobs overseas.

Capitalism of today bears little resemblance to the Jewish ideal, and contemporary aspirational tales are in short supply. We seem stuck. Andy Beckett observes that over the past decade, "it has often felt as if everything is up for grabs – from the future of capitalism to the future of the planet – and yet nothing has been decided. Between the decade's sense of stasis and sense of possibility, an enormous tension has built up. It is still awaiting release."

But maybe we can change that. Meir Tamari, former chief economist of the Bank of Israel, observes that "Judaism does not propose any specific economic theory or system; rather, it proposes a moral-religious framework within which the theory or system must operate." As we keep mentioning, haunted by events on the ground, this feature has had some unexpectedly dark implications. In practice, it has served as one of the enabling factors of the truly global phenomenon of antisemitism.

The Jew can be assailed by the left for being capitalists and attacked by the right for being socialists because of this principle. In the Jewish spiritual system, a righteous capitalist *is* as holy as a righteous socialist. A Jew can actualize their spiritual faculties in any economic structure wholly and authentically, as long as they take creative action with a desire to better the world. Which means we can always be "othered," always be seen as being on the opposing team.

But on the flip side, this feature of the Jewish tradition can inform our development of a unique spiritual strategy for work. It brings flexibility that can serve to change us for the better as we think about what work means and set out to forge new connections in our disconnected world. In this manner, spiritual work can support large scale changes to the external environment in which we work. This includes changes to the systems and institutions that may be oppressive, not only holding us down, but those that we may need to connect with, both now and down the road.

Spiritual work seeks to change all those who come into contact with us through our daily business activities. So long as it is undertaken as a transparent act of good faith, designed to encourage new relationships and expand the "we," the practice of business can serve both a moral and spiritual purpose. But given that we currently operate in a very specific type of capitalist system, it would be worthwhile to see what elements need to change in order to support our incremental efforts at reforming, without destroying, a very broken system.

Can *Mitzvahs* Repair Capitalism?

The institution of capitalism is fundamentally salvageable as a system of economic organizing. The Talmudic sages talk glowingly about the biblical forefather Jacob finding favor in the eyes of the local indigenous population through the possibility of three distinct activities: (1) establishing a stable currency for the people; (2) setting up local markets; and (3) building a working public bathhouse. In other words, they viewed offering financial services, accessible markets, and reliable social infrastructure, key activities in a capitalist environment, as the highest of moral acts.

This was the Jacob whose name was changed to Israel, meaning he wrestled with God, and won. Jacob, who like his parents and grandparents, did not believe in fate or passivity, but in moral action, decision-making, and risk-taking. And this manifested in creating a reputation around behaviors that are very much at the heart of doing good-faith work to this very day. So let's explore each of these activities and how they could be undertaken in a manner to reform crony capitalism into connected capitalism.

The Spiritual Work of Offering Financial Services

The first noteworthy act of Jacob is the spiritual work of offering financial services. This type of work was historically seen as the driver of a non-barter society's economic health. It is also the most worrisome source of societal disease. That's the truth we found Bannon honing in on in the last chapter. The finance industry in particular has created severe ruptures in our society, often leading to disconnection and alienation.

But doing the work of financial services was once viewed as a moral good – even as far back as biblical times, as we see in the praise of Jacob for stabilizing the local currency. Today, though, as the engine of a problematic institution, the work of the financial services sector appears to exacerbate the worst elements of late capitalism. Many of us can no longer defend the notion that mortgage brokers, investment bankers, credit rating analysts, or the institutions they represent are still worthy of the trust we once placed in them. This type of work seems to be the realm of bad-faith actors most interested in feeding their greed and consuming the trust of the ill-informed for exploitive ends.

In the golden years leading up to the last global financial crisis, which Bannon identified as the pivotal moment setting the stage for a populist turn, there was a belief that public policy makers had finally resolved the major economic issues associated with business cycles and volatility. This confidence that government was in effective control of the economy led to the wider public adopting a position of passivity in regards to the financial services sector. We left the work of reaction to those who were higher up in the social hierarchy. But perhaps this great trust in the new financial order led to a lapse in the critical scrutiny of the ethical posture of some financial institutions and, more importantly, the poorly understood innovations that were to change the industry, although not for the better.

Can this type of work be a good-faith activity of spiritual connection once again? There may be cause for optimism here, as research has shown that broken trust can be repaired. What is required is that the organizations and institutions perceived to be responsible for the breach in trust respond appropriately. So how can workers in the financial services sector who want to recapture the trust of a pool of potential creative cooperative partners respond to the rupture caused by past misdeeds within the industry?

In classic Jewish sources special limits are imposed on money and capital markets, born of ethical and religious principles and not an anti-capitalist bias. Specifically, these principles are rooted in the belief that spiritual work should help build greater connections across social classes. This is accomplished by limiting economic uncertainty, and being careful that the connections being made are not designed to serve the entrenched interests of the greedy or powerful. This is a radically different view than the one held by most industry practitioners. The focus of some recent financial innovations has been to work with and create wealth for a very narrow group of individuals.

In fact, some of the public anger directed against the industry has been attributed to the perception that unethical firms were using innovations to enrich their bottom line at the expense of even their customers. The insight that this behavior is ethically questionable is magnified by the limited social good associated with many recent financial innovations, coupled with the resulting social harm caused by the failure of these products in the recent economic collapse. Think of the now notorious subprime mortgages. Originally, the perspective within Fannie Mae (the Federal National Mortgage Association) was that by developing and growing the subprime market, it was working to extend the American Dream. Simultaneously, however, more mortgages, more mortgage-backed securities, and more business in general yielded higher shareholder returns and higher pay-outs to managers. These managers embraced untested financial innovations, focusing on the noble upside to their endeavors and ignoring the risk and potential large-scale social harm should things not go as they had envisioned. In the end, rather than extend the American dream, managers at Fannie Mae brought the dream of home owner-ship crashing down for many Americans.

Many financial innovations have been designed to avoid regula-tion, enable large risks whose consequences were not fully under-stood, exploit fraudulent credit ratings, and manipulate financial results for accounting purposes. Not exactly the type of work that will build connection. The public perception of the damaging nature of these products is real, as is the loss of trustworthiness. Workers in the financial services sector need to recapture the trust of the public.

The *mitzvah* perspective can help in this end. It can jump-start a process of reflection on approaches to financial innovations and on the question of whether this work leads to broader connections and greater cooperation. It is not just the fact that recent financial innovations have lacked a significant accompanying social good that warrants a response, even though that alone would disqual-ify such creative activities from being spiritual work. But it is also the fact that this apparent lack of social good, the fact that these products don't change people for the better, is coupled with a per-ceived danger of the divisive impact these innovations might have on society.

Goldman Sachs provides a compelling example of efforts to be superficially good under bad-faith capitalism. The strategic posture of Goldman Sachs prior to the global financial crisis of 2008 was de-scribed as "long-term greedy," which is to say that it would forgo prof-its in the short-term in order to build supposedly lasting trust-based relationships with its clients.

"Long-term greedy" is a strategic choice related to pursuing inno-vations that could create new wealth for its existing cooperative part-ners. So it does appear as if Goldman Sachs, at least at one point in its history, thought it could make a strategic commitment to put the needs of its clients first. Of course, numerous subsequent scandals have revealed this posture to be an unsubstantial bit of public rela-tions. One thing we can comfortably state is that greed is not good for those who hope to engage in spiritual work, whether it is framed as a long- or short-term orientation.

For example, when an investment bank like Goldman Sachs makes the decision to engage in proprietary trading as part of its business activity, as it did, the question arises as to how focused this firm can now possibly be in regards to the interests of its clients, as opposed to concern for itself and its own position in the market? A *mitzvah* activity needs to bind the active party to a community. We celebrate reactive activities provided they are undertaken with a primary responsibility to someone else. This type of conflict of interest inevitably leads to putting selfish needs first.

Complicating matters further is the fact that individual traders may have their own agenda that is at odds with the best interests of the firm as a whole. Long-term greedy is a strategy that involves a very dedicated concentration on the needs of clients and customers first. However, engaging in proprietary trading requires a shift in focus back to the needs of the firm and, more often than not, the individual trader. Working for an investment bank means wrestling with this seemingly impossible ethical and strategic challenge.

A now notorious example of the strategic choice to work in a system of bad-faith capitalism can be found in the 2007 comments of Citigroup CEO Charles Prince on the topic of why his company continued to be a player in leveraged lending despite concern for the overall health of the market. He explained, "As long as the music is playing, you've got to get up and dance. We're still dancing." In other words, he described the "music" as still "playing" because other companies were still seeking to provide loans for big-ticket private equity deals. Citigroup was not going to stand out from the herd by refusing to make these types of deals, despite the clear risks.

These types of attitudes highlight why so many of us in the workforce have such a hopeless attitude toward capitalism. A firm that pursues a spiritual strategy of reaction is forgoing many of the self-enriching opportunities that its competitors are pursuing. A good-faith financial services worker will have to explain to shareholders and other stakeholders why they are pursuing a business model that is at odds with the industry norms. In the Jewish approach to financial services, there are obligations to sometimes lend money without interest to members of your community, injunctions against usury, and specific rules on how to charge interest. The work is spiritual because the obligations extend beyond the self. The work creates new connections, designed to change all participants for the better.

However, as the former banker and Jewish ethicist Tamari notes, the dual obligation on a lender to provide a loan to those who need it and on the borrower to repay the loan promptly on the date specified reflect, perhaps, more than any other economic transaction, the ethical and moral value structure of Judaism. Because accepting the responsibility to act in a manner that builds meaning and connection to others does not necessarily mean we must act in ways that actively harm our own interests.

In a similar spirit, Rabbi Menachem Mendel of Rimanov expressed his concern for matters relating to social justice within his community by first looking out for the most vulnerable. He insisted that the weights and measures used by local merchants were frequently inspected by objective outside parties in order to insure that all transactions were transparent. He further urged the local community to financially support a school for children of the poor. But, he was also concerned that the rich not be exploited either. For example, he issued a decree banning burial societies from charging unreasonably inflated fees to the families of wealthy people. Taking connection seriously means all people are granted protection, including the elites.

The classic cases within the historic practice of Judaism of efforts to make financial services acts of spiritual work can guide contemporary capitalism to a more just paradigm. For example, Hillel the Elder instituted the *prozbul* during the Second Temple era. Like the biblical characters we have discussed, Hillel was a Talmudic sage who made independent moral decisions and acted on them, even when controversial. This novel construct was an injunction that changed the status of private loans so that they would not be annulled by the *shmita* year. In the *shmita* year, the seventh year of a cycle, personal debts are nullified and forgiven. But during his time, this was causing socio-economic harm.

The goal of the *shmita* year was to encourage economic equality. Nobody should feel burdened by eternal debt from which they cannot get out of. The bible recognizes this injunction has a price for the wealthy, but warns them against harboring base thoughts and being discouraged from lending. But the reality Hillel saw was that people were hesitant to lend because of fear of *shmita* non-repayment. This created a situation on the ground where the needy could not get the loans required for survival. Hillel saw that a divine law designed to create economic dignity and equality was having the opposite effect. And so he reacted to what he saw, not waiting for permission or hope that people change for the better. He created a tool that very craftily undermined the biblical law.

The intention was to ensure that those with capital would not be discouraged from lending, and that business transactions did not become inadvertent charitable giving due to ambiguity around timing. The *prozbul* exemplifies the need for radically rethinking lending. The weak need to be protected from exploitation, but the powerful sometimes need protection as well. The Talmudic sages were very careful to ensure that creditors had the same protection as debtors. And so, assessing risk becomes a *mitzvah*. Facilitating capital-based growth becomes a *mitzvah*. And financial services become a good-faith type of work that can change all those involved.

Douglas Rushkoff observes that an early lesson of the 2020 crisis is that resiliency requires redundancy and local capabilities. He believes that real people with actual competence will now make a comeback. In his book, *Throwing Rocks at the Google Bus*, he suggests principles for a post-growth capitalism that include ideas like optimizing for the velocity of money over the accumulation of capital and employing bounded investment strategies, like when US Steelworkers invest their retirement money in construction projects that also put steelworkers to work or the subsequent decision to invest in projects that hired them to build nursing homes for their own parents. Rushkoff argues that this triple and quadruple dipping is not a conflict of interests, but the leverage that comes with bounded investing.

Radically Transparent Markets

Jacob, who wrestled with an angel, is also credited for his wrestling with markets, the second noteworthy action he undertook. Fundamental to Judaism is the attempt to prevent the misuse of power, including market power. Good-faith work in the Jewish tradition finds great moral worth in transparency and clarity about the nature of business transactions and consequences should these transactions in any way go wrong. Considerable space in the Talmud is devoted to discussions outlining the most improbable of scenarios because the more clarity there is in the economic arena, the better markets can function.

To illustrate the great length Talmudic authorities would go to be fully transparent in their business transactions, consider the story of Rav Safra, the third-century Babylonian scholar and businessman. While deep in prayer, a potential buyer made him an offer. Rav Safra did not immediately respond as his attention in that moment was fully devoted to his religious practice. Mistaking the silence as a rebuffing of the offer, the potential buyer subsequently made a second, higher bid. When Rav Safra concluded his prayers he sold the goods for the first price offered, admitting that had he not been in prayer he would have assented and not sought to bargain.

There are a number of lessons we can learn from this tale. First, we see that Rav Safra was not always available for work, even though he was reachable. The fact that a buyer was standing in front of him

making an offer did not matter. His intention at the time was devoted to his spiritual practice. He was off the clock. Second, one of
the modern economic assumptions behind efficient markets is that
relevant information is accessible to all and flows freely. Rav Safra
believed in this principle, and sought to actualize it.

He wanted the potential buyer to know that he would not have
tried to bargain. He wanted the transaction to be completed based
on both parties having access to the same information about intent.
Much of the bad-faith effort in capitalism's current iteration is that
our most powerful tend to profit off information asymmetries ...
our markets are anything but transparent. Making work in markets
a *mitzvah* once again means doing what we can to keep information
flowing openly and honestly, especially when this means forgoing an
exploitive opportunity to profit amidst confusion.

The great twentieth-century legalist Rabbi Moshe Feinstein cites
the story of Rav Safra's radical transparency in a ruling he offered
on a somewhat different topic. In this instance, the question was not
in regards to transparency to facilitate the functioning of markets.
Instead, it was honoring a commitment to elevate work by joining a
union. In the Jewish tradition, the act of taking an oath represents
the highest expression of commitment. Breaking an oath is so severe
that average folks are discouraged from using the language of oaths
in making their general commitments.

As a consequence, the questioner asked Reb Moshe about the
status of a non-oath expression of interest in joining a union. The
answer was that any God-fearing person, even one who is not particularly pious, should make good on his verbal commitments. The
analogy to our scenario being that if Rav Safra made good on his
mental commitments, certainly we should make good on our verbal
commitments.

This commitment to radical transparency in business continued to
dominate Jewish thinking on business ethics as the laws were codified
by Joseph Karo over a thousand years after the Talmud was compiled.

In the Shulchan Aruch, a work that remains the final word on religious norms in some circles even today, Karo lists the "theft of knowledge" among the practices that violate the prohibition of theft. These prohibited practices include much of what many today consider to be smart marketing. They include feeding a cow just before a sale to make her look fat, painting old baskets to make them look new, or soaking meat in water to make it look juicy. While contemporary marketing privileges the science of persuasion, the *mitzvah* privileges transparency.

Some successful businesses today recognize this truth. For example, a few years ago McDonald's let it be known that it was revisiting aspects of its strategy as it sought to re-establish legitimacy in an environment that increasingly frowns on the fast-food industry. As a business-level strategy, McDonald's looked at the marketing and advertising components of its value chain and saw an opportunity to pursue what the company believed to be a more ethical approach by becoming more transparent. This is particularly noteworthy as McDonald's was once heavily criticized for notorious ads designed specifically to hook children's interests in its products as early as possible. In 2015, for example, McDonald's was told to change its advertising to focus on the food and not its Happy Meal toys to ensure its ads did not have the potential to enhance the appeal of its products to children.

McDonald's launched a special questions-and-answers forum on its website. One of the questions involved a request for the ingredients in their French fries, a seemingly innocent inquiry. Yet the disclosure of seventeen ingredients in what most people typically expect to be potatoes and salt created a viral sensation. Soon after, McDonald's was being invited to interact with all sorts of stakeholders that did not have the company's best interests at heart. Yet because these business-level efforts were rooted in a determined and purposeful strategic effort to increase trustworthiness, the company did not backtrack on its transparency commitments. The information is still out there, the venues for increased interactions still exist, and time will tell as to what sort of stakeholder partnerships might emerge as a consequence.

Infrastructure for the Common Good

Jacob's third noteworthy act, the building of a public bath house, represents engaging in the work of infrastructure building. Back in biblical times, a bath house would constitute both an environmental and social public good. In the Jewish tradition, we are viewed as stewards, not owners, of the planet. As a consequence, environmental concerns loom large. Humans are responsible for the well-being of the world and its natural resources. The *mitzvah* is to build, so long as we are mindful to not be causing damage or destruction in the process. We have the responsibility to protect other people's property and person. In fact, private property rights are very much contingent and not in any way absolute. Any claim of ownership must be compatible with the overall public welfare, and economic growth is not an end in itself but a means of providing for material necessities.

In simple parlance, this has been understood as a problem relating to greed. Greed is a major influence of economic roadblocks on a spiritual path. Economic activity and wealth acquisition can be viewed as virtuous undertakings depending on the purpose of the activity. We argued in the last chapter that greed rooted in economic behavior is a negative force that impedes the positive possibilities of economic exchange. When an individual seeks greater compensation than what their input should reasonably earn, and in so doing imposes costs upon others, that's greed.

The fires raging in the South American Amazon canopy are a perfect example. Brazilian President Bolsonaro has allowed the Amazon to burn, in part to make way for soy fields and beef grazing grounds that would support economic growth. This move forces the world to pay the costs of Brazil's deforestation, as it hampers efforts to counter the worst effects of global warming. Limited economic benefit for some that creates massive costs for others is greed in action. Money and power, too often presented as tools that hold us down at work or are used to keep us in line, can be tools of purpose and connection.

In contrast, Jacob's beloved child Joseph, the dreamer, took the belief in stewardship as a moral good even further. Joseph's work in Egypt after being sold into slavery by his brothers involved presenting himself as an expert in food storage, building, and forecasting, thus assuring that Egyptians would be able to weather the famine. In fact, one of his first acts was to familiarize himself with the people who managed agriculture, the locations and conditions of the fields, the crops, the roads, and the means of transportation. During the seven years of abundant harvest, Joseph had the grain stored in cities. A paradigmatic example of spiritual work: building infrastructure for the common good. Then during the seven lean years that followed, Joseph was able to distribute the grain to those affected by the widespread famine.

Connecting Is Constant

All of us need to better harness the transformational potential of cooperation. This requires vulnerability, which is the major risk of committing to a spiritual pursuit. But using power without vulnerability is a strategy that fails over the long term in all industries. Research shows that outside of monopolies, companies that rely on instrumental power, the "carrot-and-stick" mentality, to obtain desired behaviors fail in achieving their objectives over the long term as this approach has an alienating effect. There is no better example of this than Enron, the once mighty corporation that brought down many companies along with it when it was no longer able to bully or bribe its increasingly alienated stakeholders. In contrast, companies that rely on normative power, which is exercised through actions that symbolize esteem, communal relatedness, belonging, and acceptance, achieve their objectives without an aversive effect.

Think of the way Harley-Davidson, a once marginal company, became an iconic American institution with $3 billion in annual sales by using its Harley Owners Group to engender a sense of community and belonging with its customers. The Harley Owners Group was created in 1983 as a way to build longer-lasting and stronger relationships with Harley-Davidson's customers, by making ties between the company, its employees, and its consumers. Harley Owners Group members typically spend 30 per cent more than other Harley owners, on such items as clothing and Harley-Davidson-sponsored events. Much of the intent of this branding effort is presenting Harley-Davidson as an American icon. In so doing, it meets all of the above elements: esteem in being American-made, communal relatedness through exclusive events, and acceptance through a focus that celebrates authenticity. Today, there are over 1 million members.

Once again, some of us might feel the tension between a branded friendship rooted in instrumental gains for a large corporation and the *chavrusa* relationship of scholars rooted in moral and relational motivations tied to the noble objective of self-betterment. But being uncomfortable with the spectrum of possible types of friendship does not erase the conclusive fact that we need more, not fewer, efforts toward connecting in work.

Some years back, I was fortunate enough to attend a session with former Harvard Business School professor Clay Christensen on the future of universities. He had spent time talking with Harvard donor-class alumni to discover what in their experience was so meaningful that it created a lifelong bond of loyalty to the institution. Perhaps unsurprisingly, nobody spoke of the courses or the lectures. What they valued most was the personal relationships that were cultivated.

Christensen said that these findings made him nervous for the future, because when Harvard conducts faculty recruitment, it doesn't look to hire faculty who want to hang out with students or that students would want to hang out with. Between our rush to create a virtual classroom in response to technology pressures and our fear of social relationships between students and faculty, we are killing what may be our only meaningful path forward – the consecration of the traditional university as a place for human connection.

We need to connect. As we've developed in the first two-thirds of this book, meaning and connection need to be brought to the forefront if work is to be spiritual. We need business ventures that connect people and pursue an end that goes beyond economic efficiency. How do we get there? The last piece of our puzzle: wonder.

Even Meditation Is Social

Despite our earlier criticisms, wonder can come when we breathe, slow down, and take in a mindful presence. But that doesn't mean it needs to be disconnected from the social. Reb Zalman took the notion that all spiritual work must necessarily be cooperative even further, linking the Jewish idea of *chavrusa* to the mindful practices of passivity and non-judgment. For even when we choose to be in a state of non-reactivity, even when we decide to just be and not do, we must still be social.

Reb Zalman was a unique and complex figure in the landscape of contemporary Western Judaism, spending a good portion of his life dealing with the difficult challenges that come with being a spiritual innovator. Ordained as a rabbi by the leadership of the Chabad Hasidic group, he famously went on to spirit-expanding adventures that were considered taboo in the Hasidic world of his upbringing, including experimenting with LSD alongside Timothy Leary in the 1960s and counseling the 14th Dalai Lama in the 1990s on how a religious community can thrive in the diaspora.

Reb Zalman recognized decades ago that spiritual practices should not be solo endeavors, but should be work that positively affects our social situations. And so, he articulated a paradigm of socialized meditation as a way of taking our inner experiencing of wonder and sharing it among people, reaching for the possibility of spiritual intimacy.

In spiritual intimacy, we can achieve a field for mutual support that is much more than a single individual can achieve alone. It is a practice of kindness and gentleness in which we see ourselves as nurses for the wounded in our social setting. And, Reb Zalman explained, it is necessary to do these things not only in the narrow way, with the people in our own social groups, but also as outreach, looking to develop the type of future relationships that we identified as so valuable in the last chapter.

In socialized meditation, partners sit together in a state of openness and trust that inducts them into meditative states of wonder and awareness. In this form of shared discovery, we speak to our partner in a way that is quite different from the *chavrusa* exchange, which is critical and assertive. Instead, we induct each other into deepened awareness through the medium of a caring partner who acts as a mirror, a reflector of consciousness. Zalman here is using the ancient philosopher Aristotle's description of good friends as mirrors.

Because of our partner's non-judging presence and genuine interest, not simply our own passivity, we feel safe enough to drop our habitual defenses and to explore our feelings of awe and wonder. In this interactive partnership, sometimes we are the receiver, listening in silence as our partner speaks from the heart. Other times, when the roles are reversed, we become the sender while our partner listens attentively. Reb Zalman knew that even when we are passive, even when we choose to pull back after our work, we are still better off with a friend. Meaning, connection, and wonder are intimately tied. In the next part of the book, we will dive deeply into this final component.

PART THREE

Wonder at Work

7

Curiosity Isn't Relevant

When Our Frames Don't Fit

We closed the last chapter with some inspiring words from Reb Zalman. During his lifetime, he was confident that every sentient human being would be able to experience wonder with relative ease. All we had to do was be open to the experience. Reb Zalman would advise seekers on a search for deeper meaning to establish the right types of social connections. He would encourage us to find a community of folks who are equally committed to the journey, as they exist everywhere. Then, with these new spiritual friends acting as our mirror, we could use the techniques of socialized meditation to open ourselves up to the awesome wonders of existence.

It's an exciting prescription ... albeit possibly a tad overly optimistic. One of the reasons I insisted that Reb Zalman become my mentor after our late-in-life encounter is precisely because access to wonder seemed to come so easy to him. But for me, it has always been quite a challenge, even when in a spiritual state of mind. I wanted him to teach me, to the extent that it is teachable, how to find wonder in the everyday. And he did. My encounters with Reb Zalman were truly life-changing, in the most meaningful way.

So, for those reading these words thinking that experiencing wonder is impossible within the context of contemporary work, let me be a source of hope. I truly believe one of the reasons Fortune 500 companies have been so quick to introduce mindfulness into their corporate cultures is because they are cynically aware that the only way to keep their employees from jumping ship is through the distraction of inner explorations. But you can demand more. And, as we saw from the data shared in the introduction in regards to length of tenure and the earlier discussion with Michael Solomon, many millennials are doing just that.

Of the three facets we identified as central to the spiritual experience, wonder is the most difficult to manifest. As such, it is worthwhile to take these final steps of our explorations slowly. Meaning in work? That is something almost all of us have, at the very least, made an effort to pursue. And with the cognitive paradigm articulated in the first part of the book, truly everyone who seeks meaning in work has the potential to find it.

Connection through work? Perhaps a rarer outcome than meaning in work, but that is why it so highly appreciated when it happens. As our analysis has shown, all of us need cooperative friends if we are to be successful in our work. In a disruptive and rapidly changing environment, it is impossible to achieve worthwhile creative outcomes on our own. We require partners who can bring to the cooperative relationship resources we couldn't even have predicted needing just a few years earlier. Transformative encounters make us more resilient and better prepared for whatever might be coming next.

But awe and wonder? At work? Have we lost the plot? Is this book now descending into wistful fiction? That awe is a natural outcome of spiritual work and thus accessible to any who seek it might be the toughest case to make. After all, we know so little about the emotion of awe. We have a ways to go before scholars have a robust understanding of the role it plays in emerging from and contributing to our cooperative relationships, be they transformative or otherwise.

Researchers define awe as the experience of positive feelings of wonder and amazement in response to perceptions that transcend our current frames of reference. In simpler terms, this means that a feeling of wonder emerges when our existing abilities to neatly explain or categorize what we are seeing or sensing fail us. "Wow!" is, at times, an expression of wonder. Silence, at times, is an expression of wonder. It is a fleeting experience of the world that lets us concretely know how little we know. It is an indicator that our mental frames have been broken by the new content we are trying to insert, not dissimilar to the mythological shattering of the vessels in the Lurianic cosmology discussed in Part I.

The search for meaning leads to new connections. In transformative moments, these new cooperative partnerships lead to wonder. And, most critically, these feelings of wonder often lead us back once again to engaging in the hunt for meaning. This is due to the fact that after experiencing wonder, we find ourselves at a loss for words. We need new theories or narratives to help us explain and make sense of what we just perceived. In this way, the spiritual quest can be understood as an endless cycle of curiosity.

Awe and wonder is the recognition that we are part of something bigger than ourselves. Awe appears to trigger what is often described by those who experience it as a sense of smallness of the self. More importantly, awe is not only a possible outcome of increased connection, but a logical consequence of these relationships. When we become aware of the fact that we are now part of a larger community, that we have expanded the "we," that we are not alone in this big world, we are likely to feel a sense of awe, however ephemeral. Recent research undertaken by scholars in psychology has come to a somewhat unsurprising conclusion: that the feeling of wonder directs our attention to those "big-picture" entities in life. It encourages us to think more about the collective dimensions of our identity, and less about the significance we tend to attach to personal concerns and goals.

While many might find this intuitive, these research efforts on awe, self-categorization, and feelings of smallness lend scientific legitimacy to the traditional understanding in ancient spiritual traditions that awe is a force which transforms. The experience of awe and wonder changes the way we think about ourselves and our place in the world. This transient sensation shifts our long-term attention to bigger ideas, greater responsibilities, and deeper attachments. It lessens the power of our biases toward greed and selfishness. And, as we have demonstrated in the last part of the book, such a shift is critical to enabling the type of transformative cooperation required to be successful with our work.

So, perhaps even those initially resistant to the idea might now see that there is something substantive in the idea that wonder is an essential consequence to the cooperative and transformational nature of spiritual work. The feeling of wonder is as important as meaning and connection, even if we don't always pay attention to it when we experience it. Dare we say that cynicism in regards to the inclusion of wonder as a regular possible experience in work may have less to do with it not occurring and more to do with our not being mindful of the feeling when it emerges? Maybe that's an underexplored facet of the mindful*mess* explored in Part I.

In the continued spirit of taking this slowly, let's temporarily set aside the weighty term of "awe" with all of its baggage and instead settle in to its essence. The key precursor of awe and wonder is perceiving something that messes with our mental frames. It upsets our confidence in the systems we rely on for inferring meaning. Consequently, let's start by being curious about being curious. For it is curiosity that draws us to the novel and inexplicable.

But how can encountering things at work that force us to map out new frames of reference serve to benefit us? Isn't that a highly inefficient use of our time? Does actively recognizing our relative smallness actually make us better at our work?

Well, business researchers have some thoughts on the matter, and they tend to point in the direction of an affirmative response. And so did Rabbi Adin Steinsaltz.

Relevance Is the Nemesis of Innovation

Rabbi Adin Steinsaltz, recognized by *Time* magazine as a "once-in-a-millennium scholar," describes curiosity as a trait of youth. He notes that all other primates in the animal kingdom need to give up on curiosity relatively early in their lives. They need to focus on the primary challenges of existence, like finding food, shelter, safety from predators, and rearing offspring.

But, even now, in the technological era of rapid change and an upsetting of many historic social norms, many of us are blessed with a prolonged childhood. As a consequence, we are afforded the opportunity to spend more time cultivating our curiosity.

Rabbi Steinsaltz suggests that too many Western educational institutions seek to privilege "relevance" above all else. Relevance destroys the curiosity that matters most in social, political, and economic advancement. Great innovations come from curious folks who have time on their hands and objects with which to play. They play in order to satisfy their inquisitiveness, and eventually discover something interesting. Making everything relevant and practical can be helpful, but it can also kill the basic notion of curiosity. Obviously, there is value in seeking to find concrete solutions to real-world problems. But the lack of continuous curiosity slows our ability to navigate disruptive environments as we end up sitting on the sidelines as passive observers stuck in a state of being and unable to do.

Let's look at the disheartening world of academia. Many of our once-venerable institutions are suffering from mission drift, saddled with administrators who have no idea how to navigate interfering voices on all points of the political spectrum, while the general public is losing faith in higher education. Some have suggested that the solution is to increase our focus on "relevance" and practicality. Yet these proposed solutions have been tested and shown to fail.

Business academics have always made sure that our research would present itself as relevant to the practice of management. And what has emerged from these dedicated efforts to closely shape our work for "relevance"? We have probably done more to encourage business crises and immoral managerial behaviors than prevent them, a fairly insane outcome considering how often we speak of corporate social responsibility. But for academics, being "practical" often means being amoral.

We have seen recent articles in the field of business management argue that if a company is getting positive feedback about its social performance from large customers or close partners, they need to view this development as an efficiency risk. Put another way: When you get positive feedback on efforts to do *some* good, take it as a signal that you are doing *too much* good. We are telling CEOs who already buy in to the idea of corporate social responsibility that they may be going overboard, a message they are all too happy to hear. Complexity makes research confusing. So we craft simple, practical, "relevant" messages that every CEO can understand: If folks are praising your efforts to be nice, you are being too nice.

In another article, top management researchers made the argument that because robust, ethical trusting relationships with stakeholders are strategically valuable only if they are rare and difficult to imitate, most firms should not even bother trying to build them. It's just too hard. Pursue ethical business strategies, we tell corporate leaders – but not so ethical that it becomes an efficiency risk affecting your bottom line. Build trusting relationships, we tell them, but only because it will give your firm a competitive edge.

Whether we have been socialized as an academic on the left into a narrow echo chamber of specialized expertise and social justice, or socialized as an academic on the right who believes the customer is always right (with Wall Street usually being our customer), there aren't very many of us who still believe that academic institutions celebrate curiosity. If we are to prepare students for the spiritual work of connection and wonder, we need to hear more from philosophers, ethicists, theologians, or visual and performing artists. More from scientists with a sense of humor or an infectious curiosity and less from the dogmatic careerist or researcher chasing funding from a major corporation.

What Curiosity Brings to the Workplace

Business scholars have found that there are material benefits to workplace curiosity, much along the lines of what we have been arguing for. For example, we have been saying that engaging our spiritual faculties in work will lead to better strategic decisions. Well, the data confirms that once curiosity has been triggered, we make fewer decision-making errors. This result is explained by the fact that if we are curious, we are subsequently less likely to fall prey to confirmation bias.

Think back to our earlier discussion of the *chavrusa* methodology. When spiritually cooperative pairs are facing an intellectual challenge, we engage by hearing each other out and welcoming intense criticism of our expressed views. This is in opposition to the more natural tendency to seek out information that supports our beliefs. Inviting our partners to bring evidence suggesting we are wrong substantively lowers the likelihood that when we finally take action it will be motivated by errors in our decision-making. Curiosity has these positive effects because it leads us to come together and generate a wide range of alternatives.

Engaging our curiosity at work leads to a more innovative culture, because when we are curious we view tough situations more creatively. Curiosity is associated with less defensive reactions to stress and less aggressive reactions to provocation. We also perform better when we are curious. In fact, this stream of recent research offers even more support for the effectiveness of the *chavrusa* model because it identifies reductions in group conflict when participating members are curious. Why is this the case?

It relates to the feeling of connection and smallness associated with the fleeting experience of wonder. When we are curious, we are more likely to set aside our own egos and really try to imagine ourselves in the other's shoes. When we listen as intently as we talk, we can absorb our partner's ideas more robustly. When we feel deeply connected, we are less inclined to put an exaggerated amount of weight on our own perspectives.

So perhaps counterintuitively, the sustained challenging, criticism, and assertiveness in the *chavrusa* model actually causes these pairs to work together more effectively and smoothly than those who embrace the more popular passive model. Conflicts are less heated because they are welcomed and encouraged, with more open and honest communication, and, as a consequence, these groups achieve better results.

Why Aren't All Workplaces Havens for Curiosity?

Given how clear and conclusive the data seems to be in regards to the positive impact curiosity has on performance, it is fair to wonder why so many of us are disenchanted with our work environments. Why is the *chavrusa* method for transformative cooperation a novel thesis argued for by this book, and not the natural status quo?

Well, researchers have also found a few tendencies that prevent corporate leaders from encouraging curiosity in their professional spaces. The first is a bias toward "relevance" and efficiency that we discussed earlier. Rabbi Steinsaltz was on to something when he used the term "play" to describe the habits of successful innovators. To welcome curiosity means inviting play, unstructured explorations, and a bit of chaos into the workplace.

Unfortunately, many business leaders worry that the above is a recipe for a costly mess, and not a profitable innovative outcome. Furthermore, these powerful folks take Rabbi Steinsaltz's association of curiosity as a child-like trait in an ugly direction, imagining that a curiosity-positive workspace would be close to an unruly playground. They believe that their company would be much more difficult to manage if workers were empowered to go off and explore the paths they find most interesting. They also believe that disagreements would arise and that making and executing decisions would slow down, raising the cost of doing business.

And they are probably right. Meaningful innovations are rare, which is why they are so valuable. Innovative cultures are very difficult to create, and even harder to manage. That is why the most cutting-edge prescription for companies that somehow have managed to find themselves exhibiting a culture of innovation is simply to nurture it. The best advice we have is don't screw it up! While many corporations claim to value creativity as an objective, they more often than not reject creative ideas (and creative people) when they encounter them.

This is one of the personal lessons learned through my last writing. The turbulent environment businesses find themselves in today is cause for pause. There is a pressing need to reassess our understanding of what constitutes an optimal strategic posture. After nearly two decades in a business school, I decided to step out of my comfort zone and undertook a year-long effort to tackle this problem by engaging in conversations with artists.

We have heard plenty from CEOs, managers, politicians, economists, and strategists about what businesses need to do moving forward. But the current business environment is characterized by dissonance and disruption. We need to be open to creative practices and learn from them.

In many ways, the artists I spoke with for that project can be described as social entrepreneurs. Social enterprises start with a motivation to create. Musicians, for example, want to create a new soundscape, or melody, or song. They want to actualize an artistic vision. In so doing, they also want to empower all of the stakeholders who may be part of the creative process, from the manufacturers of their instruments, to the engineers that help them record, and the design people that help create the packaging for their musical output. Many musicians also want to be environmentally responsible and to create a product that working-class folks could afford to enjoy.

Put simply, working musicians are entrepreneurs who are less interested in profits and more concerned with positive social and ethical outcomes. And yet the musicians I spoke with had achieved economic success, even though it was a secondary outcome. Those of us on the frontline of contemporary capitalism have an extremely poor understanding of how entrepreneurs motivated less by commercial logics than by curiosity end up achieving successful fiscal outcomes. So I asked them.

What I discovered is that the unselfconscious romanticism that is the hallmark of many artists can facilitate a paradigm shift to allow contemporary workers to thrive amidst the chaos. These artists know how to hold on to the feelings of wonder that are so fleeting for the rest of us. How do they do it? I found that three key points kept coming up:

1 **We need to be committed to the journey, not the outcome:** Lee Ranaldo, founding guitarist of the seminal post-punk band Sonic Youth, is living proof of how a healthy dose of romanticism is a good way to keep on track amidst creative chaos and uncertainty. For him, the romantic spirit spurs the quest for ideas, which in turn encourages commitment to a project even when there is great uncertainty in regards to the outcome.

This is an important insight. Focusing on outcomes can actually be self-defeating. If we are worried about "getting off-track," if we put too much emphasis on "relevance," or if we devalue the journey of creativity while on it because we cannot see the tangible outcomes, then there is little chance of being successful in turbulent environments. For Sonic Youth, innovation came from threatening the stability of things, making creative mistakes along the way, but ultimately pushing the artistic conversation, and subsequently the culture, forward.

2 **If we're not uncomfortable, we're not creating something trans-formational:** Nels Cline, guitarist for alternative rock band Wilco, admitted to feeling the natural fear we all have of stepping off into the unknown and making a mistake, comparing it to the aversion that one might have to sounds that might be off-putting.

But embracing the feeling of wonder empowers us to stick with the discomfort, allowing for radical exploration and the possibility of creating something transformational. Nels explained that successful improvisers need to be open in their thinking. The spontaneous creation of a compelling sound world, this novel artistic innovation, can only emerge by embracing potential discomfort.

Nels hoped that non-musicians will allow themselves to experience music without overthinking, open to feeling wonder in the sounds even when weird or scary. Allowing oneself to experience the mysterious or disturbing elements of art is good practice for navigating a turbulent business environment. If we're not feeling a little uncomfortable, a little uncertain, a little insecure, then we are probably not in the process of creating something that will be truly transformational.

3 **The customer comes third:** Jeff Coffin, saxophone player for the Dave Matthews Band, shared an insight that on first blush is probably the most counterintuitive to contemporary business thinking. He talked about how the romantic instinct of musicians allows them to innovate in what is ultimately a service industry by putting the customer third. Jeff explained that the music always has to come first, no matter what. If it starts to become about something other than the music, then the group needs to reset.

In the Dave Matthews Band, it always has to be about the music, and everybody needs to have the same mindset – of serving the music first, then the musicians who are playing second, and third, the audience. This doesn't negate the importance of the customer, as Jeff acknowledged that the audience is a big part of their success.

The music would not be the same if there was nobody to listen to it or nobody who wants to hear it. But the creative process demands having wonder for the music itself, and thus by extension to the connection between the participating musicians, before it can extend to the audience.

This insight holds true for any industry or product. The primary commitment must be to honoring the mission, the value that we are trying to create and the people that we are creating with. By putting the mission and people first, we are more likely to create something worthwhile for a customer to value. But if we put the customer first in our mind, if their needs trump the beauty of our mission or the needs of our creative partners, if we push for "relevance" over wonder, then we will never find a way to innovate amidst the chaos.

Maintaining a sense of wonder is crucial to creativity and innovation. Effective leaders look for ways to nurture their employees' curiosity to fuel learning and discovery. Successful firms have participants who are always curious about each other and about the potential to be more inclusive. To be curious means to risk encountering a distressing idea. But this type of risk can be a prelude to innovation, as failure and error no longer become dirty words. A society that values order above all else will seek to suppress curiosity. A society that believes in progress, innovation, and creativity will cultivate it. Curiosity suggests a discontent with the status quo, which is why it is often viewed by those with power as a threat. The curious harbor a deep-rooted belief that things can be better.

Now Ask for Wonder

If we are comfortable with curiosity, then we are ready to make the leap toward awe and wonder. Because the highest form of curiosity is awe and wonder. The spiritual experience starts with meaning, leads to connection and peaks with wonder. This leads to an endless cycle of spiritual growth and deepening connection. Nobody has described awe and wonder better than Rabbi Abraham Joshua Heschel, so I will quote him at length:

> As civilization advances, the sense of wonder declines. Such decline is an alarming symptom of our state of mind. Mankind will not perish for want of information; but only for want of appreciation. The beginning of our happiness lies in the understanding that life without wonder in not worth living. What we lack is not a will to believe but a will to wonder ... The greatest hindrance to such awareness is our adjustment to conventional notions, to mental clichés. Wonder or radical amazement, the state of maladjustment to words and notions, is therefore a prerequisite for an authentic awareness of that which is.

"Life without wonder is not worth living." A powerful and compelling assertion. And by extension, given how much of our lives are consumed by work, we can also assert that work without wonder is not worth doing. So where can we find these feelings at work?

When There Are No Words

I promised we would take this chapter slow ... so what is the easiest (although by no means easy) and likely indicator that we may be experiencing awe? It is when we are at a loss for words. If what we have been developing thus far is accurate, not having words can be a potent experience. It's also a state which we should be seeking out more actively while working.

As social beings, one of the least appreciated tools we have at our disposal is to be wordless together. The moment where this idea really clicked for me, tying it to wonder, was while in New York City launching *Fifteen Paths* with Lee and Nels. During the Q&A, an audience member asked Nels to expand on the wisdom he gained through musical improvisation. He explained that the willingness to regularly be vulnerable in a crowded room of strangers was quite common in our religious past. We experienced a wordless feeling of wonder when we would gather in a church or synagogue to sing together. We allowed ourselves to be fully present and participate in the creation of something that was so different from the everyday interaction that we labeled this type of singing as sacred.

But in its most base, and unfortunately, most common application, our social choice to be wordless manifests in a manner quite antithetical to wonder. It shows up as a conspiracy of silence designed to further entrench us in our political and ideological silos. This conspiratorial tendency, which has been amplified by social media, is put on display most vividly when a partisan public figure makes an appallingly ignorant comment. The first, and loudest, critics to call them out for it are always ideological opponents. Rather than working to better our in-group, there emerges a wordless consensus that in an increasingly divisive political climate it is taboo to express disappointment with those who are identified as being on "our" side.

The logic is that disapproving criticism must be reserved for the "other," especially if that other is brazen enough to recognize a misstep and launch an objection from across the political divide. There is often tacit agreement that it is better to double down on attacking the other rather than bringing nuance if it means distancing yourself from a teammate's polemic. This is the opposite of the logic employed in the *chavrusa* paradigm, where criticism and objection are precisely how you demonstrate that you are a good team player.

But this is the reality of our digital age, and the reason why it is time to look for new (old) approaches to spiritual work. As we tune in to Facebook, Twitter, or cable news, our general experience of the wordless consensus is limited to the conspiracy of silence that facilitates keeping partisan arguments to a digestible soundbite quality.

While our feeds might consist of hundreds of individuals, their 280 character expressions are all variations of the same assertion.

So we need to find *chavrusa* partners who are committed to listening as carefully as we are, in turn, being listened to. Choosing to pursue the goal of achieving a wordless consensus instead of winning an argument does not mean giving up on our rational faculties. It is not that analysis and imagination cannot coexist. It is that we need to start with wonder. We need to come to a point where our comprehension of meaning and our experience of connection makes us feel awe, wonder, and curiosity. And that's when we act.

Or When We Have Just the Right Words ...

There is an ancient rabbinic commentary on the creation myth shared in the Midrash Bereishit Rabbah (17:4), which serves to emphasize that the ability to harness curiosity for the purpose of achieving spiritual work is a uniquely human trait. If we look closely at the text in Genesis 1:26, we will find somewhat peculiar language. On the sixth day of creation, prior to the forming of Adam, God says, "Let us make man." Note the usage of the plural. In the extended narrative offered by the Midrash, the commentators note that God, for the first time, is inviting the angels to partner with Him in this creative enterprise. And as the story continues, the angels were at first put off by this request. They expressed curiosity, although not for the purpose of getting things done. They were wondering what was going to be so special about humankind ... what justified making these creatures the ultimate act of creation.

To answer their curiosity, God brought forth the myriad of creatures created on the previous day. He asked the angels to name each creature, but they couldn't do it. The angels were purely spiritual beings ... they lacked the faculties to do spiritual work in the material world.

But Adam was different. When God created Adam, and asked them (the plural is used because, according to the myth, at this stage Adam and Eve were one plural being) if they could name the creatures, they readily took up the challenge. And they succeeded. Adam was able to pull out just the right words with which to name each being.

Adam was able to harness their spiritual faculties, using curiosity and wonder in order to perceive the essence of each creature. Once this code was cracked, they were able to accurately name each animal in a manner that honored the spiritual and creative essence of each individual creature. In the Jewish mystical tradition, a creature's name is its life-source. When the Hebrew letters that form the name are first put together, this act of composition creates life.

The main point of this story is that, from a spiritual perspective, we can create life with our choice of words. When we employ our sense of curiosity and wonder, we can do spiritual work on this planet that is even beyond the powers of angels. Angels are automatons. Only we can bring meaning, connection, and wonder from our work. And, as a consequence, we are once again burdened with a great responsibility.

It is true of meaning. It is true of connection. And it is true of wonder. With each facet of the spiritual experience comes an increased call to responsibility. In answering this call, author Jonathan Safran Foer has written a very beautiful, and very Jewish, book about the climate crisis. The magic of this book, and why it relates to the topic at hand, is in the author's insistence that we have a responsibility to use moral language to describe the crisis. If we all were to actively engage our sense of curiosity, wonder, and awe in assessing the current state of our planet, we would likely feel this responsibility for ourselves. But Foer understands how difficult it is for many of us to do so, and thus wrote a book to start the conversation.

Foer came to Toronto to continue said conversation right after Rosh Hashanah, the Jewish New Year, a fortuitous time to think about moral responsibility and how we can change our behavior.

After sharing some deeply personal reflections on his own struggles in aligning principles with definitive actions, he opened the floor to questions. In response, an individual rose not to ask a question but to state an assertion: The problem of climate change will be solved by engineers. We should stop framing it as a moral problem for society to wrestle with, and leave it as a practical problem that will be rectified in due course by the experts. In essence, his feeling of wonder was inspiring the opposite of spiritual work. His wonder was directed toward the scientists. He, as a non-specialist, was not curious about what he could do, and not interested in trying.

As I looked around the room, I noticed numerous heads nodding in agreement. This bothered me, as I have long felt that what most plagues contemporary Western society is the dominance of amoral language. If the climate crisis is simply a problem of engineering, then it is the responsibility of engineers to solve it, and not ours. One implication of this line of reasoning, however, is that we regular folks don't have to think about our actions, and we certainly don't need to teach our children about environmental responsibility. We can be passive in the face of the crisis. Because, much like the Zen tale shared in the first part of this book, if we can't do anything to make the water less muddy, it is a waste of both mental and physical energy to do anything. We might as well just be and let those better qualified work to resolve it.

Indeed, that very same week the Dutch chemical company DSM announced that it had synthesized a feed additive that consistently reduces cattle methane emissions by 30 per cent. Let's put aside, for the moment, questions like whether this product is effective and whether or not cows will actually eat it (it apparently tastes terrible). Assuming it does what the engineers say it will do, and given that there is no way our moral arguments will instantly convince 30 per cent of the global population to change their meat-eating habits, should we leave it to scientists and engineers to solve our global problems as they arise, and keep the language of wonder, curiosity, and responsibility out of it?

What Foer gets right, and what his critics miss, is that we cannot abdicate our responsibility to constantly bring moral language to the table. It is part of spiritual work, a necessary outcome of meaning, connection, and wonder. In fact, it is precisely due to the unprecedented power of engineers and scientists to introduce their creations into our environment that we need to be concerned about their latent biases. Specifically, the bias toward work that may involve meaning and wonder, but not connection.

We are seeing with increasing frequency how amoral endeavors can lead to immoral outcomes. And so, we as a society need to insist on explicating the moral thinking that may be latent. We need to make moral language explicitly present. We have the power to bring things to life by accurately naming them. We need to use that power in spiritual work. We need to take action and shape the world we want to emerge.

AI Is an Angel

Artificial intelligence (AI) shares many of the characteristics assigned to mythical angels – creations that are in some ways far more powerful than us, but limited in their ability to be stewards of the planet. Recently, the curtain was pulled back on some engineering processes and the revelation was both sickening and foreboding. Focusing on one example, it turns out that Uber's self-driving car, which hit and killed a woman in March 2018, detected the person six seconds before impact.

Six seconds is forever in AI time, so why didn't the car stop? As it happens, the car was not programmed to recognize the possibility of pedestrians outside of designated crosswalks. The AI did not know how to react or respond to jaywalkers *because jaywalkers are not legally there*. The algorithm was based on a framework of legal liability (prosecutors have absolved Uber of criminal liability) and efficiency, seeking to initiate braking as few times as possible. A sense of meaning, connection, or wonder was absent from this programming. It could do the work of driving a car, but unlike human Uber drivers who can bring connection to the fore, the work would never be spiritual.

Put crudely: the AI algorithm of Uber's self-driving car lacked the simple human moral intuition that a jaywalker does not deserve to die. To the AI, there was no meaning to be found in the unidentified object it struck. There was no possibility of connection with this object. And there was certainly no wonder over the frailty of life.

None of this is to say that self-driving cars won't one day become a great social good. Should the technology be perfected such that road deaths or injuries are reduced, the advancement will represent an epic innovation. But until then, we have to be very attentive to the assumptions being made in the creative process.

We are faced with a stream of global challenges as diverse as contending with climate change, like Foer does in his book, to the disappearance of privacy in our economy of surveillance capitalism, to the rise of new diseases that threaten the stability of our health-care infrastructure. The loudest and most powerful corporate and political voices tell us to leave it to machines to solve these problems. To trust the algorithms. To breathe, meditate, and then get back to programming.

But AI innovations reflect the biases and beliefs of the programmer. And a programmer who spends hours in the meditation room does not emerge better prepared to wrestle with these challenges. Claiming a morally neutral position of non-judgment does not mean that the resulting technology will necessarily be amoral. We are only beginning to see the unanticipated consequences of crafting AI algorithms from a presumption of amoral language, but the results are not encouraging.

Companies are using AI to make decisions about human resources, access to health care, and even criminal justice with an incomplete recognition of how programming biases might be manifesting.

Microsoft unleashed a bot onto the internet which quickly began spewing racist hatred. Although ... it was only reflecting the biases of the humans it interacted with. Non-judgment at its finest.

But the problem is much worse, as AI development has a global reach that cannot be regulated. Microsoft was able to immediately see the harmful behavior of the racist bot and quickly take it offline. What happens with AI whose nefarious implications are not immediately recognized, as has been the case with health-care AI? Or when it's not so easy to take the AI offline because of the inordinate costs, as with Boeing and their hesitancy to ground the Max jets?

Even more difficult ... what happens if there is no consensus on whether or not the programmed biases are immoral? As of this writing, the Committee on Foreign Investment in the United States has opened an investigation into TikTok, the popular fifteen-second video sharing app owned by a Chinese firm, to determine if it is a threat to national security after evidence emerged that the algorithm was programmed to censor information regarding the Hong Kong protests.

If we abdicate our responsibility to constantly bring moral language to social, political, economic, and technological discussions, the morals of our society will be determined haphazardly, without curiosity, wonder, or awe. But they *will be* determined – because the work of technology demands discrete, explicit instructions. And wherever there is no instance-specific moral consensus, individuals simply doing their job will make a call, often without taking the time to think where that may lead.

Much like financial and health services, tech work needs to be spiritual. It needs to be motivated by a search for meaning. It needs to build connections to those outside of their world, those who may be well equipped to provide thoroughly unambiguous answers to questions such as: Just how valuable is human life? When does one life take priority over another? What moral responsibilities must we insist a corporation answer to beyond meeting shareholder bottom-line concerns? How does a pluralistic society insist on specific moral norms that go beyond the law?

But to answer those questions, we need to discuss frankly, openly, and with a sense of wonder these questions: What is a human life? What is it that makes life valuable? What makes us responsible for one another? These are questions that were being asked, often without a satisfactory answer, during the onset of the 2020 pandemic. Authoritarian regimes were lauded in some circles for their superior outcomes, but the utilitarian calculus behind their invasive containment efforts took a human cost that, to some, may have been too high.

Responsibility Demands Action

I realize this is not a simple proposition. Secular societies have come to embrace moral relativism as an easy and convenient way to free up space in the public arena for flexibility and the accommodation of a wide array of moral viewpoints.

It's a strategy that has managed to work for us so far, but only because we come together in the politico-social sphere to discuss and debate in moral terms, reaching consensus on general, rather fuzzy parameters. But our AI can't do this … it needs explicit instructions. Our engineers, conscious or not, are making moral choices with each line of code. And as the Uber tragedy demonstrated, relying on the law or efficiency as a standard, instead of pursuing the higher objectives of spiritual work, leads to catastrophic outcomes.

So what spiritual work can those of us who are not engineers or programmers do in response? As parents and educators, the spiritual work is to teach our children that *all* problems are moral problems. As business people, the spiritual work starts with asking more questions about the social and ethical implications of the innovations we may be a part of. And it advances into pushing for the *chavrusa* model of cooperative relationships. What we cannot do is defer to the engineers – for even if we don't understand the mechanics as intricately as the experts, we may have an insight into the effects. Which also means that those who do have the technical expertise need to do their best to educate their colleagues so that sensible discussions can be had.

But perhaps most critically, we also cannot defer to the regulators. Innovative companies will always be ten steps ahead of government. We can't hope for a legal fix. Instead, we need to bring discussions of beliefs and values explicitly into the public sphere with millions of conversations between individuals. Like the sages of the Talmud, we need to be able to argue about morality openly and explicitly. We also need to come to conclusions that will be entered into the algorithmic canon, even if it does not always reflect our world view.

We're not used to these types of interactions anymore; in fact, many of us may bristle in discomfort even thinking about having these types of *chavrusa*-like exchanges. But the alternative is worse. As AI development rapidly accelerates, we may lose the battle between humanity and the machine. Remember, in the creation myth we discussed in this chapter, the angels ceded to Adam because of their ability to name, give life, and engage in spiritual work on the earthly plain. If we reduce life to standard formulas or reduce intelligence to algorithms, we are stepping away from the responsibilities of our stewardship and giving control of the planet over to the angels. It reduces thought to executable algorithms, behaviors to procedures, and ideas to formulas.

There is some appeal to this, as it liberates us from the work of repetitive tasks. But there is much spiritual work that will need to be done behind the scenes. We need to be curious enough to have these substantive and difficult conversations about the value and purpose of life. We need wonder to care, to see the magnitude, to do this right. The future of work depends on broadening the participants in this conversation, expanding the "we," and working with those whose opinion may differ strongly from our own. Can we do this?

Difficult Decisions

Language has become loaded in unexpected ways and once common terms have developed specialized meaning. Many of us are either afraid to talk to those outside of our bubble or have been burned for doing so. Successful workers spend a great deal of time and effort communicating with stakeholders about their decisions and actions. Progress only comes when we are patient with those individuals we hope to build future coalitions with. We need to approach our decision-making with a sense of awe and wonder, appreciating that they could literally have life or death ramifications.

Having the right words with which to engage others in these difficult conversations, whether in the political, economic, or cultural realm, is critical because the cognitive framework or underlying logic of action we are using is not always obvious to us during the initial reflective process. Rather, the logic of action is explicated when we try to explain or justify our decisions to others in a later process. Researchers in management and organizational studies have long recognized the critical role played by individuals' rationales in the shaping of organizational identity. Organizations are embodied in the reasons that become articulated when decisions are justified. This is the complex reality of making ethical decisions in work today. We lack the right words to justify our decisions or the curiosity to keep probing even when there is pushback.

To illustrate the complexity and uncertainty we are presented with, let's consider two recent corporate scenarios involving a business decision requiring a difficult mix of ethics and action with no clear or easy path to resolution. First, let's look at Spotify's walking-back of a policy designed to punish artists accused of sexual misconduct. The policy was positioned as a sensible response to the #MeToo movement. While Spotify wasn't going to ban the music of accused artists from its site, it decided it would no longer promote the work of those artists. Within days of the announcement, an uproar emerged over the perceived racism in the policy, as the initial targets were two Black artists.

Caught off guard, Spotify chose to back down instead of investigating who was responsible for the biased application. Those managing the company chose a mindful reset. They evidently did not know how to navigate this uncertain terrain, so they decided to breathe, observe, and take no action. A more action-oriented response would have been finding the source, determining the consequences, and making the investigation public. You can't just go with the flow of woke public opinion. But they were not curious. They thought they were throwing out the right #MeToo buzzwords, and then folded when there was resistance.

Nor can you go with the flow of Trumpist public opinion, or the opinion of President Trump himself. Consider the NFL's policy prohibiting its players from taking a bended knee during the national anthem. The "take a knee" protest started out as a comment on the clear racism present in American police forces, evident from the disproportionate targeting of Black men in police shootings. Yet through his intervention, President Trump successfully used identity politics to change the issue from the safety of Black bodies on American streets into one of patriotism and respect for the flag.

Ultimately, and without consulting the NFL Players Association, the NFL owners made a decision and took action, siding with President Trump. If players wanted to protest, they would need to stay in the locker room. This decision fails to acknowledge the complexity in ethical decision-making. Rather than judge players on the basis of their own explanations for the actions they took, alternative motivations are assigned to their behaviors. The mostly white owners were not curious about the motivations of the mostly Black players.

Both of these cases highlight the near impossible conditions workers are faced with when trying to do the right thing. In the first instance, a policy inspired by #MeToo got sideswiped by accusations of racism. In the second, a policy inspired by Black Lives Matter got hit by a presidential tweet-storm turning it into questions of patriotic loyalty. Both outcomes typify the predictably unpredictable nature of contemporary business and ethical decision-making. Both instances required action and reaction. And passivity would have nothing to offer in either situation. Non-judgment would not have led to a superior outcome. Quite the contrary, as I will now demonstrate.

Some might argue that there was nothing particularly difficult to figure out in those two examples. Some would say that the decision-makers needed to make a business decision and figure out which response was best for their bottom line. But gathering the necessary data is impossible in our competitive environment. We simply don't have the tools to predict reputational risk. Others, guided by ideological or metaphysical norms like religion, would also argue that there is nothing undecidable. So for those who follow the ideology of identity politics, it is obvious that Spotify's entire policy was rooted in institutional racism. And to conservative Christians, it is equally obvious that the NFL could never tolerate God-hating players that disrespected the flag. Just as it was obvious to this group in our earlier Hallmark example that children should not be exposed to commercials featuring same-sex marriages.

The mindful practitioner would avoid both of these traps of certainty with their position of non-judgment. But they would still face a profound difficulty in figuring out the right balance between concerns of civic responsibility, how to punish abusers with a platform, the need to be respectful of racial sensitivities, and the myriad other issues that arise in these complex, fluid, and situation-specific dilemmas that businesses and ordinary citizens must decide on. There is great difficulty in choosing between even a limited set of determined options, even if you take time to reflect mindfully. Especially because ethics is more than altruism. Creating a moral good is not as easy as putting your needs second. There is a lot to figure out.

Spotify was under attack for first not taking action, then under attack for the action it took, and it is now being questioned for retracting its action. The NFL was damned for allowing the protests to take place on its field, was then criticized for banning the protests, and then called out for hypocrisy when expressing support for the social justice protests that emerged in response to the murder of George Floyd by the police. Both of these organizations would have been under attack whether they took action or did not; whether they sought to appease the left or the right. Organizations like Spotify and the NFL need to figure out very explicitly what principles they stand for, and then stand by them when challenged. Simply being mindful will lead to an endless slew of failed expectations thrust upon them by dissatisfied customers, media, shareholders, and other stakeholders. Spotify is now scrambling for a response. And the NFL first took a knee to the president in appeasing him at the expense of their players, and then tried to reverse the position as public opinion shifted to one more aligned with the view of protesting players.

It's clear that we live in a time in which civil discussion is of critical importance. And the only way this can happen is if we learn and practice forgiveness. The next chapter will dive into the challenge that logically follows the insights we uncovered in this chapter. If civil discussion between people who disagree with each other must shift from a near impossibility to a regular necessity of spiritual work, the question of how to forgive is of the utmost importance.

8

Elevating Forgiveness

Forgiveness as a Spiritual Bypass

In many ways, this penultimate chapter echoes the first chapter, which recognizes the unique contemporary challenge of bringing a spiritual way of thinking to ordinary life. As we saw in our discussion of the mindful*mess*, contemporary psychology offers rationales for forgiveness that have an inward emphasis on personal wellness. From that perspective, forgiveness is an important step in overall health and well-being. And since research shows that holding onto anger is toxic for our health, it is in our best interest to uncritically forgive all transgressions.

Author, poet, musician, and one of my all-time favorite artists, Nick Cave, has written very eloquently on this position. I quote it at length because it really is the definitive articulation of the view that forgiveness and wellness need be inseparably intertwined. He muses:

Forgiveness is a form of self-rescue that goes, at times, against our very nature. Forgiveness can prevent us from becoming the living definition of the injury that has been inflicted upon us ... But how difficult it is to sometimes forgive; how unfair it seems to reward offence with compassion. Yet, despite our intuitions, despite the seeming insanity of the enterprise, we must try, because forgiveness can be the way to self-preservation. Forgiveness is an act of self-love where the malignancy you have endured can become the motivating force that helps enlarge the capacity of the heart.

How to forgive the unforgivable? Now there is a question. Sometimes we feel the crime is such a violation, and so egregious, that it is beyond absolution – but the struggle to forgive is where it can find its true meaning. Even the attempt to move toward forgiveness allows us the opportunity to touch the borders of grace. To try is an act of resistance against the forces of malevolence – a form of defiant grace.

There are some who have found ways to forgive all manner of horrors and we look at them with awe.

These words are beautiful and inspiring. They contain within them the wisdom of a man who has personally faced unimaginable tragedy and has found a way to continue to do spiritual work. Recently, when Cave was in Toronto, I had the opportunity to question him on this thinking. But I couldn't do it. We weren't in a *chavrusa* relationship, and I feared the exchange would not be transformational. So instead, I am left to wonder: Is this strategy for thinking about forgiveness a spiritual bypass? We can't forgive all transgressions. We need to forgive, yes, but we need to do it in a skilled and thoughtful way.

The importance of forgiveness at work has been well documented. A classic example is contrasting the socio-economic conditions in South Africa under Nelson Mandela, who embraced forgiveness, with the conditions in Zimbabwe under Robert Mugabe, who did not. Fred Kiel, CEO of KRW International, found that the character trait of forgiveness is predictably correlated with higher profitability performance by CEOs and the companies they lead. Harvard University's Rosabeth Moss Kanter discussed how the decision by South Korea's Shinhan Bank to forgive 3,500 employees of an acquisition target that protested the takeover in an embarrassing way by giving them everything they asked for instead of taking revenge led to unprecedented corporate success for the new combined entity within three years.

We need to develop a coherent and contingent framework for forgiveness that recognizes the importance of judgment and reaction, not just the type advocated by wellness experts. The forgiveness of mindfulness is an exercise of non-judgment and presence undertaken primarily for our own emotional well-being. The forgiveness we need is a well-considered tactic designed to achieve a specific end. But on the last point, Cave is absolutely correct: those who can forgive are looked upon with awe. And maybe, as a corollary, those who can access awe can access forgiveness.

How to Forgive

Within the ancient Jewish spiritual tradition, there are a number of explorations of the topic of forgiveness between individuals, along with related discussions around atonement, absolution, and forgiveness granted from God. For the purpose of our considerations, two categories of forgiveness seem particularly relevant.

The first idea is that of "*selicha.*" The word literally means forgiveness, but is perhaps better understood as the act of freeing the party who has wronged us from an emotional obligation. *Selicha* signifies a process that begins with a sincere and concerted effort by the individual seeking forgiveness to express remorse, followed by a determination to make meaningful amends. The aggrieved party can then assess these efforts and choose to grant a release from guilt or further emotional obligation.

Forgiveness in this sense is an active judgment made in response to reactive efforts by the offender that are both internal, in that the offender comes to feel remorse, and external, in that the offender expresses that remorse and seeks to right the wrong. It is the opposite of the wellness type of forgiving. This type of forgiveness is born of a pragmatic calculation. It suggests that the forgiver has not forgotten the wrong-doing but allows the parties to exist in the present moment, not the past. The act of atonement, whatever it was, is deemed sufficient to enable the two parties to once again work together and move forward.

Forgiveness in contemporary psychology is defined as the release of resentment or anger. Note how the focus is exclusively on the inner state of the victim. Forgiveness, in this model, doesn't involve any sort of reconciliation. It doesn't depend on the offender apologizing and/or accepting forgiveness. There is no spiritual work here ... psychological forgiveness is not tied to meaning, connection, or wonder. It is framed as an important exercise for the mental health of those who have been victimized, having been shown to elevate mood, enhance optimism, and guard against anger, stress, anxiety, and depression.

In the reactive model of ancient Judaism, forgiveness is akin to granting a pardon. The victim observes a meaningful effort to make amends, and so a release from obligation is granted. The wrongdoing remains, but the offender has done the necessary work to pay off their emotional debt. And to be clear, within the system of spiritual work forgiveness is not granted if the offender is not sincere in their repentance or does not take the appropriate steps to correct the wrong done.

And really, why should it be otherwise? Spiritual work is about meaning, connection, and wonder. Where is the meaning or connection if forgiveness is nothing more than a release from anger? The crime, as it were, was born of a social interaction. It came from doing something particular with others. How can a passive retreat into non-judgment be a constructive response? Are there no other ways to lower our blood pressure and cope with the biological responses to stress? Repentance should be active. Words of apology that are not accompanied by sincere feelings of regret and resolve to change remain empty, bereft of the crucial element that lends them meaning.

Rabbi Soloveitchik describes two processes that lead to the resolve to change. The first is motivated by emotion, resulting from the wrongdoer's spontaneous inner feelings of shame, which instinctively lead to remorse. The individual's sense of utter remorse is what automatically brings about the resolve never to commit the same wrongs. The second is motivated by intellect. Here, the individual understands the impropriety and negative effects of their behavior and resolves not to engage in such behavior in the future. In such a case, the individual does not immediately experience passionate feelings of remorse; rather, remorse will grow out of the individual's continued determination not to repeat the wrongful actions in the future.

The second idea is that of "*mechila*," a forgiveness of the heart, usually translated as "wiping away." *Selicha* operates at the intersection of meaning and connection. *Mechila* is situated at the intersection of connection and wonder. Here, the spiritual work is putting the relationship back to the level it was at before the offending incident. It involves empathy, rooted not in a selfish desire to make ourselves feel better by releasing our anger, but born of work and reaching the conclusion that human frailty is forgivable. This is the forgiveness of renewal.

Can we forgive those who have exploited their economic power? Might we consider a new transformative cooperative relationship with them? Can we forgive those at our own company who made unethical decisions and tarnished all of us who work there? Can we forgive those on the other side of our political divide, those who we believe supported immoral political positions in order to enter a deep and trusting relationship with them? Can we forgive those who once subscribed to or benefited from discriminatory practices? In our highly polarized times, where civil discussions between people who disagree with each other is a near impossibility and deplatforming has come to replace civilized debate, the question of how to forgive is of the utmost importance. What cannot be in question is the possibility of forgiveness.

In fact, David Frum addressed this issue in our conversation:

Reform coalitions need to safeguard themselves against the very understandable temptation to cultural retaliation. I don't blame it, but I do condemn it. Pro-tip: If you find yourself about to use the phrase "white males" or "old white males" in a sentence in any tone other than respect – stop immediately and revise your work. When Franklin Delano Roosevelt ran against Alf Landon in 1936, he reproved an associate mocking Kansas, the state of which Landon was governor. He told him, in politics never speak disparagingly of any group of people and particularly not a group with which your opponent can claim identity. The associate had referred to Kanas as a "typical flat prairie state." Roosevelt corrected him that he should have referred to Kansas as "one of our magnificent prairie states," as Roosevelt himself habitually did. Roosevelt carried Kansas in 1936. There's a lesson for us all.

In other words, if we are committed to the pragmatic process of reform, we need to remember that this is an exercise in coalition building. We live in a time of identity politics when "old," "white," and "male" and any combination thereof are considered pejoratives. Any attempt to disparage by identity is a mistake, opening up the possibility for those against our reforms to invite the aggrieved party into their coalition. And this holds true even if we achieve our reforms. Whether the challenge is changing capitalism on a macro/social level or changing work on a micro/company level, we need to resist the urge to alienate those who we disagree with, especially if we are successful. Cultural retaliation is antithetical to achieving long-term objectives in a dynamic environment. Forgiveness is thus a useful tactic in our long-term strategy of hope. And by the way, it is not only others that at times we need to forgive; the spiritual work starts with forgiving ourselves.

How We Forgive in the Rehearsal Room

There is one more individual that I needed to have a *chavrusa* exchange with for this project. Her name is Amelia Sargisson, a brilliant actress and playwright who has found, through an enormous amount of sustained and dedicated effort, meaning, connection, and wonder in her creative spiritual work. She is wise beyond her years, and it is fitting to close our explorations with the thoughts of a younger mind.

I first experienced a transformative encounter as a result of her work through her portrayal of Eve in a production of Erin Shields's *Paradise Lost*. One of the tools she used to prepare for the role was plastering her walls with every portrait she could find of Eve, from the earliest stone carvings onward, "just to have all that iconography dancing in my subconscious."

The performance that subsequently emerged changed me. It made me rethink a conception I had taken for granted since childhood. As Amelia would explain, "almost everyone in the Western world has an idea or image of a figure as iconic as Eve. So really my task was to focus on realizing Erin's version of Eve, knowing that the 'classical' counterpoint would inevitably be conjured by that very undertaking, and would also be very alive in the minds of the viewers."

When we first sat down together for lunch, I could not have anticipated how we would touch upon almost every theme of this work. It validated the universality of spiritual truths. For while we each approached the big-picture questions of spiritual work from the perspective and influence of differing traditions, we ended up with the same conclusions.

We began our conversation with my suggestion that she seems to be something of an expert in inspiring transformational cooperation. She was humble in her response, but insightful in how she deflected: "Not aware that I can prompt transformation. But my passion and commitment may be infectious or contagious and that is what people are energized by ... Heart energy, brain energy, body energy in the rehearsal room will feed the whole collective and then in turn feed me as well." It is not by accident that Amelia chose to emphasize that transformative encounters are stimulated by doing, not being. It is not her persona that elicits a willingness in others to cooperate with her; it is her active assertiveness. She decides that there is something special in a particular project, tied to her desire to find meaning in her work and thus commits to it with passion. Seeing this commitment inspires the other participants to react in kind, thus creating connection among the cast. The output of these endeavors brings a sense of wonder, experienced not only by the creative team but the audience as well.

In her brief explanation, Amelia hints at all three motivations for social influence that we talked about earlier. What she terms "heart energy" is the relational motivation. Her fellow creatives are motivated to commit to the project, in part, because of the need for identification through social relationships. Personal satisfaction from the relationship is based on either reciprocity or modeling. Only actions that signal authenticity, friendship, esteem, and relatedness will work to convince; that is, the "heart energy."

"Brain energy" is the moral motivation. Moral motivations are based on the internalization of a set of values that guide our work decision. What Amelia brings to the project stimulates an internal assessment by each team member of the correspondence between her world view and their own internal system of values. It is "brain energy" because each player adopts an evaluative perspective toward the ongoing collaboration. Even as they continue to work together, it is conditioned on continued positive assessments of the outcomes.

Finally, "body energy" hints at the instrumental motivation. Instrumental motivations are based on the desire to obtain a specific reward, whether material or, in this case, symbolic. The reward is the metaphorical interplay of energy exchanged by bodies in motion.

We then shifted to a discussion on the importance of curiosity. In the introduction, we identified the alarming statistics suggesting that a majority of millennials are failing to find meaning in work. Without meaning, work becomes a soul-crushing exercise of repetitiveness. Amelia shared that as her acting career has picked up steam, she finds herself facing new challenges. For example, in the early days of her career, a play would run for a few weeks. Now the runs will sometimes last for months. How does she manage to bring that same amount of passion, commitment and energy, so critical to the success of the project, to each performance in these circumstances?

How do you maintain your stamina? How do you find the passion to do it over and over again? Curiosity ... Get curious about this moment ... I took an art class at the AGO and the first thing that we were to do was drawing, and that's the thing which I am worst at. But my mother, who is an artist, said to me, you are as good a drawer as you are an observer. And I'm sure that what you'll find is that you can observe things infinitely ... you can ask infinite questions about any given moment ... We give ourselves a point of focus for every show. Yesterday it was new beginnings. The one prior to that was commitment. Prior to that was awe. Prior to that forgiveness. You put a new little spice in your stew with every iteration of it.

With this comment, Amelia raises two insights that are helpful to our project. The first is the infinite possibilities of questioning. Throughout this work, I have almost presented the search for meaning as a search for answers. But what might have gotten lost is that it should be a search for questions. Rabbi David Hartman recognized that the role of the rabbi in America today is to instill a desire to ask questions and be bothered by Judaism. Amelia is highlighting the same point.

Her second, and related, point is on the exercise of giving ourselves a unique point of focus each time we engage in a repetitive activity. As we see, there is much overlap between the themes she highlights and our own earlier explorations. We have argued that something special can happen when we look for connection as we engage in the tasks of the everyday. Something unexpected might occur when we seek out awe in the ordinary activities that we have done so many times before. Our philosophy of reaction, the *mitzvah* approach, creates the possibility that this experience, what happens in this moment, can always be different from what happened before.

It is contingent on the surprising changes that may emerge as a consequence of our focus.

Pushing further, we came to agree that spiritual work is a call to action, not contemplation. Amelia admits the heaviness she finds in the weight of sacred work:

> What I do is a deeply spiritual thing, and sometimes my language around it is almost biblical. Like, "I was unworthy of Desdemona that night, I failed her," and it's not good for me. I'm trying to eradicate that language because it doesn't make me a better actor. It puts a yoke on my freedom and the best acting requires us to be free. When there's less of a higher calling, it's easier for me because I feel free. But when I feel like through this I'm participating in whatever platonic social function the arts may have, that's when I feel the sandbags on my shoulders. I have to balance the fact that this work is sacred to me.

This honest confession is moving. It's easier for us to do work without a higher calling because then we are free. She's right in recognizing that it is not easy on the mind or body to accept the challenge of spiritual work. We've emphasized repeatedly that once we engage we are answering a call to responsibility. Responsibility to those affected. Responsibility to the past. Responsibility to the future. It is not light and it is not easy.

Finding meaning, connection, and wonder in work will not make work easier. It will make it harder. There is a certain amount of freedom available to those who resist the call and do not think about the infinite responsibility of action.

But that is not the path of creativity. A sense of wonder used to be a hallmark of leadership. Leaders get excited by emotional and imaginative language that challenges us to overcome mediocrity, outlining a romantic view of the future with a demanding attitude toward the present. When we embrace wonder, curiosity, and the power of our imagination to move the world forward we model the paradigm of doing and then being. First we do the work, and only then do we earn the right to rest.

> Every time I cross that threshold to make my first entrance as Desdemona I'm trying to transform the whole room … in that moment, with her first speech, I'm saying to everyone, "Awaken your dream, for your best possible world." And that's just the imaginative exercise I give myself. Can I, through what I'm doing, invite all of these other sentient beings in that room today to be with me in this moment to explode their technicolour dream for a better world? That's a lot. That's a huge thing to carry with your first entry … If I want that to be my imaginative condition, I need to make sure there's joy underneath it, so that it doesn't kill me.

We have not spent enough time on her last point. We have not considered deeply the important role that joy can play. The Hasidic Master Rabbi Simcha Bunim exclaimed that joy is a wisdom that prepares one for prophecy. The spiritual lessons of joy can be learned from the smiling Buddha, the Holy Laughter of Christianity, or the Hindu practice of Hasya yoga.

In Deuteronomy 29:9, Moses opens up praising the Israelites with this observation, "You are standing today." Given what we have developed about the reactive philosophy he lived by, we know this is the highest praise he can offer the people. Even after the punishments, the negativity, the efforts to push us down, to demean us, we are strengthened in our resolve to stand firm. And what is the aspiration Moses has for the people that are still standing? What does he hope they become? He ends by stating that the life of spiritual work is near and "not beyond the sea." The Ishbitzer Rebbe draws on a similar metaphor. Not beyond the sea means we need not distance ourselves from the joy in this world as we engage in our spiritual work. The Ishbitzer says that the metaphor of "the sea" in Jewish sources is meant to allude to bodily desire. As I noted earlier in our discussion of *mitzvah*, the Ishbitzer believes that one needs fences and boundaries when we do not have a mature understanding. We need to be "dry" to start learning. But when the words and ideas are natural to us, a life of spiritual work means embracing the joys of the world. To achieve our work, we need not reach beyond our desire for joy.

Finally, Amelia and I built the conversation to the topic of this chapter. How do we make forgiveness a practice of spiritual work, one that goes beyond wellness?

> I just want to say that I am intrigued by this assessment of yours that forgiveness is selfish. That we forgive to feel better. I feel that we as a society are in a moment right now that avoids forgiveness. And our culture has become extremely punitive and litigious. When people err, which is human, the quickness with which we indict, rather than examine, what are the causes for this, what prompted this behavior, disappoints me. Especially on the part of major institutions on whom it is incumbent to correct the ways of the world and unravel some of these power structures, but the quickness with which they are trying to do that, for me, means we are not looking holistically at any of these situations.

There is so much depth to unpack here. Amelia is correct in observing that we are living through a social moment that rejects forgiveness. The past few years have seen the rise of "cancel culture." Zealous individuals rush to assign purity tests and immediately seek to punish those that fail. Forgiveness seems to be a conversational non-starter.

Writing for the *New York Times*, Loretta Ross states that as a Black feminist, she finds cancel and call-out culture a toxic practice where "people attempt to expunge anyone with whom they do not perfectly agree, rather than remain focused on those who profit from discrimination and injustice." She observes that most public shaming is horizontal, meaning that it is not done to justifiably criticize people who are seriously dangerous, but to score points against people who mean no harm. The people doing the canceling become the self-appointed guardians of political purity.

These self-appointed puritans are incredibly dangerous to the possibility of spiritual work. Rabbi Menachem Mendel Morgensztern of Kotzk is said to have observed that "the suppressed cry of someone who needs to shout but can't – that is the loudest cry of them all." The Kotzker Rebbe had little patience for false displays of piety like those that make up cancel culture. I believe that his quote, consistent with his philosophy as a whole, is meant to teach the idea that the unexpressed spiritual feelings of the sincere individual, forced to remain silent because of a lack of training in the norms of "acceptable" expressions of piety, is deeper and more meaningful than the noisy, self-righteous expressions of observance made by the powerful. I think the Kotzker would much prefer an honest laugh to an off-color comment from a simple person than an uninvited pontification by a cancel culture zealot.

One of the surprising turns of this era is how cultural and artistic expressions are greeted carefully by an impossibly complicated analysis. Before one can assess if a play is worth seeing, for example, one needs to first engage in some background research and an algorithmic calculus involving the cultural/social/racial/sexual/religious/political/biological identity of the playwright, the actors, the audience, and all possible intersections. We need to analyze before we can feel. This, to an accomplished artist like Amelia, is a strange turn:

> For me, forgiveness is tethered to, or even indistinguishable from, really, empathy. If I can empathize with somebody, if I can dare to put myself in their shoes, if I dare to try and understand their motivations, then I am more likely to forgive. And that is the job of the actor. We do it for characters all the time. We train that capacity within ourselves, to get in there, to understand what motivated this, what are the factors influencing this person's heart, mind, body, behavior in this moment. And I believe that is an essential skill. One that everybody needs to be practicing as devotedly as the actor does.

Amelia explains that forgiveness is tethered to empathy. Empathy is a feeling of essential connection with all that is. It's the thing we feel if we dare to walk a mile in someone else's shoes. It's when we consider "being" from their perspective, even if we don't agree with the choices they have made or the actions they have taken, especially if those actions brought us harm. While, she notes, that is the job of the actor, it is a skill all of us can use. Rather than cancel, we need to work on developing our capacity for understanding.

Actors train to develop that capacity, knowing there is a danger in doing so. Throughout history we have turned to artists to be our social guides for a reason. Artists look for integration, and can assimilate a multiplicity of viewpoints more naturally than others. The type of art being discussed by Amelia celebrates the deep possibilities of our humanness:

> We're motivated to do it, in fact we're called to do it for "unsympathetic" characters all the time ... In a way it's dangerous what we do. But in a way if we were willing to make that investment with, say, our political opponents, the art of discourse and problem solving would not be going the way of the dodo bird, as it is now. We're not being uncritical. "Why did you do that? Why did you think that?" If we cannot get curious and creative, given the problems facing the planet, we are all doomed.
>
> Drama is only interesting because of conflict. But to be the vessel for that, you have to have the mind and spirit to know that, in the creative context, we're all working towards the same thing. I think that so much of what we do in the rehearsal room could serve the world at large.

At an event I hosted last year, the conversation turned to the question of how we can create an educational environment that nurtures this type of creativity and spirit of innovation. We were exploring how to enact what Amelia calls for, bringing what artists do in their creative spaces to the world at large. Lee Ranaldo, guitarist and founding member of Sonic Youth, is an artist most closely associated with the DIY aesthetic of the post-punk no-wave movement. He said to me at the time:

> You don't want the sheep, you want the innovative thinkers that are put down because they're not playing by the rules ... they're not safe ... they're making waves ... but it's hard to nurture those people ... Our

institutions are businesses and that's why they fall on the wrong side of the line ... they are not there to impart wisdom, they are there to collect your money and perpetuate their model, whether it's the university business or the democratic nation business ... The people making the waves are put down because they threaten the status quo and they threaten the stability of things ... but that's where innovation comes ... when you are threatening the stability of things and knocking some plates off their spindles you are potentially pushing the conversation, and therefore the culture, forward.

These words obviously resonated with the punk rock folks who were in attendance, consistent with a philosophical outlook that they have come to expect from Lee over the four decades that he has been creating dissonant art. But speaking to the converted was not the point of this gatherings. And at the end of the panel discussion, a self-described Fox-News-watching Trump voter approached me and asked to be introduced to Lee. He was moved by Lee's thoughts and wanted to talk more about the challenge of educating in a manner that nurtures independence of thought and the innovative spirit. Liberal talking heads never reached him – but an artist did.

If we stop and think about this for a moment, it should not necessarily be a surprising outcome. That Lee's words would speak to a Trumpist is unexpected only because we are so used to being isolated in our cultural silos that we have reduced those we disagree with to caricatures. Lee's words encourage resistance to that which has become mainstream. These words are constructed to empower those who are making waves. As such, I should have expected that Lee's thoughts would spark something in an individual who views himself as a marginalized conservative in a way that is not viscerally dissimilar from how his ideas inspire liberal punks. The details around which aspects of the status quo these two different types of individuals may wish to overturn will vary substantively, and that is no small point. But they share an overall desire for freedom from an oppressive culture that doesn't value them and an overwhelming desire for change. And I must confess … that moment gave me hope for America's future.

The Surprise of Being Forgiven

How realistic is this undertaking? Impossible to know. But a central element in Jewish spiritual thinking on forgiveness that we have not yet discussed is the divine delight in surprise. It is the final piece to this section, and vitally necessary to set the stage for bringing a Jewish spiritual metaphor into mainstream work practice.

Western capitalism has morphed into a religion that encourages greed, self-interest, and callousness as innovations are more often than not construed in zero-sum terms instead of mutual wins. In this spirit, we have sought to get down to some of the essential principles of Judaism, the core ideas that we need to repair our broken world. And sure, it may surprise some readers that we are turning to Judaism at this particular historical moment, in this particular political climate. Others may be surprised that we are exerting efforts to save capitalism, while others still may be OK with either topic in isolation, but uneasy with the pairing of the two.

But in Judaism, questioning everything is a virtue. Surprise is a virtue. There is a famous story in the Talmud capturing a debate between Rabbi Eliezer ben Hyrcanus, a prominent Judean sage who was as notorious for his intractable religious conservatism as lauded for his intellect, and the rest of the rabbinic academy. At issue in this situation was the ritual status of an oven that was broken into pieces. Rabbi Eliezer ruled that this oven was not susceptible to ritual impurity. But every other sage disagreed with him. In simple terms, they were debating whether or not this oven might be considered *kosher*. All of the local rabbis believed that the oven was not *kosher*. Eliezer believed it was. And so, he unleashed a torrent of arguments, proofs, and supporting evidence to convince his colleagues that he was right. But his fellow experts wouldn't budge. They felt he was wrong.

Frustrated, exhausted of rhetorical tools, but utterly convinced of his rightness, this Eliezer, the son of Hyrcanus, decided to invoke mystical forces on his behalf. If you can't persuade people to change their minds using rhetoric and argument, then see if the powers of the supernatural can help. Eliezer announced that if the law was in accordance with his reasoning, and the oven was indeed *kosher*, then the carob tree will prove it (not an accidental choice of species – guess where this is going). Immediately, a carob tree that was hundreds of feet away became uprooted and miraculously crashed through the study hall. Clearly, Eliezer was right. But his fellow sages were not impressed by this bit of magic. The study hall was a space for rational debate, and the behavior of a carob tree, no matter how unusual or spectacular, was not a convincing proof of anything relating to the topic at hand.

Enraged and emboldened, Eliezer continued to draw on his mystical powers. He caused the water in the local aqueducts to visibly flow backwards, as the forces of water would testify to his rightness. He then caused the walls of the study hall to start caving in, as stones were called in to give evidence on his behalf.

But neither water nor stone subverting the laws of nature had a persuasive effect on his fellow scholars. To the contrary, one sage, Rabbi Joshua, used his own mystical abilities to rebuke … the walls. He yelled that if scholars are in the middle of debating the law, what qualifications does a wall have to intervene? And as the tale goes, the wall remains at a slant. It did not fall down, in deference to Rabbi Joshua, but it also did not straighten up, in deference to Rabbi Eliezer.

Finally, Rabbi Eliezer summoned the highest authority his mystical powers could materialize. He shouted out, "If the law is as I say it is, let this be proven from heaven!" And in the rarest of miracles, a voice from heaven was heard by all who had gathered in the study hall. And the voice stated definitively: "What do you want of Rabbi Eliezer – the law is as he says …"

One would think that in a classic religious story, a cameo appear-
ance by God to directly intervene in the narrative with His opinion
would constitute the grandest of finales. One might assume that
Rabbi Eliezer had won the day, that the oven was to be deemed *kosher*
and his humbled peers were put in their place conclusively. But such
assumptions indicate a misunderstanding of Judaism and the glori-
ous role of surprise.

For as the story is recounted, in fact, Rabbi Joshua got up on his
feet, having just put the wall in its place, and turned his attention
to God himself, quoting a passage from Deuteronomy and exclaim-
ing: "The Torah is not in heaven!" Rabbi Yirmeya expanded on his
reasoning, explaining that the council will be taking no notice of
heavenly voices, since God has already said to us during the Revelation at Mount Sinai that on matters of law we are to follow the will of
the majority. The holy council of rabbis essentially told God to stay
in His lane.

And with that, Rabbi Eliezer was booted from the academy, sent
into exile, and lived the rest of his life mostly in isolation. He apparently continued to use his supernatural powers to remotely set angry
fires that burned one-third of the planet's crops. But the coda is the
best part of this story. Sometime later, one of the academy members,
Rabbi Nathan, was on a mystical journey of his own. In this state, he
encountered Elijah the Prophet, who according to Jewish mythology
ascended to heaven without dying, and thus acts as an intermediary,
wandering freely between the realms of the living and the dead. Nathan asked him for some gossip on what was happening in heaven
during the whole ordeal of Eliezer and his miracles. How did God react in that moment when the sages rejected His intervention? Elijah
replied: "God smiled and said, 'My children have bested me.'"

This to me represents something absolutely novel. This sense of
awe and wonder, the enjoyment of surprise, extends to God himself.
At the heart of Jewish theology is the belief that God wants us to
surprise Him. It's an idea that can be found throughout the Jewish

canon, and one which I explored in *Fifteen Paths* in a conversation with Rabbi Tzvi Freeman. To build on Amelia's insight that rehearsal room exercises are useful to all walks of life, we can view the rules compiled in the Torah as God presenting humanity with a script of how to behave. According to that script, everybody is called on to act good. We've all been given this nice little task of enacting a very specifically defined type of morality. So long as we follow that script we are good.

But the problem with this script is that it's kind of boring. Not only to us, but to God. That was the dilemma captured in the Rabbi Eliezer story. Both sides were sort of right. On a purely rational level, Rabbi Eliezer had the correct argument. And so when Rabbi Eliezer called for divine intervention, God acceded because this was an interesting play. But Rabbi Eliezer was also sort of wrong for trying to bring God into this. Which was Rabbi Joshua's point. Which was sort of right. But arguing against a rational truth, and standing up to God, seems also sort of wrong.

It's a stunning story because it captures the messy reality of life. We're always somewhat messing up. So what happens next? My friend Rabbi Freeman explains that in those moments God says, "Well, it's not in the script. So I guess you're going to have to write your own script." And that is spiritual work. We take action. We make connections. We engage in transformative cooperation. We come out changed. We marvel with awe at the new world. We both seek and enact forgiveness and try something new. And God says, "That is amazing!"

This narrative of surprise is one of the earliest in the Bible, featured in the story that Amelia brought to the stage. While Adam and Eve are in Paradise, they have all of their wants and needs met without effort. Adam and Eve are given but one injunction: do not eat the fruits of the Tree of Knowledge on penalty of death. But Eve's burgeoning moral consciousness led her to conclude that while it is possible that her creator would destroy her for being curious, she did not want to live in a world where judgment trumped compassion. So she bit into the fruit as an act of protest, breaking the rules in hope that a better, more loving, moral truth would emerge.

God was surprised, but convinced. He changed the rules and forgave. Eve was punished, but not with death. Adam, who was at an earlier developmental moral stage, didn't get it. To him, rules were made to be followed. That's what his creator told him. But Eve wanted a better world for herself and her future children. This account of the classic biblical story offers a Hasidic interpretive twist that may make it slightly less familiar to some. But it is a reading with deep insight into the psychology of virtuous rule breaking and a feminine twist on the mythological birth of wisdom. Eve was going to become a partner in creation, so she broke a specific rule because of her deep respect for the notion of rules. And the rule she hoped would be dominant was love and compassion. She set the paradigm for later rule breakers.

The downfall of Rabbi Eliezer ben Hyrcanus is tied to misplaced awe. Rabbi Eliezer did not view cooperation as a transformative encounter. Rabbi Eliezer did not understand this type of cooperative project. He did not understand why God would hand over the responsibility for legal interpretation to the humans that would be governed by it.

For here was a living partnership, where a group of mortals could take a divine system, come to radically different conclusions than the classic intent, and have all parties pleased by that outcome. God liked being surprised. Rabbi Eliezer could have responded to this realization with awe. But to him, there was only "the truth." He needed to be exiled because he could not be part of this project. He could not find wonder in this community of equals. He was too obsessed with being right. Not curious about how he might be wrong. Not knowing how to forgive. Always thinking that verbal exchanges need to end with a winner or loser. For Rabbi Eliezer, there was no hope.

9
Strategize for Hope

What have we been trying to build with this project?

A plan to reform capitalism from the inside through spiritual work. A philosophy of reaction to empower the disenchanted. A practical map for making assertiveness and action the foundation for stability amidst the confusing chaos of everyday work in the era of big data, surveillance capitalism, global pandemics, racial injustice, and cronyism amongst the elite.

Through the language of *mitzvah* and *chavrusa* we have shown how spiritual work can be expressed through agile risk-taking designed to expand the boundaries of our community. We have explained the moral good in taking ownership of complex challenges that are beyond our capabilities to solve, in an environment best characterized by an accelerated rate of change, in the hopes of doing our part to craft a better world. We do all this as we search for meaning, connection, and wonder in our ordinary everyday experiences. We do this in partnership with others, former strangers who become part of our "we," as we create something of value through transformational change.

Even in the most hopeful of scenarios, the paradigm we have developed in this book will not solve all of the problems of contemporary capitalism overnight. But it places us firmly in the company of the reform coalition devoted to making this a better place for the next generation, if not our own. It is the work of dreamers.

The COVID-19 global public health crisis has certainly accelerated this momentum. For example, the *Financial Times*, a conservative publication, offered this editorial:

> Despite inspirational calls for national mobilisation, we are not really all in this together ... Sacrifices are inevitable, but every society must demonstrate how it will offer restitution to those who bear the heaviest burden of national efforts. Radical reforms – reversing the prevailing policy direction of the last four decades – will need to be put on the table. Governments will have to accept a more active role in the economy. They must see public services as investments rather than liabilities, and look for ways to make labour markets less insecure. Redistribution will again be on the agenda; the privileges of the elderly and wealthy in question. Policies until recently considered eccentric, such as basic income and wealth taxes, will have to be in the mix.

Change is likely coming, of the type that we have outlined in this book and called "connected capitalism." But in the meantime, many of us may still find ourselves in contingent and precarious employment situations despite our shift to a spiritual frame. The sort of economic system that exploits rather than empowers workers is not sustainable anymore. And maybe, we have a unique opportunity where Westerners are more open to crafting a spiritual community. Maybe the pressure on those who are being taken advantage of to keep quiet and carry on will be lifted. Maybe those with power will finally be motivated to follow the lead of Feuerstein's *mitzvah* capitalism and recognize that efficiency is not always the smartest corporate objective to pursue.

A spiritual approach to work has the potential to increase productivity, innovativeness, agility, and other traits we need to develop in order to thrive in the current economic order. It will bolster our ability to initiate positive change from within the failing institutions so desperate for revitalization.

The message of those who partake in spiritual work is that we are not temporary and replaceable cogs in a global machine. We are not nuisances for corporations to tolerate until automation improves and smarter artificial intelligence can be deployed in our stead. And if reform does not work, we are not without the power to bring about radical, revolutionary transformation instead, as made evident by the tens of thousands who spontaneously took to the streets demanding social justice in the aftermath of the George Floyd murder.

We have the opportunity to elevate our vulnerabilities to sources of strength. We can harness our physical, mental, and emotional faculties in a practical and uplifting way. Our model seeks to make creating new value a spiritual task, through a higher-order of cooperation rooted in the privileging of transformative human relationships, filled with curiosity and wonder. We deliberately engage with those who were once strangers, deploying forgiveness for the wrongs of the past where appropriate and tapping into a confident hope for the future.

Through our explorations of meaning, connection, and wonder, we now have a holistic framework for solving the large-scale socio-economic problems of modernity with spiritual work. We can once again deploy all of our faculties and capabilities in the context of ordinary work. And by embracing a different type of sacred, we can raise up that which currently seeks to hold us down. We can make better strategic decisions. We can think differently about purpose in work. We can build a stronger, more deeply connected social order.

It all starts with a strategy for hope.

Where Can We Learn Hope?

The questions we explored in this book are as pressing to those of us who work in academia as those in financial services. It is somewhat uncontroversial to assert that the perception of the university as a credible institution for shaping the minds and characters in a manner that will allow future generations in Western society to thrive is in trouble. Greg Lukianoff and Jonathan Haidt do a good job outlining some of the problems with our current educational paradigms in their recent best-seller *The Coddling of the American Mind*. Lukianoff and Haidt link many of the contemporary problems found on campuses across North America to a culture of safetyism that prevents individuals from speaking honestly, sheltering students from confrontational views, and encouraging an educational climate of fear and resentment that leads to polarization and dysfunction in the socio-political arena. In short, coddled minds make for bad democratic citizens.

The phenomenon identified by Lukianoff and Haidt is real, and sometimes manifests in unexpected ways. For example, many critics presume this coddling supports an exclusively liberal bias amongst students on campus. While this may be true in the humanities, this was certainly not my experience teaching in a business school. I'll never forget an in-class discussion that occurred during a student presentation for a strategy class I was conducting. It was the winter semester of 2014 and the Olympics in Sochi were making headlines. The student presenter made a comment about a bill that had passed earlier in the summer banning the distribution of information about homosexuality to children in Russia, leading to the fear that visiting LGBT athletes may be prosecuted for an act as simple as waving a rainbow flag.

Almost immediately, the presenter was interrupted by a classmate of Russian origin who decided to helpfully pipe in that there were no gay people in Russia, and the law in question was a reasonable effort to protect Russian children from Western propaganda that may turn them gay. At which point, a number of Middle Eastern students joined the conversation, explaining that homosexuality was not found in their home countries either, followed by students from India and Eastern Europe. The presenter, who happened to be Asian, expressed surprise by this new data, but began to accept the possibility that homosexuality only occurred naturally in citizens of North America, parts of Asia, and Western Europe.

While my pedagogical bias is to let students work through bad ideas on their own, I had to jump in and redirect. I brought up websites of LGBT organizations in Russia, the Middle East, and elsewhere, asking which constituencies they were advocating for. Informed by the vocal majority in the classroom that these organizations were Western propaganda fronts, I brought up pictures of self-identified LGBT nightclubs in those same locales, inquiring about who was frequenting the establishments. Tourists, they answered.

Realizing that the advocates of this theory were not open to the possibility of falsification, I gave up on further arguments, hoping to move on. But I had to throw out a closing thought. I commented that despite the obvious ethnic diversity in the classroom, there appeared to be very little intellectual diversity. I was not convinced that our learning environment was enhanced by the presence of a diversity of skin colors if they were all expressing homophobic sentiments. Still flustered later in the day, I shared this story with a colleague in the business ethics department. Listening carefully, he let me know that what bothered him most was *my* comment. "You can't say things like that in the classroom," he informed me, "you can't criticize their diversity or their culturally based opinions, even if they are illiberal, or you will get in trouble."

Protecting the feelings of students has become a de facto priority in the mission of universities. It was not always that way, certainly not when I was a student in the 1990s. And many critics attribute the emergence of this zeal toward cultural deference and safetyism to viewing moral responsibility through one lens. As Haidt notes elsewhere, "Many students are given just one lens – power. Here's your lens, kid. Look at everything through this lens. Everything is about power ... This is not an education ... It's a paranoid worldview that separates people from each other ..."

While I would tend to agree that such ideas have caused a lot of our current problems, mainly based on the obvious evidence that my colleagues trained in such thinking are enacting these new approaches, I also think that ideas around power taken seriously can help get us

out of this mess. The questioning of power structures, all power structures, and a radical sense of responsibility to the "other" need not
lead to a culture of coddling and safetyism. In fact, an authentic commitment to questioning everything would have the opposite effect. It
would empower people to build deep and meaningful relationships
even with those they fiercely disagreed with. It could be spiritual work.

Let's think about responsibility in multicultural environments
where we do not share the same dogmas or first principles. What does
it look like when the university becomes a place where we can say anything? If academics embraced spiritual work, what would follow would
be a radical sense of responsibility and transparency. It would flip the
academic/professional distinction so favored by university administrators on its head. It would remind academics that they too have a
professional responsibility. It would undo the administrative processes
that coddle students and stifle their development while frustrating
professors. Our professional responsibility would not be to enforce
processes; it would be to respond, in real time, to moral failures and
keep a conversation going. It would replace safetyism with care.

In a responsible university, the status of rules would be fluid. Both
students and administrators would trust professors to adhere to a
professional sense of responsibility that would seek the ever elusive
goals of truth and justice. Universities could become safe places for
experimentation and knowledge creation under this paradigm, but
less safe for corporatism, customers who want to buy a degree and
those who fear failure. There is still much spiritual work to be done
in our educational institutions.

Immediate Next Steps

I have been researching and teaching business strategy and holistic decision-making for over two decades. The questions I most
commonly hear from leaders, managers, entrepreneurs, and those

waiting in the wings for their turn to ascend in reflective moments are, How do I make better decisions in these confusing times? How do I unlock my full cognitive potential? Can you help me upgrade my thinking toolkits? The folks asking these questions are increasingly aware of the need to make decisions whose impacts will reverberate throughout the organizations they work for, the industries they compete in, and the communities they live in.

They see a world characterized by proceleration, which is defined as the acceleration of acceleration. This means oftentimes they need to react quickly, making critical business decisions of significant consequences without necessarily having sufficient time for research and reflection. They need to make good-faith efforts at tackling what the classic lenses of economic and political agency demands of them: take action, often quickly, based on predictions of what resources might prove valuable in an uncertain future or what capabilities will be required to exploit these currently unknown resources down the line.

This book has laid out a long-term strategy for accomplishing these ends. But what tactics can be offered that will make a difference right now? In recognition of the unique stressors brought about by living through proceleration, here are some practical exercises that can be undertaken right now in order shape a unique strategy for hope:

Craft a plan for forgiveness. In times of social upheaval and episodic change, thinking about how to forgive should be a critical activity for those negotiating power shifts. Unfortunately, that doesn't seem to be happening right now. So here is where those of us wanting to operationalize spiritual work can make a near immediate contribution. In this book, we explored a number of ways to approach forgiveness. There is a psychological paradigm that identifies a direct connection between the decision to forgive and an improvement in our health and wellness. We forgive because it is good for us. This doesn't mean that we necessarily want to be in the same room as those that hurt us ever again, but we let go of the anger and resentment.

There is a related religious conception of forgiveness, where we forgive because we are mandated to do so by our belief system. Once again, we forgive because we believe that in the greater scheme of things it is good for us to do so.

A more pragmatic approach to forgiveness is one where we wait for some level of atonement before we forgive. In this instance, we judge the atonement sufficient to allow us to move forward. We don't forget, but we are comfortable moving on.

Perhaps the highest level of forgiveness is rooted in an act of renewal, where through our forgiveness we wipe the slate clean. We forgive and forget. Or maybe we embrace a paradigm of forgiveness that is a mix of any of the above approaches.

What is critical to take away from this discussion is the recognition that a course of action involving some notion of forgiveness is the only path that will allow us to operate most effectively in the present. It is a necessary tactic in achieving a hopeful outcome. So taking the time to map out a plan of forgiveness is probably the most impactful action that one could take right now in the service of spiritual work.

Forgive yourself. When we think of forgiveness, we usually frame it as something that we grant to others. We rarely think of it as something that we need to give to ourselves. Survival is messy. One of the unhelpful beliefs many of us carry is a commitment to a monolithic notion of our "true selves." We believe that most of our traits are immutable, and we judge ourselves harshly for our failings.

If we are to engage in meaningful spiritual work, we need to be comfortable finding new ways to describe our past and selves that better serve the living present. And as noted above, the only way to be effective in the present is to forgive for the past. The self is provisional, made up of changing values and beliefs acquired through social interactions. We need to actively forgive our past selves.

The Jewish spiritual tradition is filled with stories of transformation. Abram became Abraham after his spiritual journey of smashing the idols of his father and leaving his childhood home forever. Jacob became Israel after he wrestled all night with an Angel, refusing to cede until he received a blessing. Moses the adopted child of privilege became Moses the leader of the downtrodden after he encountered the burning bush.

My friend, artist, and healer Dany Lyne brilliantly calls the temporary parts of ourselves that help us through crisis our "architects of survival." It's an empowering concept that names the parts of our personality that we create in response to specific situations faced at particular points in time. For many of us, we will need to construct new pieces of ourselves to get through new challenges. Which means we will need to forgive and let go of other parts of ourselves, particularly those that we created to help us contend with a world that may no longer exist.

Give up on algorithms. Some of us may have come to this book thinking that the essence of a spiritual practice is primarily manifested by embracing a specific set of rules. Hopefully, by this point, we have given up on still believing that there is an algorithm for the enlightened waiting to be unearthed.

Rules only work when the challenge we face is difficult but solvable. For example, if the problem we see is that "life is suffering," then "just breathe" is a reasonable solution. But what if the problem cannot be reduced to a quantifiable set of truths?

Usually, we view spiritual discussions as a focus on what is good in a complicated world. Complicated problems might be difficult to wrestle with, but ultimately they come down to figuring out what rules need to be applied. The challenges we face in an era of disruption and rapid change require us to think about what is complex, and how spiritual work can empower us to respond to complexity.

Strategic, political, and ethical dilemmas require contemplation followed by action. Unfortunately, the reality is such that all the time in the world would not be enough to meet the responsibility of thinking before acting in these instances. But what is open is the space for an authentic decision to be made. We are not like artificial intelligence, programmed to follow algorithms. Sometimes, the greatest difficulty can be found in having to choose between two determined options, two competing choices that seem to have an equal amount of truth value.

When we are faced with those situations, we do not have access to any resources that will aid us in objectively justifying one decision over another. We get stuck. And we often choose passivity.

Our rules and recipes for life in a complicated world don't work for complex challenges. Complex problems are full of ambiguity, unknown variables, and innumerable moving and interrelated parts. We are not machines. Give up on algorithms. We need to trust our forgiven selves and take action.

We can co-create or we can manage. We cannot do both simultaneously. One of the biggest mistakes I see corporations making as they try and figure out an appropriate response to the racial justice reckoning is believing that the best solution is to be found by hiring equity and diversity officers. Essentially, they are simply kicking the can down the road, although they obviously don't see it as such.

They think that efforts to make our workspaces more inclusive must involve the creation of whole new industries of professionals, brought in to manage the needs of employees through power and an extension of the corporate hierarchy. This is the wrong approach. Spiritual work means becoming a partner in co-creation. And meaningful change can only be enacted by transformative efforts across hierarchies and other power structures.

Each of us reading this book can encourage a shift away from the stifling, controlling, and outdated paradigm of management and towards a more robust cooperative effort of value creation. Especially for those of us who still believe in capitalism, the shift towards co-creation is an absolute must for capitalism to survive the current justified and long-coming social unrest. And we can start the process rather simply by using the language of friendship in our professional exchanges.

Granted, "simply" may be an unfair descriptor. Some of us may be very uncomfortable with embracing this paradigm shift because using a language of friendship where we once used the language of management means expanding the boundaries between the social/professional/personal that we have been clinging to for so long. But real change will emerge when our workplaces have fewer officers and more *chavrusas*.

Spiritual work is a constant negotiation. We need to be curious even while under duress. It can be a prelude to a break-through. In times of crisis, failure and error are no longer dirty words. The standard is doing the best we can as we negotiate change. But we need to participate in these negotiations armed with the deep-rooted belief that things can be better.

In stable times we can get hyper-focused on outcomes. Many of us right now might be justifiably worried that our lives or our societies are getting "off-track." But it's precisely in these conditions that we need to find value in the journey we are on, because that's all we have. We cannot comfortably predict the material outcomes in turbulent environments. We need to find a way to be empowered by the instability, allow ourselves to make mistakes along the way, but ultimately keep negotiating a way forward.

Spiritual work is the cultivation of a life in the ordinary world bearing the holiness once associated with sacred space and time. It is not a station we are trapped in. We can read these words and fit them nicely into our existing mental frames. But maybe that is a mistake. What habits or biases are preventing us from defining any particular ordinary activity as sacred? What parts of us have not undergone change? How can we better shape the game we are playing?

Do a mitzvah. A *mitzvah* is a moment of *doing* that creates a space of *being*. It opens up a space where we can create a meaningful moment with other people. The essence of spiritual work is to energize our activities with purpose, preferably one that will lead to greater communal connections and creative outcomes.

As such, there is no reason to wait to do this. Define a problem and take action. On the surface, the problem could be practical, rational, financial, emotional, spiritual, or relational. But thinking of a *mitzvah* response blurs the lines between the left/right brain, rational/emotional, internal/external perceptions. It pushes us into an experimental frame of mind, encouraging us to describe and re-describe ourselves and those around us.

As we discussed, spiritual work demands qualities and character traits that do not, at first glance, have overtly moral significance. Traits like an entrepreneurial tolerance for risk, an innovative spirit, or a mathematical mindset. What are our unique traits? What sort of immediate action can we take that is likely to create multiple types of value? How do we feel after?

Answer a tough question. Spend some extra time and effort communicating with the folks you work with, or hope to work with, about your decisions and actions. Think about the fact that prior to its historic downfall, in some circles Enron was viewed as a paradigm of ethical business for having created an extensive and ambitious code of conduct. In fact, the strategy textbook we used at our business school at the time used the Enron code as a model for other firms to follow. And it took two years after the fall of Enron for them to revise the chapter (which says a lot as well)!

The sense was that because Enron managers were able to so eloquently articulate an ethical position on one facet of their business, it must be a good company. But could they explain how they were making money? Not at all. In fact, when challenged, they would bully the questioner into doubting their own intellectual capacity. Enron managers positioned themselves as "the smartest guys in the room." They felt no need to explain their value proposition to those beneath them. Right until the end, when Jeff Skilling, Enron's CEO, famously said in a March 28, 2001, *Frontline* interview: "We are the good guys. We are on the side of angels."

When telling the stories of our spiritual work, we will likely be called upon to answer some tough questions. We need to provide thoroughly unambiguous answers to questions such as: Just how valuable is human life? What is a human life? What is it that makes life valuable? What makes us responsible for one another? When does *one* life take priority over another? What moral responsibilities must we insist a corporation answer to beyond meeting shareholder bottom-line concerns? How does a pluralistic society insist on specific moral norms that go beyond the law?

We Can't Know, but We Can Hope

This book has mapped out a journey designed to change the way we think about work and encourage us to seek the spiritual sparks hidden in our complex world. This means that we are now thinking about the spiritual potential in all of our ordinary activities. It means that our efforts in the economic, political, or cultural arenas will have the potential to be moral callings in and of themselves because we are using our minds, spirits, and bodies to seek engagement with an expanding "we," and not simply resigning ourselves to only changing our inner landscapes.

Collectively, the thought processes described throughout this book make up a strategy for hope, concerned with engaging in work, politics, and culture in ways that change the individual, change the environment in which individuals work, and change all those who come into contact with these individuals through their ordinary daily activities.

So long as ordinary activities are undertaken as transparent acts of good faith, the practice of business or politics can serve both a moral and spiritual purpose. This paradigm pushes for the development of qualities and character traits that do not, at first glance, have overtly moral significance, like an entrepreneurial tolerance for risk, an innovative spirit, or a mathematical mindset.

If there are sacred sparks needing to be unleashed in economic interactions, then the individual who takes the risk in starting a new business has performed an act of equal (or greater) moral content as an individual who makes a charitable contribution.

If we believe that cooperation can be transformational, then the innovator who creates a new platform that brings about the opportunity to engage has exhibited moral leadership.

If finding new financial models that allow for greater access to capital is a necessary task in mitigating the challenge of greed, then the mathematical minds that can come up with these models are as morally important as our philosophers and theologians.

Through this framing, practitioners create a story of transformation through the seemingly simple acts of good faith. This is ultimately a hopeful act because we, like Moses when he smashed the stone, are uncertain about potential outcomes as we make our spiritual choices, but we are optimistic. There is no more critical, spiritual, or hopeful a task than to actively engage in making choices. On the surface, this assertion seems simplistic and obvious. Yet, if we pause and reflect, we'd realize that spiritual decision-making is rarely easy.

A spiritual decision is not the application of an algorithm. There is freedom to choose between distinct paths that lead to unique outcomes. Effective decision-making in times of uncertainty has always been challenging, but perhaps never more so than in our turbulent age. Disruptive technological innovations are emerging at a faster pace than our decision-making frameworks are able to adapt. Yet we are called upon to continue to plan, predict, and decide as we always have.

What far too many business schools, management experts, and political gurus are afraid to admit is the ultimately undecidable nature of our strategic choices. To assume that most strategic situations are inherently decidable, which is to say, that with the right data or tools one can objectively decide A over B without controversy, oversimplifies the reality facing leaders and everyday citizens today and the choices that we must make.

That's why the strategic is spiritual. As we noted from the outset, there is little practical difference between what might be called ethical decision-making, political decision-making, strategic decision-making, or even business decision-making. Strategic decisions are necessarily spiritual decisions. And spiritual decisions are not simply leisurely normative speculations or abstract contemplations of what is right or wrong.

Things Break ... Let's Fix Them

As I write the closing words to this book, six months have passed since the initial discussion with my Google-based friend on spirituality at work. That conversation was the *chavrusa*-like interaction that stimulated the exploration that would become this book. In what can only be described as a fortuitous turn, he and I found ourselves back at the same synagogue, this time celebrating a *bat mitzvah* on a Monday morning. As this book started with a synagogue chat, it seems only fitting to end the same way. And the timing was perfect. I had gone on the journey of crafting this book, and my friend had just returned from Google's mythical "Search Inside Yourself" two-day mindfulness course. Would we find common ground as we got together to debrief?

There is no doubt that my friend was particularly energized by the experience of the corporate retreat. His energy was off the charts. I pushed him to explain to me why the Google mindfulness program was so impactful. He had completed an MBA degree at a well-known university and had taken many professional development courses over the years as he climbed the corporate ladder. What was so unique about this particular experience? And what my friend shared with me in that moment was a restating of the idea that started this book: we are still very much a spiritual people, with spiritual needs, even though few of us take the time to feed these needs in our overly busy lives.

Our desire for meaning, connection, and wonder is still paramount. We may be living through a period of extreme disruption, but our longing for spirituality and community based on meaning, connection, and wonder has not been extinguished. What struck my friend most profoundly about his experience in Google's mindfulness course was how hungry all of the diverse participants were for spiritual nourishment.

My friend explained to me that Google's course leader offered a brief fifteen-minute introduction, and then went around the room asking all those gathered to share their name and one word to describe themselves in that moment. One by one, the describing words offered up were all variances of a theme: curious, inspired, interested, and so on. To my friend, and I agree with him completely, this alone was incredibly impressive. Despite decades in the industry, he had never before seen a crowd of tech folks move into alignment so quickly.

Those of us who regularly work with roomfuls of people know that bringing a large group along with us on an intellectual journey can require weeks of preparation. And, quite frankly, even with all the extensive preparation, if one is fortunate enough to have the entirety of the group fully engaged even for a single ten-minute period that session would be considered an absolute success. On this mindfulness retreat, the whole group was engaged for the full two days. They wanted to express their spiritual feelings to colleagues in a work setting. My friend observed, "Anytime you have a chance to think about slowing down, stop being a crazy person, it's very powerful. Is it durable? I hope."

And that's the key point, isn't it? Is mindfulness more durable for cooperation than the *chavrusa* methodology we offer? I don't think so. It reminds me of an ongoing conversation I have been having with a very senior psychologist about the therapeutic possibility of psychedelics, in particular for changing behaviors that impede a healthy work/life/relational balance. There is no doubt that anecdotally we are hearing more and more stories from people who have an incredible, exciting experience micro-dosing in a therapeutic setting where they emerge feeling ready to make meaningful changes to their lives.

And, indeed, there is a logically sound premise at work here. If injurious experiences like trauma can have lasting negative consequences for mental health, it is also plausible that positive, cathartic experiences might be able to induce a positive mental health outcome. But the question that lingers for this seasoned psychologist is whether the changes inspired by the *psychedelic* experience are durable without the hard work of therapy? Is being in a psychedelic moment enough for lasting change to occur? Similarly, is being in a mindful moment, even somewhat regularly, enough to get these wired, alpha-tech workers to slow down *over the long-term*, change the way they work, and ultimately not burn out? Or do meaningful, lasting changes only come through the more difficult work of spiritual doing? And, equally important, is not burning out a sufficient goal of a spiritual work practice?

As we explained, the *chavrusa* model of interacting is a long-term, cooperative, intellectual endeavor featuring both a social and practical component. It is designed to force reaction while building a social bond. It emphasizes that collaboration needs to be reactive, assertive, even confrontational, while also friendship-driven. Key to the *chavrusa* exchange is communication and clarity, but it is achieved through challenge and intellectual innovation. Within a *chavrusa* exchange, the stage is set to facilitate surprise, friendly opposition, and truly radical interpretations. Put on display will be both the power and the limits of each individual's reactive faculties. In a *chavrusa*, we are actively pushed to do, not just be. And isn't that a better description of what happens at Google when workers are at their best?

My friend took a breath, then a pause, as he thought about this idea. He wanted to answer carefully, and warned me that his experiences were limited, and that what he is describing is a work culture as it was, not as it is. Google is in the process of a cultural shift at present, but at its origins it had been a bottom-up type of organization. And in that iteration, it would seem that a lot of the *chavrusa* principles were in play.

When Google wanted to grow their organization, folks would be hired into a team. These teams would then pick the projects to work on based on what interested them, a cultural orientation described as "leading by interest." As has been stated repeatedly in this book, spiritual work is a social endeavor powered by curiosity. When Google is at its best, it offers an environment that is people-driven and led by the idiosyncratic interests of independent teams. This approach to management is a clear and unambiguous rejection of asking workers to accept the limitations of their station and trust in a big-picture plan. It is a rejection of the workist instinct to disregard our all-too-human need for social connection. It is a rejection of the mindfulness message telling workers to disregard their reactive instincts and just be where they are. It is why there is a tension between what is expected in the meditation rooms and what happens elsewhere on the Google campus.

It is far more closely aligned to the approach to spiritual work described in the Jewish tradition. It is reminiscent of Abraham and Moses and other biblical figures who discovered meaning by throwing themselves head on into complexity and ambiguity, took action, and then dealt with the fallout. My friend explained to me that this work culture of leading by interest meant that if a team was interested in the grandiose project of mapping out the entire world, they were empowered to do so.

Google supported seemingly crazy projects like these, even when there was no immediately apparent link to the firm's corporate objectives. And the approach paid off. True, some of Google's success can be attributed to a bit of luck because the strategic importance of technological devices has descended as the importance of the web has ascended. Leading by curiosity paid off because many of the folks who joined Google in the early years were very curious about what the web might be able to do.

This revelation also ties back to our earlier discussion of relevance as the nemesis of innovation. Workers need to be afforded the opportunity to spend sufficient time cultivating and indulging their curiosity. This is consistent with Rabbi Steinsaltz observing that great innovations come from curious folks who have time on their hands and objects with which to play. They play in order to satisfy their curiosity, and eventually discover something interesting. Making everything relevant and practical can be helpful, but it can also kill the basic notion of curiosity. My friend observed, "At Google, the expectations on engineers is like 3.5 days per week productivity. The rest is learning. It's slower but faster."

And from this curiosity, comes wonder. For those still suspicious about the possibility of the third pillar of the spiritual experience, I share what I can only describe at this point as a form of testimony. My Google friend got serious and careful, measuring his words for the public record:

> I see this all the time … We have a meeting scheduled with a client after about a year has passed since they engaged us for a project. The client had asked us to develop all of these features for them, and they wanted to check in and see how far we had come after a year of work. The product manager leads the meeting, describing what the team has done. And the first thing the owner asks is, "OK. But what about all of these things that I asked you to do? What about these features that are so critical to the success of my business?" And the product manager is like, "Look, we

forgot to work on all those things that you asked for, but let me show you this ..." And the owner sees what the team has done and exclaims, "That's amazing! Wow!" Not a lot of companies operate like this. We forgot to look at what is critical, but look at this cool thing we ended up doing on the side. And the owner is ecstatic because their mind is blown.

My friend is speaking about the enduring power of wonder. Identified in this book as the third pillar of a spiritual experience and defined as when our existing abilities to neatly explain or categorize what we are seeing or sensing fail us. "Wow!" is, at times, an expression of wonder. Silence, at times, is an expression of wonder. It is a fleeting experience of the world that lets us concretely know how little we know. It is an indicator that our mental frames have been broken by the new content we are trying to insert. Wonder is a force that transforms. This shift that Google seems to do so often is critical to enabling the type of transformative cooperation required to be successful with our work. The *chavrusa* work at Google, at times, and seemingly a lot of times, inspires wonder.

So what is the strategy that allows so many of my friend's colleagues and clients in the tech world to get to that point so often? What is the strategy of hope that empowers these teams to confidently walk into a meeting after a year of work and announce that while they forgot what was important to the client, they are confident that the work they have done is valuable?

In one sentence? It is the ability to challenge conventional thinking and work together as a team to achieve intellectual innovations. What I have been calling transformational cooperation. This is a big part of the reason why my friend believes that Google has become so successful over the years. Perhaps more so than other companies, Google has built a culture that can be characterized by the widespread ability to see things differently than the norm. As a culture, Google has come to accept things that nobody else will accept. And this is true even today ... more than twenty

years after the company was founded. My friend enthusiastically
continued:

> I'll give you one example. Let's say you are designing for McDonald's.
> And you notice that the tables are breaking. How do you solve the prob-
> lem? Most people would say that the solution is to build a stronger ta-
> ble. That approach represents the popular way of thinking about this
> problem. Tables are probably breaking because people are heavier and
> more pressure is being put on them, so let's solve the problem by get-
> ting some better metal and building a stronger table. They approach
> the solution by thinking about the structure. Now in tech, the structure
> is "the cloud." You are running the compute. And when things break,
> people can't compute. So the traditional way of thinking is to buy things
> that don't break as much. Find better suppliers, build better infrastruc-
> ture, etc. But the people who built Google originally looked at this and
> said that is a mistake. Because things break.

Abraham smashed the stone idols of his father. Moses smashed
the stone to get water flowing for his people. Things break. Reactive spiritual work means accepting this reality. The above example
shared unprompted by a Google executive connects to our message
that we need to expect failure, but act anyway. We need to keep
trying, no matter what conditions we are facing. Our only hedge
is to connect more widely, find others to work with so that when
things break, when we break things, we have a coalition of allies
that can help us move forward. This is the spiritual paradigm we
need in contemporary work. One that allows for mistakes, because
innovations come from trial and error, as long as the intentions
are good. One that encourages reaction, not passivity, because in
a disruptive, fast-paced, ever-changing environment it's easy to be
overwhelmed. And one that empowers individuals to keep moving
forward. My friend summed up his thinking on the matter with this
final insight:

This is the paradigm behind Google's approach to the challenge of innovations: The conventional approach just exacerbates the problem. The cost of replacing things is exponential. A hard drive that lasts 2x as long costs 4x more to replace. And to put in one 2x as good as the last one costs 10x to replace. Nobody can afford to do this. So Google went against the conventional logic. They bought cheaper components that break more frequently and invested in resilience. If I replace the table with one 2x as strong, it will last 2x as long. But when it does break – because things break – nobody will remember how to fix it. They will call suppliers who will be out of parts. They will find new suppliers who will have to look overseas. The problem will take forever to be resolved. So instead, going back to our problem, I'm going to instrument every table. The second a table breaks it will send a signal to HQ that will automatically load a new table and that replacement table will be in the restaurant by the next morning. I'm willing to accept 10x more failures and it's still going to reduce my down time. This is not an instance of technological innovation. It's fully looking at the problem. It rejects the traditional solution, which is effectively ignoring the problem. Nothing succeeds the first time. That's a technology mindset.

What my friend calls here a "technology mindset" is a critical part of what we have been calling the *mitzvah* mindset. Things break. The world is broken. Contending with that truth is the work of a lifetime. Those who embrace the *mitzvah* mindset commit themselves to try and make the world function a little bit better. The work is often repetitive and uncertain, but it is also a source of meaning, connection, and wonder.

We are resilient. We are in this together, and for the long haul. We are always looking for new partners who don't think that we have to throw away a socio-political system that has provided much good for generations, but want to work to reform from within. As my friend explained, if you replace a good system that fails with a newer, more elaborate, more expensive system, you are simply running away from the real problem.

What we need to do instead is find a *chavrusa*, sit in our current reality, realize that we are facing significant problems, see how we and others have messed up and commit to fix whatever *it* turns out to be. This sort of work may make some of us feel uncomfortable in the near term, but only through this type of process can we hope to start to solve the actual problems we are facing. As the Lubavitcher Rebbe has famously stated:

If you see something that is broken, fix it.

If you cannot fix all of it, fix some of it.

But do not say there is nothing you can do.

Because, if that were true, why would this broken thing have come into your world?

Notes

Introduction: It's Time for a Different Spirituality

5 *dozens of countries ignored* S. Gebrekidan, "The World Has a Plan to Fight Coronavirus. Most Countries Are Not Using It," *New York Times*, March 12, 2020, https://www.nytimes.com/2020/03/12/world/coronavirus-world-health-organization.html.

6 *#MeToo movement* Stefanie K. Johnson, Ksenia Keplinger, Jessica F. Kirk, and Liza Barnes, "Has Sexual Harassment at Work Decreased Since #MeToo?" *Harvard Business Review,* July 18, 2019, https://hbr.org/2019/07/has-sexual-harassment-at-work-decreased-since-metoo.

6 *pledges from Corporate America* Tracy Jan, Jena McGregor, Renae Merle, and Nitasha Tiku, "As Big Corporations Say 'Black Lives Matter,' Their Track Records Raise Skepticism," June 13, 2020, *Washington Post*, https://www.washingtonpost.com/business/2020/06/13/after-years-marginalizing-black-employees-customers-corporate-america-says-black-lives-matter/?arc404=true.

6 *Reb Zalman, wrote* Z. Schachter-Shalomi and J. Segel, *Jewish with Feeling: A Guide to Meaningful Jewish Practice* (New York: Penguin, 2005), 140, emphasis mine.

8 *September 2017 Pew Research survey* M. Lipka and C. Gecewicz, "More Americans Now Say They're Spiritual but Not Religious," Pew Research Centre, September 6, 2017, https://www.pewresearch.org/fact-tank/2017/09/06/more-americans-now-say-theyre-spiritual-but-not-religious/.

10 *The rabbinic sages decided* Babylonian Talmud, Tractate Shabbat, 31a.

13 *"The simplest way ... "* D. Rushkoff, *Team Human* (New York: WW Norton, 2019).

14 *Millennials are the largest* D. Fry, "Millennials Are the Largest Generation in the U.S. Labor Force," Pew Research Centre, April 11, 2018, http://www

.pewresearch.org/fact-tank/2018/04/11/millennials-largest-generation
-us-labor-force/.

14 *make up a full 75 per cent* A. Mitchell, "The Rise of the Millennial Workforce," *Wired*, August 2013, https://www.wired.com/insights/2013/08/the
-rise-of-the-millennial-workforce/.

14 *Their entry into working life* C. Kurz, G. Li, and D.J. Vine, "Are Millennials
Different?" Finance and Economics Discussion Series, Federal Reserve
Board, Series 2018-080. Washington, DC: Board of Governors of the Fed-
eral Reserve System, 2018. https://doi.org/10.17016/FEDS.2018.080.

14 *"The Deloitte Global Millennial Survey 2019"* "The Deloitte Global Millennial
Survey 2019," accessed June 29, 2020, https://www2.deloitte.com/global
/en/pages/about-deloitte/articles/millennialsurvey.html.

15 *Generation C* A. Mull, "Generation C Has Nowhere to Turn," *The Atlantic*,
April 13, 2020, https://www.theatlantic.com/health/archive/2020/04
/how-coronavirus-will-change-young-peoples-lives/609862/.

1. Mindful*mess*

22 *Sociologist Max Weber argues* M. Weber, *The Protestant Ethic and the Spirit of
Capitalism* (New York: Scribner, 1958).

23 *The Protestant Work Ethic held* M. Benefiel, L.W. Fry, and D. Geigle, "Spirituality and Religion in the Workplace: History, Theory, and Research,"
Psychology of Religion and Spirituality 6 (2014): 175–87.

24 *According to David W. Miller* D.W. Miller, *God at Work: The History and Promise
of the Faith at Work Movement* (New York: Oxford University Press, 2007).

24 *"workism," defined as* D. Thompson, "The Religion of Workism Is Making
Americans Miserable," *The Atlantic*, February 24, 2019, https://www
.theatlantic.com/ideas/archive/2019/02/religion-workism-making
-americans-miserable/583441/.

25 *recent Pew Research report* J. Menasce Horowitz and N. Graff, "Most U.S. Teens
See Anxiety and Depression as a Major Problem Among Their Peers," Pew
Research Centre, February 20, 2019, https://www.pewsocialtrends.org
/2019/02/20/most-u-s-teens-see-anxiety-and-depression-as-a-major-problem
-among-their-peers/.

29 *National Health interview survey* D. Kachan et al., "Prevalence of Mindfulness
Practices in the US Workforce: National Health Interview Survey," *Preventing
Chronic Disease* 14 (2017): 1–12.

30 *While there is a demonstrable link* J. Horgan, "Buddhist Retreat," *Slate*,
February 12, 2003, https://slate.com/culture/2003/02/why-i-ditched-
buddhism.html.

33 *mindfulness as an "umbrella term"* J.M.G. Williams and J. Kabat-Zinn, "Mindfulness: Diverse Perspectives on Its Meaning, Origins, and Multiple Applications at the Intersection of Science and Dharma," *Contemporary Buddhism* 12 (2011): 1–18.

33 *In experimental and clinical psychology* A. Lutz, A.P. Jha, J.D. Dunne, and C.D. Saron, "Investigating the Phenomenological Matrix of Mindfulness-Related Practices from a Neurocognitive Perspective," *American Psychologist* 70 (2015): 632–58.

34 *the critical distinguishing feature* D.J. Good et al., "Contemplating Mindfulness at Work: An Integrative Review," *Journal of Management* 42 (2016): 114–42.

34 *"Attention" means* K.W. Brown, R.M. Ryan, and J.D. Creswell, "Mindfulness: Theoretical Foundations and Evidence for Its Salutary Effects," *Psychological Inquiry* 18 (2007): 211–37.

35 *understanding mindfulness as attention to* D.J. Good et al., "Contemplating Mindfulness at Work."

37 *"experiential processing"* K.W. Brown et al., "Mindfulness."

38 *In experiential processing,* D.J. Good et al., "Contemplating Mindfulness at Work."

38 *"decentering"* K.W. Brown et al., "Mindfulness."

39 *Those who push for mindfulness* D.J. Good et al., "Contemplating Mindfulness at Work."

39 *But mindfulness also carries a risk* J.A. Austin, *Zen and the Brain: Toward an Understanding of Meditation and Consciousness* (Boston: MIT Press, 1999).

40 *Researchers Richard Davidson ... and Alfred Kaszniak* R.J. Davidson and A.W. Kasniak, "Conceptual and Methodological Issues in Research on Mindfulness and Meditation," *American Psychologist* 70 (2015): 581–92.

40 *a mindfulness practice has been connected* D.J. Good et al., "Contemplating Mindfulness at Work."

41 *mindfulness may alter* G. Desbordes et al., "Moving Beyond Mindfulness: Defining Equanimity as an Outcome Measure in Meditation and Contemplative Research," *Mindfulness* 6 (2014): 356–72.

41 *mindfulness can be seen as conferring* T.M. Glomb et al., "Mindfulness at Work," *Research in Personnel and Human Resources Management* 30 (2011): 115–57.

41 *researchers at the University of Minnesota* A.C. Hafenbrack and K.D. Vohs, "Mindfulness Meditation Impairs Task Motivation but Not Performance," *Organizational Behavior and Human Decision Processes* 147 (2018): 1–15.

42 *Hafenbrack, explains* S. Berinato, "Mindfulness Is Demotivating," *Harvard Business Review,* 97 (2019): 32–3.

42 *mindfulness may support* D.J. Good et al., "Contemplating Mindfulness at Work."

43 *Silent Thunder Order advised* "Zen and Politics," Silent Thunder Order, 2016, https://storder.org/2016–06-01-02-26-21/dharma-bytes/419-zen-and-politics.

43 *"I take great solace ... "* International Campaign for Tibet, "In Message on COVID-19 Pandemic, Dalai Lama Says It Is Natural to Feel Anxious," March 30, 2020, https://savetibet.org/in-message-on-covid-19-pandemic -dalai-lama-says-it-is-natural-to-feel-anxious/.

2. Be Spiritual or Do Spiritual Work?

44 *great corporate scandals of our age* D. Hakim, A.M. Kessler, and J. Ewing, "As Volkswagen Pushed to Be No. 1, Ambitions Fueled a Scandal," *New York Times,* September 26, 2015.

44 *Recent revelations demonstrate* G. Gates et al., "How Volkswagen Is Grappling with Its Diesel Scandal," *New York Times,* November 18, 2016.

46 *open letter advocating for* "Open Letter Advocating for an Anti-racist Public Health Response to Demonstrations Against Systemic Injustice Occurring During the COVID-19 Pandemic," accessed July 20, 2020 https://drive .google.com/file/d/1Jyfn4Wd2i6bRi12ePghMHtX3ys1b7K1A/view.

46 *conservative commentators* Dan Diamond, "Suddenly, Public Health Officials Say Social Justice Matters More Than Social Distance," Politico, June 4, 2020, https://www.politico.com/news/magazine/2020/06/04/public -health-protests-301534.

46 *majority of Americans recognize* Giovanni Russonello, "Why Most Americans Support the Protests," *New York Times,* June 5, 2020, https://www.nytimes .com/2020/06/05/us/politics/polling-george-floyd-protests-racism.html.

50 *Rabbi Shalom Dovber Schneersohn* S.C. Kesselman, "Moses Strikes the Rock: The Full Story," Chabad.org, accessed June 29, 2020,https://www.chabad .org/library/article_cdo/aid/3839434/jewish/Moses-Strikes-the-Rock-The -Full-Story.htm.

55 *Tiffany Shlain argues* T. Shlain, *24/6: The Power of Unplugging One Day a Week* (New York: Simon and Schuster, 2019).

55 *"a palace in time"* A.J. Heschel, *The Sabbath* (New York: Farrar, Straus and Giroux, 1951), 13.

56 *Kabbalist Rabbi Isaac Luria* "Sefer Etz Chaim 8:1," Sefaria, accessed June 29, 2020, https://www.sefaria.org/Sefer_Etz_Chaim.8.1?lang=bi.

56 *Rabbi Menachem Mendel of Rimanov suggests* D. Levine, trans., *The Torah Discourses of the Holy Tzaddik Reb Menachem Mendel of Rimanov 1745–1815* (New York: Ktav Publishing, 1996).

57 *spirituality as a dialectic* D. Hartman, *From Defender to Critic: The Search for a New Jewish Self* (Woodstock: Jewish Lights Press, 2012).

58 *Rabbi Joseph Soloveitchik* D. Hartman, *From Defender to Critic.*

58 *"Do* Shabbos ... *first"* Z. Schachter-Shalomi and J. Segel, *Jewish with Feeling: A Guide to Meaningful Jewish Practice* (New York: Penguin, 2005).

59 *Rabbi David Hartman further notes* D. Hartman, *From Defender to Critic.*

60 *Jonathan Sacks identifies* J. Sacks, "The Leader's Call to Responsibility," The Office of Rabbi Sacks, September 22, 2014, http://rabbisacks.org/haazinu -5774-leaders-call-responsibility/.

62 *"the ethics of the shepherd"* Y. Hazony, *The Philosophy of Hebrew Scripture* (Cambridge: Cambridge University Press, 2012), 138, emphasis mine.

64 *underestimate ethical risks and associated social harm* D. Weitzner and J. Darroch, "The Limits of Strategic Rationality: Ethics, Enterprise Risk Management and Governance," *Journal of Business Ethics* 92 (2010): 361–72.

64 *the attractiveness of alternatives* K.R. MacCrimmon and D.A. Wehrung, *Taking Risks: The Management of Uncertainty* (New York: Free Press, 1986).

64 *as argued by the late James March* J.G. March and Z. Shapira, "Managerial Perspectives on Risk and Risk Taking," *Management Science* 33 (1987): 1404–18.

66 *"Rather than applying mindfulness ..."* R. Purser and D. Loy, "Beyond McMindfulness," *The Huffington Post,* July 1, 2013, http://www.huffingtonpost .com/ron-purser/beyond-mcmindfulness_b_3519289.html.

66 *"The mighty 'Mindfulness' juggernaut ..."* G. Wallis, "Elixir of Mindfulness," Speculative Non-Buddhism, July 3, 2011, http://speculativenonbuddhism. com/2011/07/.

3. *Mitzvah* in the Workplace

67 *Choura Events* A. Brown, "They Were Supposed to Build Stages for Coachella. Now They're Building Coronavirus Triage Tents," *LA Times,* March 30, 2020, https://www.latimes.com/entertainment-arts/music/story/2020-03-30 /coronavirus-event-companies-coachella-pivot-covid-19-testing.

69 *Aaron Feuerstein, the CEO* R. Leung, "The Mensch of Malden Mills," *60 Minutes,* July 3, 2003, https://www.cbsnews.com/news/the-mensch-of -malden-mills/.

70 *Rabbi Art Green ... "spirituality"* A. Green, *Radical Judaism: Rethinking God and Tradition* (New Haven: Yale University Press, 2010).

70 *Reb Zalman ... "commandment"* Z. Schachter-Shalomi and J. Segel, *Jewish with Feeling: A Guide to Meaningful Jewish Practice* (New York: Penguin, 2005).

70 *Rabbi Tzvi Freeman notes* T. Freeman, "What Is a Mitzvah?" Chabad.org, accessed June 29, 2020, https://www.chabad.org/library/article_cdo/aid /1438516/jewish/Mitzvah.htm.

71 *Rabbi Mordecai Kaplan* M.M. Kaplan, *Judaism as a Civilization: Toward a Reconstruction of American Jewish Life* (New York: The Jewish Publication Society, 2010).

71 *Rabbi Mordechai Yosef Leiner* B.P. Edwards, trans., *Living Waters – The Mei HaShiloach: A Commentary on the Torah by Rabbi Mordechai Yosef of Isbitza* (New York: Jason Aronson, 2001).

72 *the guide to sainthood* Babylonian Talmud, Tractate Berachot, 63b.

73 *Moses Pava … argues* M.L. Pava, "The Substance of Jewish Business Ethics," *Journal of Business Ethics* 17 (1998): 603–17.

73 *Rebbe Menachem Mendel Schneerson* T. Freeman, *Wisdom to Heal the Earth – Meditations and Teachings of the Lubavitcher Rebbe* (New York: Ezra Press, 2018).

74 *Freeman … ray of conscious thought* T. Freeman, "Who Came Up with Tikkun Olam?" Chabad.org, September 20, 2016, https://www.chabad.org/library /article_cdo/aid/3433653/jewish/Who-Came-Up-With-Tikkun-Olam.htm.

76 *"In a fast-changing retail environment … "* T. Hsu, "Ikea Enters 'Gig Economy' by Acquiring TaskRabbit," *New York Times*, September 28, 2017, https://www .nytimes.com/2017/09/28/business/ikea-taskrabbit.html?_r=0.

77 *The presence of trust allows* A.C. Wicks, S.L. Berman, and T.M. Jones, "The Structure of Optimal Trust: Moral and Strategic Implications," *Academy of Management Review* 24 (1999): 99–116.

77 *Sabel's definition of trust* C.F. Sabel, "Studied Trust: Building New Forms of Cooperation in a Volatile Economy," *Human Relations* 46 (1993): 1133–70.

77 *Jay Barney has defined* J.B. Barney and M.H. Hansen, "Trustworthiness as a Source of Competitive Advantage," *Strategic Management Journal* 15 (1994): 175–90.

79 *"crushing the economy … "* L. Blankfein, Twitter Post, March 22, 2020, 9:59 PM, https://twitter.com/lloydblankfein/status/1241907502662418437.

81 *Rabbi Jonathan Sacks talks* J. Sacks, "Morals: The One Thing Markets Don't Make," *The Times*, March 21, 2009, https://www.thetimes.co.uk/article /morals-the-one-thing-markets-dont-make-ft958b0sqzd.

81 *Researchers at the University of Virginia* L. Dunham, R.E. Freeman, and J. Liedtka, "Enhancing Stakeholder Practice: A Particularized Exploration of Community," *Business Ethics Quarterly* 16 (2006): 23–42.

82 *The Apple Store was not created* C. Gallo C. "How Apple Store Seduces You with the Tilt of Its Laptops," *Forbes*, June 14, 2012, https://www.forbes. com/sites/carminegallo/2012/06/14/why-the-new-macbook-pro-is-tilted -70-degrees-in-an-apple-store/#87172855a987.

84 *Starbucks outlets nationwide shut down* M. Stevens, "Starbucks C.E.O. Apologizes after Arrests of 2 Black Men," *New York Times*, April 15, 2018, https://www.nytimes.com/2018/04/15/us/starbucks-philadelphia-black -men-arrest.html.

84 *a barista in Arizona* "Starbucks Apologizes to Police after Six Officers Were Asked to Leave Arizona Store," Reuters, July 7, 2019, https://www.reuters .com/article/us-starbucks-arizona-police/starbucks-apologizes-to-police -after-six-officers-were-asked-to-leave-arizona-store-idUSKCN1U20I9.

84 *training videos posted online* "The Third Place: Our Commitment, Renewed," Starbucks Stories, May 30, 2018, https://stories.starbucks.com/stories /2018/thethirdplace/.

85 *a day that cost $12 million* Z. Meyer, "Starbucks' Racial-Bias Training Will Be Costly, but Could Pay Off in the Long Run," *USA Today*, May 26, 2018, https://www.usatoday.com/story/money/2018/05/26/starbucks-racial -bias-training-costly/642844002/.

86 *wedding planning company Zola* H. Waller, "Hallmark Channel Apologizes for Pulling Ad Featuring Two Brides after Backlash," *Bloomberg News*, December 15, 2019, https://www.bloomberg.com/news/articles/2019-12-15/hallmark -pulls-kissing-brides-and-netflix-degeneres-push-back.

87 *CEO John Mackey* E. DeJesus, "Whole Foods CEO Suggests Employees Donate Sick Days to Each Other as Way to Get through Coronavirus Outbreak," Eater, March 13, 2020, https://www.eater.com/2020/3/13/21179075/amazon -whole-foods-want-employees-to-donate-sick-days-amid-coronavirus-pandemic.

87 *Whole Foods employee Matthew Hunt* A. Leonardi, "Whole Foods Says Employees Should Consider Donating Paid Vacation Days during Coronavirus," *Washington Examiner*, March 13, 2020, https://www.washingtonexaminer.com/news /whole-foods-says-employees-should-consider-donating-paid-vacation-days -during-coronavirus.

88 *Rabbi Abraham Joshua Heschel* A.J. Heschel, *Who Is Man?* (Stanford: Stanford University Press, 1965), 50.

4. Transformational Cooperation

95 *US Senator Richard Burr* L. Markay, W. Bredderman, and S. Brodey, "Sen. Kelly Loeffler Dumped Millions in Stock After Coronavirus Briefing," *The Daily Beast*, March 19, 2020, https://www.thedailybeast.com/sen-kelly -loeffler-dumped-millions-in-stock-after-coronavirus-briefing.

96 *the gloomy data* "The Deloitte Global Millennial Survey 2019," accessed June 29, 2020, https://www2.deloitte.com/global/en/pages/about-deloitte /articles/millennialsurvey.html.

97 *"good team player"* S. Shellenbarger, "You Could Be Too Much of a Team Player," *Wall Street Journal*, July 23, 2018, https://www.wsj.com/articles/you -could-be-too-much-of-a-team-player-1532352464.

99 *three distinct motivations* D. Weitzner and Y. Deutsch, "Understanding Motivation and Social Influence in Stakeholder Prioritization," *Organization Studies* 36 (2015): 1337–60.

100 *"acquire a friend"* B.Z. Bokser, *The Maharal: The Mystical Philosophy of Rabbi Judah Loew of Prague* (New Jersey: Jason Aronson, 1994).

101 *recent research coming out of Harvard Business School* N. Torres, "It's Better to Avoid a Toxic Employee than Hire a Superstar," *Harvard Business Review*,

December 9, 2015, https://hbr.org/2015/12/its-better-to-avoid-a-toxic
-employee-than-hire-a-superstar.

101 *We know that elite cultures* J. Eades, "Research on Hundreds of Companies
Showed Toxic Cultures Have These Characteristics," *Inc.*, February 13, 2018,
https://www.inc.com/john-eades/research-on-hundreds-of-companies
-showed-that-toxic-cultures-have-these-characteristics.html.

102 *cooperation is defined* D.G. Rand and M.A. Nowak, "Human Cooperation,"
Trends in Cognitive Sciences 17 (2013): 413–25.

102 *The Gates of Repentance* J. Gerondi, *The Gates of Repentance* (New Jersey: Jason
Aronson Press, 1999).

103 *the decision to engage in pro-social behavior* D.G. Rand et al., "Social
Heuristics Shape Intuitive Cooperation," *Nature Communications* 5 (2014):
3677.

104 *Rabbi Yossi bar Chanina says* Babylonian Talmud, Tractate Berachot, 63b.

105 *Reish Lakish* Babylonian Talmud, Tractate Bava Metzia, 84a.

113 *Psychologist Dr. Christian Jarrett* C. Jarrett, "Why Meeting Another's Gaze Is
so Powerful," *BBC*, January 8, 2019, https://www.bbc.com/future/article
/20190108-why-meeting-anothers-gaze-is-so-powerful.

114 *"safe space"* Merriam-Webster, *s.v.* "safe space," accessed June 29, 2020,
https://www.merriam-webster.com/dictionary/safe%20space.

114 *philosopher Liz Swan* L. Swan, "Safe Spaces Can Be Dangerous," *Psychology
Today*, March 20, 2017, https://www.psychologytoday.com/ca/blog
/college-confidential/201703/safe-spaces-can-be-dangerous.

115 *Van Jones* F. Rose, "Safe Spaces on College Campuses Are Creating Intolerant
Students," *Huffington Post*, March 30, 2017, https://www.huffpost.com/entry
/safe-spaces-college-intolerant_b_58d957a6e4b02a2eaab66ccf.

118 *Alexander Nehamas argues* J. Beck, "Why Friendship Is Like Art," *The Atlantic*,
May 4, 2016, https://www.theatlantic.com/health/archive/2016/05/why
-friendship-is-like-art/481083/.

119 *the Revelation at Mount Sinai* D. Levine, trans., *The Torah Discourses of the
Holy Tzaddik Reb Menachem Mendel of Rimanov 1745–1815* (New York: Ktav
Publishing, 1996).

5. All "WE"s, Always

122 *Choni ha-M'agel* Babylonian Talmud, Tractate Ta'anit, 23a.

125 *Rabbi Hyim Shafner* H. Shafner, "The Dream of Exile: A Re-reading of Honi
the Circle-Drawer," *Kerem*, 2011, http://kerem.org/wp-content/uploads
/2011/01/Kerem-12-Hyim-Shafner-....-The-Dream-of-Exile.pdf.

126 *Management researchers have* D. Kiron and G. Unruh, "Business Needs a
Safety Net," *MIT Sloan Management Review* 59 (2018): 1–6.

127 *LVMH ... decided to use* A. Lee, "Luxury Perfume Makers Dior and Givenchy Will Produce Free Hand Sanitizer for French Health Authorities," CNN, March 15, 2020, https://www.cnn.com/2020/03/15/business/coronavirus -lvmh-dior-hand-sanitizer-trnd/index.html.

128 *Mark Lilla observes* M. Lilla, *The Once and Future Liberal* (New York: Harper, 2017).

129 *As I wrote for Tablet* D. Weitzner, "I Chose to Spend Shabbat with Steve Bannon," *Tablet*, November 6, 2018, https://www.tabletmag.com/scroll /274371/i-chose-to-spend-shabbat-with-steve-bannon.

133 *Bernanke and Paulson made no apologies* J. Cox, "Bernanke, Paulson and Geithner Say They Bailed Out Wall Street to Help Main Street," *CNBC*, September 12, 2018, https://www.cnbc.com/2018/09/12/bernanke -paulson-and-geithner-say-they-bailed-out-wall-street-to-help-main-street.html.

133 *I had written a paper* D. Weitzner and J. Darroch, "Why Moral Failures Precede Financial Crises," *Critical Perspectives on International Business*, 5 (2009): 6–13.

135 *As Frum has stated elsewhere* D. Frum, "How Republicans Can Fix American Healthcare," *The Atlantic*, June 30, 2017, https://www.theatlantic.com /politics/archive/2017/06/how-republicans-can-fix-american-health-care /532251/.

136 *Andrew Sullivan suggests* A. Sullivan, "How to Live With COVID-19," *New York Magazine*, April 3, 2020, https://nymag.com/intelligencer/2020/04 /andrew-sullivan-how-to-live-with-the-coronavirus.html?utm_source=tw.

141 *Rabbi Jonathan Sacks explains* J. Sacks, "Rabbi Sacks on 'The Politics of Hope,'" The Office of Rabbi Sacks, January 8, 2018 http://rabbisacks.org/ the-politics-of-hope/.

6. Connected Capitalism

144 *A 2018 survey* R. Browne, "70% of People Globally Work Remotely at Least Once a Week, Study Says," *CNBC*, May 30, 2018, https://www.cnbc.com /2018/05/30/70-percent-of-people-globally-work-remotely-at-least-once-a -week-iwg-study.html.

144 *a Gallup poll* A. Mann and A. Adkins, "America's Coming Workplace: Home Alone," Gallup, March 15, 2017, https://news.gallup.com/business journal/206033/america-coming-workplace-home-alone.aspx.

145 *over 20 per cent of remote workers* A. Hickman, "How to Manage the Loneliness and Isolation of Remote Workers," Gallup, November 6, 2019, https://www.gallup.com/workplace/268076/manage-loneliness-isolation -remote-workers.aspx.

145 *Prithwiraj Choudhury* D. Gerdeman and P. Choudhury, "How the Coronavirus Is Already Rewriting the Future of Business," *Harvard Business Review*, March 16,

2020, https://hbswk.hbs.edu/item/how-the-coronavirus-is-already-rewriting
-the-future-of-business.

147   *More young Americans than ever* F. Newport, "Democrats More Positive About
Socialism than Capitalism," Gallup, August 13, 2018, https://news.gallup
.com/poll/240725/democrats-positive-socialism-capitalism.aspx.

148   *"How to Get Americans ... "* H.M. Paulson and E.B. Bowles, "How to Get
Americans to Love Capitalism Again," *New York Times,* December 11, 2019,
https://www.nytimes.com/2019/12/11/opinion/america-capitalism.html.

148   *"SNC-LAVALIN PLEADS GUILTY ... "* Nicolas Van Praet et al., "SNC-Lavalin
Unit Pleads Guilty to Fraud Charge, to Pay $280-million Fine," *Globe and Mail,*
December 19, 2019, https://www.theglobeandmail.com/business/article
-snc-lavalin-reaches-agreement-to-plead-guilty-to-charges-of-corruption/.

149   *"While it's fair to argue ... "* Editorial, "SNC-Lavalin Got What It Wanted. It's
Still a Win for the Rule of Law," *Globe and Mail,* December 19, 2019, https://
www.theglobeandmail.com/opinion/editorials/article-snc-lavalin-got-what
-it-wanted-its-still-a-win-for-the-rule-of-law/.

150   *"it has often felt ... "* A. Beckett, "The Age of Perpetual Crisis: How the 2010s
Disrupted Everything but Resolved Nothing," *The Guardian,* December 17,
2019, https://www.theguardian.com/society/2019/dec/17/decade-of
-perpetual-crisis-2010s-disrupted-everything-but-resolved-nothing.

150   *"Judaism does not propose ... "* M. Tamari, *With All Your Possessions: Jewish Ethics
and Economic Life* (New York: Free Press, 1987).

152   *public policy makers had finally* D. Weitzner and J. Darroch, "Why Moral
Failures Precede Financial Crises," *Critical Perspectives on International Business*
5 (2009): 6–13.

153   *respond appropriately* N. Gillespie and G. Dietz, "Trust Repair After an
Organization-Level Failure," *Academy of Management Review* 34 (2009): 127–45.

153   *In classic Jewish sources* M. Tamari, *With All Your Possessions.*

153   *some of the public anger* "Vampire Squished? What Is Bad for Goldman Is
Bad for Wall Street, but Good for Regulatory Reformers," *The Economist,*
April 22, 2010.

153   *the perspective within Fannie Mae* D. Listokin et al., "The Potential and
Limitations of Mortgage Innovation in Fostering Homeownership in the
United States," *Housing Policy Debate* 12 (2002): 465–513. https://www
.innovations.harvard.edu/sites/default/files/hpd_1203_listokin-1.pdf.

154   *Many financial innovations have* F. Partnoy, "Do CDOs Have Social Value?"
New York Times, April 27, 2010, https://roomfordebate.blogs.nytimes.com
/2010/04/27/do-c-d-o-s-have-social-value/.

154   *"long-term greedy"* S.M. Sears, "Goldman Sachs: A Long-Term-Greedy Trade,"
Barron's, February 8, 2017, https://www.barrons.com/articles/goldman
-sachs-a-long-term-greedy-trade-1486578735.

155   *"As long as the music ... "* D. Wighton, "What We Have Learned 10 Years
after Chuck Prince Told Wall St to Keep Dancing," *Financial News,* July 14,

2017, https://www.fnlondon.com/articles/chuck-princes-dancing-quote
-what-we-have-learned-10-years-on-20170714.

156 *Jewish ethicist Tamari notes* M. Tamari, *With All Your Possessions.*

157 *Throwing Rocks at the Google Bus* D. Rushkoff, *Throwing Rocks at the Google Bus: How Growth Became the Enemy of Prosperity* (New York: Portfolio, 2017).

158 *Rav Safra* Babylonian Talmud, Tractate Makkot, 24a.

159 *Rabbi Moshe Feinstein cites* M. Feinstein, *Igrot Moshe, Hoshen Mishpat* (New York: M. Feinstein, 1964).

160 *In 2015 … McDonald's was told* L. O'Reilly, "McDonald's Slapped Down for Focusing Its Happy Meal Advertising on the Toy and Not the Food," *Business Insider*, May 15, 2015, https://www.businessinsider.com/mcdonalds -told-to-change-ads-by-childrens-advertising-review-unit-2015-5.

160 *McDonald's launched* "Small World Famous Fries," McDonald's, accessed June 30, 2020, https://www.mcdonalds.com/us/en-us/product/small -french-fries.html.

161 *Brazilian President Bolsonaro has allowed* C. Pires, "The Trump Ally Who Is Allowing the Amazon to Burn," *The New Yorker*, August 28, 2019, https:// www.newyorker.com/news/news-desk/the-trump-ally-who-is-allowing-the -amazon-to-burn.

163 *Harley Owners Group* R. Clifton, J. Simmons, and S. Ahmad, *Brands and Branding: The Economist Series*, 2nd ed. (New York: Bloomberg Press, 2004).

165 *In socialized meditation* Z. Schachter-Shalomi and R.S. Miller, *From Age-ing to Sage-ing: A Revolutionary Approach to Growing Older* (New York: Time Warner Books, 1997).

7. Curiosity Isn't Relevant

170 *Researchers define awe* P.K. Piff et al., "Awe, the Small Self, and Prosocial Behavior," *Journal of Personality and Social Psychology* 108 (2015): 883–99.

173 *Rabbi Adin Steinsaltz … describes curiosity* A. Steinsaltz, "Curious Jews," *The Times of Israel*, May 18, 2015, https://blogs.timesofisrael.com /curious-jews/.

173 *focus on "relevance" and practicality* D. Weitzner, "The Customer Is Not Always Right," *Quillette*, September 20, 2018, https://quillette.com/2018/09/20 /the-customer-is-not-always-right-a-reply-to-elliot-berkman/.

174 *view this development as an efficiency risk* R.S. Nason, S. Bacq, and D. Gras, "A Behavioral Theory of Social Performance: Social Identity and Stakeholder Expectations," *Academy of Management Review* 43 (2018): 259–83.

174 *management researchers made the argument* T.M. Jones, J.S. Harrison, and W. Felps, "How Applying Instrumental Stakeholder Theory Can Provide Sustainable Competitive Advantage," *Academy of Management Review* 43 (2018): 371–91.

175 *Business scholars have found* G. Francesca, "The Business Case for Curiosity," *Harvard Business Review*, 96 (2018): 48–57.

177 *This is one of the personal lessons* D. Weitzner, *Fifteen Paths: How to Tune Out Noise, Turn On Imagination and Find Wisdom* (Toronto: ECW Press, 2019).

181 *"As civilization advances … "* A.J. Heschel, *God in Search of Man: A Philosophy of Judaism* (New York: Farrar, Straus and Giroux, 1976), 46.

184 *Jonathan Safran Foer has written* J.S. Foer, *We Are the Weather* (New York: Farrar, Strauss and Giroux, 2019).

186 *Uber's self-driving car* A. Marshall and A. Davies, "Uber's Self-Driving Car Didn't Know Pedestrians Could Jaywalk," *Wired*, November 5, 2019, https://www .wired.com/story/ubers-self-driving-car-didnt-know-pedestrians-could-jaywalk/.

191 *Spotify's walking-back of a policy* L. Shaw, "Spotify Plans to Change XXXTentacion Policy After Outcry," *Bloomberg*, May 24, 2018, https://www .bloomberg.com/news/articles/2018-05-24/spotify-said-to-plan-to-restore -xxxtentacion-music-after-outcry.

192 *The "take a knee" protest* A. Beaton, "How Trump's Pressure Influenced the NFL to Change Its Anthem Rules," *Wall Street Journal*, May 30, 2018, https://www.wsj.com/articles/how-trumps-pressure-influenced-the-nfl-to -change-its-anthem-rules-1527685321.

194 *the NFL first took a knee* Dakin Andone, "Roger Goodell Saying Black Lives Matter Is 'Almost Like a Slap in the Face,' Michael Bennett Says," CNN, June 13, 2020, https://www.cnn.com/2020/06/13/us/michael-bennett -roger-goodell-black-lives-matter-trnd/index.html.

8. Elevating Forgiveness

195 *"Forgiveness is a form … "* N. Cave, "How Do You Forgive Somebody Whom You Love Very Much but Has Done Something Truly Terrible?" *The Red Hand Files*, Issue 58, September 2019, https://www.theredhandfiles.com /how-do-you-forgive/.

196 *Fred Kiel … found* F. Kiel, "Measuring the Return on Character," *Harvard Business Review*, April 2015, https://hbr.org/2015/04/measuring-the -return-on-character.

196 *Rosabeth Moss Kanter discussed* R. Moss Kanter, "Great Leaders Know When to Forgive," *Harvard Business Review*, February 26, 2013, https://hbr.org /2013/02/great-leaders-know-when-to.

198 *Forgiveness in contemporary psychology* "What Is Forgiveness?" *Psychology Today*, accessed June 30, 2020, https://www.psychologytoday.com/ca/basics /forgiveness.

198 *Rabbi Soloveitchik describes* S.J. Levine, "Teshuva: A Look at Repentance, Forgiveness and Atonement in Jewish Law and Philosophy and American

Legal Thought," *Fordham Urban Law Journal* 27 (2000): 1676–93, https://
ir.lawnet.fordham.edu/ulj/vol27/iss5/43/.

203 *Rabbi David Hartman recognized* D. Hartman and C. Buckholtz, *The God Who Hates Lies: Confronting & Rethinking Jewish Tradition* (New York: Jewish Lights Publishing, 2014).

205 *"not beyond the sea"* B.P. Edwards trans., *Living Waters – The Mei HaShiloach: A Commentary on the Torah by Rabbi Mordechai Yosef of Isbitza* (New York: Jason Aronson, 2001).

206 *"people attempt to expunge anyone …"* L. Ross, "I'm a Black Feminist. I Think Cancel Culture Is Toxic," *New York Times*, August 17, 2019, https://www
.nytimes.com/2019/08/17/opinion/sunday/cancel-culture-call-out
.html.

207 *"the suppressed cry …"* S. Raz and E. Levin, *The Sayings of Menahem Mendel of Kotsk* (New York: Jason Aronson, 1995).

210 *There is a famous story in the Talmud* Babylonian Talmud, Tractate Bava Metzia, 59a–b.

9. Strategize for Hope

216 *"Despite inspirational calls …"* The Editorial Board, "Virus Lays Bare the Frailty of the Social Contract," *Financial Times*, April 3, 2020, https://www
.ft.com/content/7eff769a-74dd-11ea-95fe-fcd274e920ca.

218 *The Coddling of the American Mind* G. Lukianoff and J. Haidt, *The Coddling of the American Mind* (New York: Penguin, 2018).

219 *"Many students are given …"* J. Haidt, "Notable & Quotable: Jonathan Haidt on Identity Politics," *Wall Street Journal*, November 23, 2017, https://www
.wsj.com/articles/notable-quotable-jonathan-haidt-on-identity-politics
-1511464920.

223 *"architects of survival"* D. Weitzner, *Fifteen Paths: How to Tune Out Noise, Turn On Imagination and Find Wisdom* (Toronto: ECW Press, 2019).

227 *"We are the good guys …"* "Interview: Jeff Skilling," *Frontline*, PBS, March 8, 2001, https://www.pbs.org/wgbh/pages/frontline/shows/blackout/interviews
/skilling.html.

231 *therapeutic possibility of psychedelics* E.E. Schenberg, "Psychedelic-Assisted Psychotherapy: A Paradigm Shift in Psychiatric Research and Development," *Frontiers in Pharmacology*, July 5, 2018, https://www.frontiersin.org/articles
/10.3389/fphar.2018.00733/full.

237 *"If you see something …"* T. Freeman, *Wisdom to Heal the Earth – Meditations and Teachings of the Lubavitcher Rebbe* (New York: Ezra Press, 2018).